Ubuntu® Linux®
TOOLBOX

Ubuntu® Linux®
TOOLBOX

1000+ Commands for Ubuntu
and Debian Power Users

Christopher Negus
François Caen

Wiley Publishing, Inc.

Ubuntu® Linux® Toolbox:
1000+ Commands for Ubuntu and Debian Power Users

Published by
Wiley Publishing, Inc.
10475 Crosspoint Boulevard
Indianapolis, IN 46256
www.wiley.com

Copyright © 2008 by Wiley Publishing, Inc., Indianapolis, Indiana
Published simultaneously in Canada
ISBN: 978-0-470-08293-5
Manufactured in the United States of America
10 9 8 7 6 5 4 3

Library of Congress Cataloging-in-Publication Data

Negus, Chris, 1957–
  Ubuntu Linux toolbox : 1000+ commands for Ubuntu and Debian power users / Christopher Negus,
François Caen.
    p. cm.
  Includes index.
  ISBN 978-0-470-08293-5 (pbk.)
  1. Linux. 2. Operating systems (Computers) I. Caen, François. II. Title.
  QA76.76.O63N42676 2007
  005.4'32—dc22

                              2007041567

As always, I dedicate my work on this book to my wife, Sheree.

— Christopher Negus

To my wife, Tonya, for supporting me in all my endeavors.

— François Caen

About the Authors

Christopher Negus is the author of the best-selling *Fedora and Red Hat Linux Bibles*, *Linux Toys, Linux Troubleshooting Bible*, and *Linux Bible 2007 Edition*. He is a member of the Madison Linux Users Group. Prior to becoming a full-time writer, Chris served for eight years on development teams for the Unix operating system at AT&T, where Unix was created and developed. He also worked with Novell on Unix development and Caldera Linux.

François Caen, through his company Turbosphere LLC, hosts and manages business application infrastructures, with 95 percent running on Linux systems. As an open source advocate, he has lectured on OSS network management and Internet services, and served as president of the Tacoma Linux User Group. François is a Red Hat Certified Engineer (RHCE). In his spare time, François enjoys managing enterprise Cisco networks.

Credits

Acquisitions Editor
Jenny Watson

Development Editor
Sara Shlaer

Technical Editor
Thomas Blader

Copy Editor
Michael Koch

Editorial Manager
Mary Beth Wakefield

Production Manager
Tim Tate

**Vice President and
Executive Group Publisher**
Richard Swadley

Vice President and Executive Publisher
Joseph B. Wikert

Project Coordinator, Cover
Lynsey Osborn

Compositor
Laurie Stewart,
Happenstance Type-O-Rama

Proofreader
Kathryn Duggan

Indexer
Melanie Belkin

Anniversary Logo Design
Richard Pacifico

Contents at a Glance

Contents

Contents

Contents

Contents

Contents

Contents

Acknowledgments

I would like to acknowledge Canonical Ltd. and the Ubuntu community for their ongoing excellent work producing the Linux-based Ubuntu operating system.

Special thanks to François Caen for giving up most of his free time over the past year, while juggling his existing professional obligations, to co-author the book with me. Thomas Blader went far beyond his technical editor title, providing excellent insights and meticulous testing throughout the book. Eric Foster-Johnson came in near the end of the process and provided Ubuntu feature enhancements throughout the book.

At Wiley, I'd like to thank Jenny Watson for sticking with us through the development of the book. And, last but not least, thanks to Sara Shlaer for keeping us on track with schedules and supplying the never-ending ToDo lists we needed to accomplish to get this book published.

— *Christopher Negus*

I would like to thank Chris Negus for giving me the opportunity to co-author this book with him. We had wanted to write together for the last couple of years, and this Toolbox series was the perfect fit for our collaboration.

I couldn't have worked on this book without the unrelenting support from my wife, Tonya. Thank you for emptying the dishwasher all these times even though we both know it's my job.

Thanks to Thomas Blader for his detailed tech editing. Thanks to Eric Foster-Johnson for adding his Ubuntu expertise to this book. Thanks to Sara Shlaer for her guidance throughout the authoring process, and to Jenny Watson for being the most patient cat-herder out there. Special thanks to Wayne Tucker for sharing his Debian experience with me over the years, especially when it came to cutting-edge features like kernel 2.4.

Finally, I would like to express my gratitude to Mark Shuttleworth, Canonical Ltd., and the Ubuntu community for making Ubuntu possible and helping spread Linux to the masses.

— *François Caen*

Introduction

The huge, enthusiastic Ubuntu community has swept up thousands and thousands of new Ubuntu Linux users. If you are one of them, you will probably soon find yourself wanting to dig beneath the surface of Ubuntu's applications and graphical tools. You'll want to become a power user.

Becoming a power user with any Linux system means being able to work from the command line. Few graphical interfaces will provide you with the options and flexibility you get with commands that address the same features.

Ubuntu Linux Toolbox provides you with more than 1000 specific command lines to help you dig deeply into Linux. Whether you are a systems administrator or desktop user, the book will show you commands to create file systems, troubleshoot networks, lock down security, and dig out almost anything you care to know about your Linux system.

This book's focus for your Linux command-line journey is Ubuntu, the community-based Linux distribution sponsored by Canonical Ltd., and the Debian GNU/Linux system on which it is based. Tapping into the skills needed to run those systems can help you to work with your own Linux systems and to learn what you need as a Linux professional.

Ubuntu Takes Linux by Storm

Since its inaugural release in 2004, Ubuntu (www.ubuntu.com) has become the most popular and, arguably, best loved of the Linux distributions. From its name, which translates to *humanity toward others*, to its focus on support for many languages and special needs, Ubuntu has reflected its ideals of spreading free software beyond the standard Linux target markets of geeks and corporate servers.

The Ubuntu project does everything it can to help ease new users into using its Linux-based Ubuntu operating system. Ubuntu live CDs let a new user try out Ubuntu before installing it. If the user likes Ubuntu, a single click can start an Ubuntu install to hard disk. And because Ubuntu is based on Debian GNU/Linux, Ubuntu has been able to make massive amounts of software from the Debian software repositories available free to Ubuntu users.

Although it's true that Ubuntu focuses on ease-of-use desktop systems, that doesn't mean Ubuntu has no commercial Linux value. In fact, Canonical offers paid enterprise-quality support for its systems through its Canonical Global Support Services team (www.ubuntu.com/support/paid). Canonical also offers training courses to help you become an Ubuntu Training Partner (www.ubuntu.com/support/training). In other words, there are professional opportunities for those who learn to operate Ubuntu.

Who Should Read This Book

This book is for anyone who wants to access the power of a Linux system as a systems administrator or user. You may be a Linux enthusiast, a Linux professional, or possibly a computer professional who is increasingly finding the Windows systems in your data center supplanted by Linux boxes.

The bottom line is that you want to find quick and efficient ways of getting Ubuntu and other Debian-based systems working at peak performance. Those systems may be a few desktop systems at work, a file and print server at your school, or a home web server that you're doing just for fun.

In the best case, you should already have some experience with Linux. However, if you are a computer professional with skills managing other types of operating systems, such as Windows, you should be able to easily adapt your knowledge to be able to use the specific commands we cover in the book.

What This Book Covers

This is not a beginner's Linux book. Before you jump in, it would be best if you have a basic working knowledge of what Linux is, how the shell works, and what processes, files systems, and network interfaces are. The book will then supplement that knowledge with information you need to do the following activities:

❑ **Get software** — Ubuntu offers the Add/Remove Applications GUI tool for getting software. With tools such as apt-get, you'll learn the best ways to search for, download, install, update, and otherwise manage software from the command line.

❑ **Use the shell** — Find neat techniques and tips for using the shell.

❑ **Play with multimedia** — Play and stream multimedia content from your computer. You can also modify audio and image files, and then convert the content of those files to different formats.

❑ **Work with files** — Use, manipulate, convert, and secure a wide range of file types in Linux.

❑ **Administer file systems** — Access, format, partition, and monitor your file storage hardware (hard disks, CD/DVD drives, floppy disks, USB flash drives, and so on). Then create, format, and check the file systems that exist on those hardware devices.

❑ **Backup and restore data** — Use simple commands to gather, archive, and compress your files into efficient backup archives. Then store those archives locally or on remote computers.

❑ **Work with processes** — List running processes in a variety of ways, such as by CPU use, processor use, or process ID. Then change running processes to have them run in the background or foreground. Send signals to processes to have them re-read configuration files, stop and resume processing, or stop completely (abort).

❏ **Manage the system** — Run commands to check system resources, such as memory usage, run levels, boot loaders, and kernel modules.

❏ **Monitor networks** — Bring wired, wireless, and dial-up network connections up and down. Check routing, DNS, and host information. Keep an eye on network traffic.

❏ **Get network resources** — Connect to Linux and Windows remote file systems using FTP, NFS, and Samba facilities. Use shell-based commands to browse the Web.

❏ **Do remote administration** — Access and administer other computers using remote login (ssh, telnet, and so on), and screen. Learn about remote administration interfaces, such as Webmin, SWAT, and CUPS.

❏ **Lock down security** — Set up firewalls and system logging to secure your Linux systems.

❏ **Get reference information** — Use the appendixes at the end of this book to get more information about the shell (such as metacharacters and shell variables) and the state of the system (from /proc).

Hopefully, if we have done it right, it will be easier to use this book than to Google for the command lines or GUI tools you need.

After you have mastered many of the features described in this book, you'll have gained the following advantages:

❏ **Hundreds of commands** — By compressing a lot of information into a small space, you will have access to hundreds of useful commands, in over 1000 command lines, in a handy form to carry with you.

❏ **Critical Linux information** — This book lists connections to the most critical information on the Web for succeeding with Linux in general and Ubuntu in particular.

❏ **Transferable knowledge** — Most of the same commands and options you use in Ubuntu will work exactly the same way on other Linux systems. Different Linux distributions, on the other hand, offer different graphical administration tools. And even within a particular distribution, graphical tools change more often than commands do.

❏ **Quick problem solving** — By the time others have started up a desktop and launched a graphical administration tool, you will have already run a half dozen commands and solved the problem.

❏ **Enduring value** — Many of the commands described in this book were used in early Unix systems. So you are gaining tools that reflect the experience of thousands of computer experts for more than 30 years.

Because the full documentation for commands used in Linux consists of thousands of man pages, info text, and help messages, you will surely want to reach beyond the pages of this book from time to time. Luckily, Ubuntu and other Linux systems include helpful information installed on the system itself. Chapter 1 contains descriptions of how to access that information that is probably already installed on your Ubuntu system.

How This Book Is Structured

This book is neither a pure reference book (with alphabetically listed components) nor a guide (with step-by-step procedures for doing tasks). Instead, the book is organized by topics and aimed at including as many useful commands and options as we could fit.

Chapter 1 starts by giving you a basic understanding of what Ubuntu is and how it relates to other Linux systems, such as various Debian-based distributions. Then it describes some of the vast resources available to support your experience with this book (such as man pages, info material, and help text). Chapter 2 provides a quick overview of installation and then describes useful commands such as apt-get for getting and managing your Ubuntu software.

Commands that a regular user may find useful in Linux are described in Chapters 3, 4, 5, and 6. Chapter 3 describes tools for using the shell, Chapter 4 covers commands for working with files, and Chapter 5 describes how to manipulate text. Chapter 6 tells how to work with music and image files.

Starting with Chapter 7, we get into topics relating to system administration. Creating and checking file systems are covered in Chapter 7, while commands for doing data backups are described in Chapter 8. Chapter 9 describes how to manipulate running processes, and Chapter 10 describes administrative tools for managing basic components, such as hardware modules, CPU use, and memory use.

Chapter 11 begins the chapters devoted to managing network resources by describing how to set up and work with wired, wireless, and dial-up network interfaces. Chapter 12 covers text-based commands for web browsing, file transfer, file sharing, chats, and email. Tools for doing remote system administration are included in Chapter 13.

The last chapter (Chapter 14) tells you how to lock down security using features such as firewalls and logging. After that there are three appendixes that provide reference information for text editing, shell features (metacharacters and variables), and system settings (from the /proc file system).

What You Need to Use This Book

Although we hope you enjoy the beauty of our prose, this is not meant to be a book you curl up with in front of a nice fire with a glass of wine. We expect you will be sitting in front of a computer screen trying to connect to a network, fix a file system, or add a user. The wine is optional.

In other words, the book is meant to be a companion as you work on an Ubuntu or Debian operating system. If you don't already have an Ubuntu or Debian system installed, refer to Chapter 2 for information on getting and installing those systems.

All of the commands in this book have been tested against Ubuntu on *x*86 or *x*86_64 architecture. However, because many of these commands have been around for a long time (some dating back over 30 years to the original Unix days), most will work exactly as described here on Debian systems, regardless of CPU architecture.

Many of the commands described in this book will work on other Linux and Unix systems as well. Because this book focuses on Ubuntu, descriptions will differ from other Linux systems most prominently in the areas of packaging, installation, and GUI administration tools.

Conventions

To help you get the most from the text and keep track of what's happening, we've used a number of conventions throughout the book. In particular, we have created styles for showing commands that allow us to fit as many command lines as possible in the book.

With command examples, computer output (shell prompts and messages) is shown in regular monofont text, computer input (the stuff you type) is shown in bold monofont text, and a short description (if included) appears in italics. Here is an example:

```
$ ls *jpg          List all JPEG files in the current directory
hat.jpg
dog.jpg
...
```

To save space, output is sometimes truncated (or skipped altogether). Three dots (. . .) are used to indicate that additional output was cut. If a command is particularly long, backslashes will appear at the end of each line to indicate that input is continuing to the next line. Here is an example:

```
# oggenc NewSong.wav -o NewSong.ogg \
    -a Bernstein -G Classical        \
    -d 06/15/1972 -t "Simple Song"   \
    -l "Bernsteins Mass"             \
    -c info="From Kennedy Center"
```

In the example just shown, you can literally type the backslashes to have all that information included in the single command. Or, you can simply put all the information on a single line, excluding the backslashes.

Although a regular user can run many commands in Ubuntu, to run some commands the user must have root privilege. Because Ubuntu is installed without a root password, you are expected to use the sudo command from an Ubuntu user session to run administrative commands. Here's an example:

```
chris@host1:/tmp$ sudo useradd -m joe
```

For clarity, and to save space, we typically show a regular user prompt as simply a dollar sign ($):

```
$              Indicates a regular user prompt
```

On occasion, you will also see a pound sign prompt (#), indicating that you probably need to run the command with root privilege. So, if you see a # prompt you can either type the sudo command in front of the command line or gain root privilege using one of the ways described in Chapter 3.

Notes and warnings appear as follows:

> **NOTE** *Warnings, notes, and tips are offset and placed in italic like this.*

As for styles in the text:

❑ We *highlight* new terms and important words with italics when we introduce them.

❑ We show keyboard combinations like this: Ctrl+a. If the command requires you to type an uppercase letter, the combination will show this: Ctrl+Shift+a.

❑ We show file names, URLs, and code within the text like so: persistence.properties.

One final technique we use is to highlight text that describes what an upcoming command is meant to do. For example, we may say something like, "use the following command to **display the contents of a file**." Highlighting descriptions in this way is done to provide quick visual cues to the readers, so you can easily scan the page for that command you just knew had to be there.

1

Starting with Ubuntu Linux

Whether you make extensive use of Ubuntu Linux at work every day, or just putter around with it once in a while, a book that presents efficient and comprehensive ways to maintain, monitor, secure, and enhance Ubuntu can be an invaluable resource.

Ubuntu Linux Toolbox is that resource.

Ubuntu Linux Toolbox is aimed primarily at power users and systems administrators. To give you what you need, we will show you how to quickly find and install software for Ubuntu, as well as how to update, maintain, and monitor the health and security of your system. In short, we will show you the most efficient ways of using Ubuntu by working with some of the powerful tools that are at your fingertips.

The goal of this book is to pack as much useful information as possible into a small package that you can carry around with you. To that end, we describe:

❏ **Commands** — Tons of command line examples demonstrate clever and useful ways to navigate the often daunting command line.

❏ **GUI tools** — Quick tips for using graphical interface tools to administer and configure your Ubuntu system.

❏ **Software repositories** — Methods for downloading and installing the software which is custom made for your Ubuntu system.

❏ **Online resources** — Where to find useful and helpful information about Ubuntu, such as mailing lists that you can subscribe to, IRC channels, and other online resources.

❏ **Local documentation** — Tools for working with the man pages, the standard Linux and Unix reference volumes, as well as specific documentation for the software you install.

IN THIS CHAPTER

Introducing Ubuntu Linux

Finding Ubuntu resources

Learning quick and powerful commands

Referencing useful utilities

Working as Linux gurus do

Because this book is for people already familiar with Linux, there won't be a lot of screenshots of icons and menus. What you get instead is the quickest path to using your Ubuntu system to its fullest extent.

What you learn in this book will help you become more adept at working with your Ubuntu or Debian system, as well as Linux in general. If this sounds useful to you, please read on.

Ubuntu, Debian, and Linux

Ubuntu is an operating system based on Debian GNU/Linux (www.debian.org/). Debian has been around since the early 1990s, and because of its maturity, is regarded as a leading Linux distribution in terms of stability and security. Debian is also known for its strict adherence to free software (www.debian.org/intro/free). It is on this foundation that Ubuntu has been formed.

If you think of Linux as a cake in a bakery, the Linux kernel and operating system files would compose the soft spongy cake material itself. Not a whole lot to look at, but extremely functional as far as cake goes. Linux distributions, in contrast, take that spongy cake and add top and bottom borders, colors, tiers, side trim, frostings, flavors, decorations, designs, candles, nuts, and sprinkles. As diverse as cakes are in a bakery window, so are Linux distributions. Ubuntu, designed by the Canonical Group (www.canonical.com/), is the icing and color of a Linux distribution built on top of a Debian cake center.

Debian has given rise to not only Ubuntu, but many other Linux distributions (www.debian.org/misc/children-distros):

❑ Xubuntu — An Xfce-based desktop system based on Ubuntu.

❑ Kubuntu — A KDE-based desktop system based on Ubuntu.

❑ Edubuntu — An Ubuntu derivative focused on schools.

❑ Knoppix — A KDE desktop-oriented live CD based on Debian.

❑ Kanotix — A Debian-based live CD.

❑ Damn Small Linux — A tiny (50MB) live CD based on Knoppix.

❑ Mepis — A desktop live CD based on Ubuntu and Debian.

Xubuntu, Kubuntu, and Edubuntu are the same Debian-based Ubuntu distribution under the hood. The only difference in these is the default desktop they run, or the collection of applications bundled with them. For example, Kubuntu features the KDE Desktop and Adept package manager, which are not installed on Ubuntu. Edubuntu is geared towards educational applications, many of which are not installed by default on the other *ubuntu distros.

Because Debian and Ubuntu are open source systems with many parts built on the GNU General Public License (www.gnu.org/copyleft/gpl.html), anyone is free to take the GPL-based source code, or any part of the GPL'd system, and modify, strip down, build upon, extend, embed, reverse-engineer, and freely distribute those changes or modifications. Generally, the only requirement is that you abide by the terms of the GPL, which basically states that any changes you make to existing GPL works must be made available for others to utilize in the same way (see www.debian.org/social_contract for other licenses Debian recognizes).

In the end, you have not only a superior system with a free, online, worldwide support base, but a product which is constantly evolving and driven by people with a passion for what they do. Many other Linux distributions offer these same advantages; however, Ubuntu has certainly pulled out in front in terms of popularity.

> **NOTE** *Ever wonder where Ubuntu (Edgy Eft) and Debian (Woody) get those odd naming conventions from? Find out at* https://wiki.ubuntu.com/ DevelopmentCodeNames *or* www.debian.org/doc/manuals/project-history/ch-releases.en.html.

Ubuntu Compared to Other Linux Distributions

If you log into the command line of both an Ubuntu system and a Red Hat Enterprise Linux or Fedora system, very little will look different. There are common directories and utilities between the two, and functionality is fundamentally the same. So what makes Ubuntu different from other Linux distributions? One difference is the installer.

The complexity of booting and installing Ubuntu has been narrowed down to a handful of mouse clicks, making many of the install decisions automatic based on assumptions as to what the average user may need and want. In contrast, a Red Hat system presents the user with many install options, such as setting up a workstation or server, individually selecting packages to install, and setting administrative options.

Another major difference among Linux distributions is in software management tools. The aim of the utilities and packaging systems is the same for Debian as for other Linux distributions, however the operation and implementations are significantly different. Ubuntu and most other Debian-based systems use the APT (Advanced Package Tool) family of utilities for managing software. You use APT to install, remove, query, and update Debian (deb) packages. Red Hat uses an RPM packaging system to handle the same tasks with its rpm packages.

Another big difference is the way the systems look in regards to initialization, login screen, default desktop, wallpaper, icon set, and more. From this look-and-feel perspective, there are a lot of differences. Although Red Hat and Ubuntu both use the GNOME desktop as the default Window Manager, the GUI tools used for administering the system and their locations on the drop-down menus are entirely different.

The login screen and autumn-colored theme of a default Ubuntu system set it apart from other distributions as well. When you drop down the menus of an Ubuntu desktop, you are not presented with a huge list of applications and utilities. What you get is a rather simple and elegant mixture of some of the best and most functional applications available for the Linux desktop. This approach is characteristic of Ubuntu and is done with the intent of keeping the user from feeling overwhelmed.

Another unique characteristic of a Ubuntu system is the intentional practice of locking the root user account, and instead implementing the use of sudo (www.gratisoft .us/sudo/intro.html), which allows you to run one command with root permissions, for system administration tasks (see Chapter 3 for details on the sudo command). The root login on a Linux system has privileges that allow unrestrained access to nearly every component of the system. It would be trivial to remove an entire file system as the root user, so Ubuntu tries to limit use of this account to only times when it is prudent. Most Linux distributions require the user to log in or *su* to root to perform administration tasks, however a user on a Ubuntu does this through sudo using their own login password, and not a separate one for the root user.

Ubuntu has unique features that have their advantages and disadvantages, but they are far from limiting. Ubuntu has the tools in place to allow you to customize, modify, experiment, and hack to your heart's content if that is what you want to do. Otherwise, the idea is to be an easily maintainable, secure system with a clear and concise application set which is neither limiting nor overwhelming. This makes Ubuntu a very fluid system so you can jump right in and become familiar with it very quickly.

Finding Ubuntu Resources

The Ubuntu community has a vast pool of knowledge you can draw from in the form of online resources. The following is a list of links to some of the most popular and useful venues.

❑ http://ubuntuforums.org — In this searchable web forum and moderated social network is a diverse, talented, and moderated community of Ubuntu users and support staff. Here people share their success and setbacks with each other as well as offering assistance and guidance. Chances are good that if you're having difficulty with something in Ubuntu, someone has already run into the same problem and found a solution.

❑ www.ubuntu.com/support — This site offers paid support from Canonical Ltd., the company behind Ubuntu. If you don't want to spend time searching through the forums, or waiting for responses, Canonical Ltd. is one avenue for telephone, e-mail, and web support costing around $20 a month. There is also Ubuntu training available aimed at companies and corporate users.

❑ https://help.ubuntu.com — This site contains the official, up-to-date, online documentation for each Ubuntu release. As newer Ubuntu releases come out, you can come here to find out what's new.

❑ http://screencasts.ubuntu.com — View recorded desktop sessions on how to do different things with Ubuntu, from setting up a printer, to setting up Samba file sharing, to installing updates to keep your Ubuntu system in top shape. Ubuntu users are encouraged to join the Ubuntu Screencasts Launchpad Team (https://launchpad.net/~ubuntu-screencasts) to contribute.

❑ https://lists.ubuntu.com/mailman/listinfo/ubuntu-users — Join the Ubuntu-users mailing list and interact with Ubuntu users over e-mail to discuss and solve problems that come up with everything from implementing mysql databases to setting up a problematic network devices. An archive of past threads can be viewed at https://lists.ubuntu.com/archives/ubuntu-users.

❑ https://wiki.ubuntu.com/IRCResourcePage — If you are interested in live IRC chat support, you can visit the Ubuntu IRC resource page to find guidelines, clients, and chat servers which are an available source of support, free at any time. It is advisable to visit the Ubuntu Code of Conduct page (www.ubuntulinux.org/community/conduct/) if you have not taken part in IRC chat before.

If you plan on buying hardware to use with your Ubuntu or other Linux system, these sites may be helpful in determining where to spend your money:

❑ www.linux-usb.org — This web site aims to maintain a working knowledge of USB devices known to be Linux-friendly. There is a search utility where you can plug in the name or model of a manufacturer and get an instant status report on the usability of that device with Linux.

❑ www.linux-foundation.org/en/OpenPrinting — The CUPS (http://cups.org) printing system is the standard printing system used on most Linux systems these days. If your printer model is not listed when you attempt to add a new printer to your Ubuntu system, you may need to search this site for an updated PPD file to add to your CUPS system. Vendors who make Linux-friendly printers can also be found at www.linux-foundation.org/en/OpenPrinting/Database/SuggestedPrinters.

❑ www.sane-project.org — Scanner Access Now Easy (SANE) is a site devoted to the topic of document scanning on Linux. If you are looking for a scanner or multifunction printer, check here to see how well the vendors stack up in terms of Linux support.

❑ http://tldp.org — The Linux Documentation Project is a culmination of Guides, How-To articles, and FAQS covering everything from how to make coffee with Linux to setting up QoS and Traffic Control.

Certainly this is not a complete list, but these are good places to look first. You can also try searching for Linux-related support on a hardware vendor's web site prior to making your purchase. If they intend their hardware to work with Linux, they may have drivers or instructions available. And don't forget the wealth of information you can find by searching for Linux on your favorite search engine.

Lastly, look for a local Linux User's Group (LUG) in your area. A LUG is a local community of people keenly interested in Linux and its implementations. You will find people with a wide range of experience, from system administrators to casual Linux users, to distro maintainers, to CEOs of companies. LUGs generally meet on a regular basis for group discussions and hold presentations to demonstrate ways they've found to implement Linux and other related technology.

Some LUGs sponsor local events like install fests (http://en.wikipedia.org/wiki/Install_fest) or other Linux advocacy–type events. Chances are good that if you ask a question at a LUG meeting, someone (but more likely several) will have an answer. A search engine should help you locate a LUG in your area if you decide to pursue this. Most LUGs have web sites or mailing lists that can be easily found online.

Ubuntu Software

Most Ubuntu software can be found on the Ubuntu package web site (http://packages.ubuntu.com). The standard tools — Synaptic, APT, and Update Manager — are the most common ways of installing software on your Ubuntu system (Chapter 2 provides details on finding and installing software).

Someday though, you may want to experiment and look for software that is not available in the Ubuntu packages. Most packages will have an MD5sum or GPG key you can use to verify that downloaded software hasn't been tampered with (www.debian-administration.org/articles/375). You can also run into compatibility issues with non-standard software, making upgrades a difficult task. The key to experimenting with non-standard software is to test it out in ways that do not alter your system. The following list includes some web sites you can check out to see what other software is out there.

> **WARNING!** *You should be careful about how you go about mixing the software on your Ubuntu system with software from non-Ubuntu sources. We advise you to check carefully the authenticity of anything you download.*

❑ www.happypenguin.org — The Linux Game Tome. A collection of games, games, and more games for Linux, varying from experimental demos to commercial game companies that have provided source code or binaries to run their games under Linux. (Thanks, commercial game companies!)

❑ www.freshmeat.net — Boasts the Web's largest collection of Unix and cross-platform software, themes, eye-candy, and Palm-OS software. It also sports a discussion board for each software entry to facilitate discussions and feedback. These guys have been around for a very long time.

❑ http://sourceforge.net — When open source developers get together to start a new project, many go to SourceForge to get their project hosted there. SourceForge offers web space as well as tools for managing projects, resources, communications, and code. If you are looking for software, certainly try some searching here.

❑ www.linux.org/apps — Linux.org has been around since 1994; it was born out of the need for housing information about the Linux movement. This web site is a growing source of information on everything Linux. The apps section of Linux.org will direct you to a wide variety of software available for Linux systems.

Focusing on Linux Commands

These days, many important tasks in Linux can be done from both graphical interfaces and from commands. However, the command line has always been, and still remains, the interface of choice for Linux power users.

Graphical user interfaces (GUIs) are meant to be intuitive. With some computer experience, you can probably figure out, for example, how to add a user, change the time and date, and configure a sound card from a GUI. For cases such as these, we'll mention which graphical tool you could use for the job. For the following cases, however, you will probably need to rely on the command line:

❑ **Almost any time something goes wrong** — Ask a question at an online forum to solve some Linux problem you are having and the help you get will almost always come in the form of commands to run. Also, command line tools typically offer much more feedback if there is a problem configuring a device or accessing files and directories.

❑ **Remote systems administration** — If you are administering a remote server, you may not have graphical tools available. Although remote GUI access (using X applications or VNC) and web-based administration tools may be available, they usually run more slowly than what you can do from the command line.

❑ **Features not supported by GUI** — GUI administration tools tend to present the most basic ways of performing a task. More complex operations often require options that are only available from the command line.

❑ **GUI is broken or not installed** — If no graphical interface is available, or if the installed GUI isn't working properly, you may be forced to work from the command line. Broken GUIs can happen for lots of reasons, such as when you use a third-party, binary-only driver from NVIDIA or ATI and a kernel upgrade makes the driver incompatible.

The bottom line is that to unlock the full power of your Linux system, you must be able to use shell commands. Thousands of commands are available for Linux to monitor and manage every aspect of your Linux system.

But whether you are a Linux guru or novice, one challenge looms large. How do you remember the most critical commands and options you need, when a command shell might only show you this:

```
$
```

Ubuntu Linux Toolbox is not just another command reference or rehash of man pages. Instead, this book presents commands in Ubuntu Linux by the way you use them. In other words, instead of listing commands alphabetically, we group commands for working with file systems, connecting to networks, and managing processes in their own sections, so you can access commands by what you want to do, not only by how they're named.

Likewise, we won't just give you a listing of every option available for every command. Instead, we'll show you working examples of the most important and useful options to use with each command. Then, we'll show you quick ways to find more options, if you need them, from man pages, the info facility, and help options.

Finding Commands

Some of the commands in this book may not be installed by default on your Ubuntu distro, but will certainly be available through APT or other sources. When you type a command that the bash shell cannot find, you will see an error message similar to this:

```
$ sillycommand
-bash: sillycommand: command not found
```

There are a few reasons why the command not found message is returned:

❏ You may have mistyped the command name ("fat-fingered" it).

❏ The command is not in any of the directories the shell has been instructed to look in (PATH variable).

❏ The command may only be available to root (through the use of sudo or a similar method).

❏ The command, or Ubuntu package containing the command, is simply not installed.

Table 1-1 shows some shell commands you can run on any Linux distribution to check whether the command you typed is on the system. Table 1-2 shows similar commands specific to Ubuntu and Debian systems.

> **NOTE** *You may see an ellipsis (...) used in code output to note where non-essential information has been omitted for the sake of brevity.*

If you find a command listed in the output of apt-cache search or suspect that the command you want is not installed, you can install it from the Internet by running the command

```
$ sudo apt-get install packagename
```

where *packagename* is the name of the package you want to install.

Table 1-1: Generic Linux Commands for Finding Installed Commands

Command and Sample Output	Description
`$ echo $PATH` `/usr/local/sbin:/usr/local/bin:/usr/sbin:/usr/bin:/sbin:/bin:/usr/games`	Show the current PATH.
`$ which mount` `/bin/mount`	Find the first occurrence of the mount command in the PATH.
`$ find /usr -name umount` `/usr/lib/klibc/bin/umount`	Search the /usr file system for a filename or directory named umount.
`$ whereis mount` `mount: /bin/mount /usr/share/man/man8/mount.8.gz`	Show where the first binary and man page are for the mount command.

`$ locate mount`
`...`
`/usr/bin/fdmountd`
	Use the locate command to search its list of (configurable) directories for mount.

`$ apropos umount`
`...`
`umount (8)        - unmount file systems`
	Search the man page descriptions for instances of a keyword; in this example, umount.

`$ man 8 umount` `Reformatting umount(8), please wait...`	View section 8 of the man page for umount (type q to quit).

Table 1-2: Ubuntu/Debian-Specific Commands for Finding Installed Commands

Command and Sample Output	Description

`$ apt-cache search umount`
`gnome-mount - wrapper for (un)mounting and ejecting storage devices`
`--`
	Search the cached list of packages that may contain a command or description of umount.

`$ dpkg-query -S umount`
`...`
`initscripts: /etc/init.d/umountnfs.sh`
`--`
	Search the list of installed packages for the filename umount, revealing the package it is in.

`$ dpkg -L initscripts`
`...`
`/bin/mountpoint`
`--`
	List all the files contained in the initscripts package

`$ sudo apt-get update`
`Password:`
`Get:1 http://security.ubuntu.com feisty-security Release.gpg [191B]`
`...`
`--`
	Refresh the list of cached packages.

Reference Information in Ubuntu

Original Linux and Unix documentation was all done on manual pages, generally referred to as *man pages*. A slightly more sophisticated documentation effort came a bit later with the GNU *info* facility. Within each command itself, help messages are almost always available.

This reference information is component oriented. There are separate man pages for nearly every command installed on the system. Man pages also document devices, file formats, system, developer info, and many other components of a Linux system. Documentation more closely aligned to whole software packages is typically stored in a subdirectory of the /usr/share/doc directory.

Ubuntu compresses much of this documentation, so it needs to be uncompressed before it can be read. You can use the gzip program to do this, but instruct gzip to only print the contents of the file and not decompress the files to disk. Here's the command to unzip the documentation for the mount command:

```
$ gzip -dc /usr/share/doc/mount/README.mount.gz
mount/umount for Linux 0.97.3 and later.
...
```

The man pages, info facility, and /usr/share/doc directories are all available on most Linux systems.

Using help Messages

Nearly all commands on a Linux system print some form of brief usage information if asked to. Frequently, the way to ask for this usage info is by way of the -h or --help argument to the command, and nothing more. The following command shows how to ask the ls command to print its usage information.

```
$ ls --help
Usage: ls [OPTION]... [FILE]...
List information about the FILEs (the current directory by default).
...
```

Since there is so much information printed by the --help flag, you can again use a pager to limit the output to one screen at a time:

```
$ ls --help | more
...
```

> **NOTE** *The* more *command is a popular pager command, which you will find on nearly every Unix system in use. Linux systems favor a command called* less *which is whimsically named and ironically more functional than the* more *command. It allows paging backwards in the output as well as forwards, allows the use of the arrow keys to scroll, and understands vi editor keystrokes for navigating and searching through text.*

The preceding examples show how to output the `ls` command help to the screen. You can also format the help output with the use of the `card` command, which will print directly to the default printer, or can be saved to a Postscript file to be viewed later with something like the `evince` utility, or converted into a PDF file with the `ps2pdf` utility.

Using man Pages

Table 1-1 briefly covered using the `apropos` command for finding the man page section for the `umount` command. You can use the `apropos` command to search the man page database for any keyword or group of characters. The output will show man page sections which contain the word you supply to `apropos`.

```
$ apropos crontab
/etc/anacrontab (5) [anacrontab] - configuration file for anacron
anacrontab (5)        - configuration file for anacron
crontab (1)           - maintain crontab files for individual users (V3)
crontab (5)           - tables for driving cron
```

The `apropros` output here shows the section and man page where the word `crontab` was found. Sections of man pages are ways of grouping man pages by topic. Man pages in section 1 are *Executable programs or shell commands*. Man pages in section 5 fall under the topic of *File formats and conventions*. The man page sections will be the same on all Linux systems, but may vary a bit on other Unix-type systems. You should be able to view the man page for man to find out which sections are represented on the system you're on:

```
$ man man
Reformatting man(1), please wait...
...
```

Table 1-3 shows the section numbers of the manual followed by the types of pages they contain.

Table 1-3: man Page Sections

Number	Types of Pages
1	Executable programs or shell commands
2	System calls (functions provided by the kernel)
3	Library calls (functions within program libraries)
4	Special files (usually found in /dev)

Table 1-3: man Page Sections (*continued*)

Number	Types of Pages
5	File formats and conventions such as /etc/passwd
6	Games
7	Miscellaneous (including macro packages and conventions), such as man(7), groff(7)
8	System administration commands (usually only for root)
9	Kernel routines [Non standard]
. . .	. . .

Given this information, we can see the crontab word we searched for has an entry in section 1 (*Executable programs or shell commands*) as well as section 5 (*File formats and conventions*). We can view the man pages from those sections by passing the section number as an argument to the man command.

```
$ man 5 crontab
Reformatting crontab(5), please wait...
CRONTAB(5)                                              CRONTAB(5)

NAME
       crontab - tables for driving cron

DESCRIPTION
       A  crontab file contains instructions to the cron(8) daemon of
the general form: ``run this command at this time on this date''.
...
```

If we omit the section number, man will return the man page from the first section it finds. In the next example, man returns section 1 of the crontab man pages.

```
$ man crontab
Reformatting crontab(1), please wait...
CRONTAB(1)                                              CRONTAB(1)

NAME
       crontab - maintain crontab files for individual users (V3)
...
```

In addition to section numbers, the man command takes several arguments to perform different tasks. Table 1-4 shows some examples.

Table 1-4: man Command Options

Option	Description
man -a crontab	Shows all man page sections, in succession, for crontab
man 5 crontab	Shows the section 5 man page for crontab
man crontab -P more	Uses the pager program more for paging through the crontab man page
man -f crontab	Equivalent to the whatis command
man -k crontab	Equivalent to the apropos command

The whatis command is another man page searching utility. It is different from apropos in that it only prints man page descriptions that match the keyword you type in. Running the apropos command for the route command returns three different man pages where a reference to the word route was found:

```
$ apropos route
NETLINK_ROUTE (7)      - Linux IPv4 routing socket
route (8)              - show / manipulate the IP routing table
traceroute6 (8)        - traces path to a network host
```

In running whatis for the route command, only the section 8 man page for the route command is returned:

```
$ whatis route
route (8)              - show / manipulate the IP routing table
```

Using info Documents

In some cases, developers have put more complete descriptions of commands, file formats, devices, or other Linux components in the info database, a sort of linked set of online manual pages. You can enter the info database by simply typing the info command or by opening a particular component (use the q key to quit the info utility).

```
$ info ls
```

The previous command shows information on the ls command. You can navigate around the info utility using the up, down, left, and right arrow keys, as well as the Page Up and Page Down keys. Table 1-5 shows more about navigating in info.

Software packages that have particularly extensive text available in the info database include gimp, festival, libc, automake, zsh, sed, tar, and bash. Files used by the info database are stored in the /usr/share/info directory.

Table 1-5: Moving through the info Screen

Keystroke	Movement
?	Display the basic commands to use in info screens.
Shift+l	Go back to the previous node you were viewing.
n , p, u	Go to the node that is next, previous, or up, respectively.
Enter	Go to the hyperlink that is under the cursor.
Shift+r	Follow a cross reference.
q or Shift+q	Quit and exit from info.

Summary

In one short chapter, we've covered some of the differences and similarities of Ubuntu Linux as compared to other Linux distributions and other Unix-like systems. You've learned about several online resources specifically for Ubuntu as well as those for Linux in general.

You found out where to find Ubuntu-specific software as well as other Linux software. You installed a few packages using the Debian Advanced Package Tool (APT) and worked with ways of searching for commands and man pages on the system. You also worked with the stdin and stdout I/O streams by redirecting command output (stdout) to temporary files as well as the input streams (stdin) of other commands.

While you certainly can read this book from cover-to-cover if you like, it was designed to be a reference to hundreds of features in Ubuntu and Debian Linux that are the most useful to power users and systems administrators. Because information is organized by topic, instead of alphabetically, you don't have to know the commands in advance to find what you need to get the job done.

Most of the features described in this book will work equally well in all Linux-based systems, and many will carry over to legacy Unix systems as well.

2

Installing Ubuntu and Adding Software

Time-tested tools for initially installing Ubuntu, and later adding and managing software, include the APT (Advanced Package Tool) and dpkg (Debian package) utilities. These are some of the standard packaging utilities that serve as a back-end to the more familiar Desktop GUI tools for managing software on Ubuntu and other Debian-based systems. These package utilities interact with .deb files from online repositories, or local .deb files you've downloaded and have sitting on your hard disk.

This chapter highlights critical issues you need to know during Ubuntu initial installation. It covers information about online Ubuntu software repositories. Detailed examples of APT, dpkg, and related command line utilities including aptitude are given later in this chapter.

IN THIS CHAPTER

Installing Ubuntu

Working with software repositories

Getting software with APT

Managing software with Debian package tools

Extracting files from other package formats

Obtaining and Installing Ubuntu

Ubuntu and its close cousins Kubuntu, Xubuntu, and Edubuntu are all designed with ease of use and familiarity in transition in mind. These distributions focus on keeping things simple and clean to help smooth out the learning curves when you are adapting to a new system.

The Ubuntu installer (Ubiquity) is a prelude to the simplicity of the Ubuntu system, breaking down the install process into about 10 clicks. Canonical Ltd., the support company behind Ubuntu, has even made it easy for people to obtain installation media by offering to mail CD-ROMs, free of charge if needed (https://shipit.ubuntu.com/login). If you have a fast Internet connection however, you can download one of the many ISO images for free from one of the many mirrors around the world (www.ubuntu.com/getubuntu/downloadmirrors). The list of mirrors is huge to make sure there are plenty of servers available for people to download from. If one is not available, or unresponsive, try another.

The download mirrors can be a bit confusing, so there is also an enhanced download page (www.ubuntu.com/getubuntu/download) available to make things more clear. The current, stable offering at the time of this writing is Ubuntu 7.04 (Feisty Fawn). Ubuntu 7.10 is scheduled for October 2007, so you may have that option available instead. The enhanced download page currently offers the following Ubuntu install media in both Desktop and Server options. The Server option is geared towards people who do not need a full-blown Desktop system.

❏ **Ubuntu 7.04** — The current stable release of Ubuntu. This is the most commonly selected version.

❏ **Ubuntu 6.06 LTS** — The Long Term Support offering of Ubuntu for people who purchase three-year Desktop support, or five-year Server support options.

Other options you need to select on the enhanced download page are:

❏ **Standard personal computer** — This option is the typical choice for most users. 64-bit desktop and laptop CPUs from both AMD and Intel will run this fine if you don't have special RAM or application requirements.

❏ **64-bit AMD and Intel computers** — This option is for computers that have a need for large amounts of RAM, or specifically, a 64-bit platform to run applications.

❏ **Sun UltraSPARC–based** — This is Ubuntu for hardware based on the Sun Micro-systems UltraSPARC RISC platform. A nice alternative to Sun Solaris (works fine on an Ultra 60).

The Alternate Desktop CD option has some extra functionality built in, such as Logical Volume Management (LVM) support (LVM is covered in Chapter 7). If you need LVM, at least at the time of this writing, you will need to check this box. Lastly, click the Download button.

After your download is complete, you may want to browse through the list of mir-rors above and obtain the MD5SUM file for the version of Ubuntu you downloaded (https://help.ubuntu.com/community/HowToMD5SUM). This can help verify the integrity of the ISO image. Most open source software will have such a digital signa-ture available, and we recommend that you verify this prior to installation, or before burning the ISO image to CD-ROM or DVD.

> **NOTE** *If you desire more security for your downloads beyond the MD5 checksums, look at SecureApt. For more information on how APT uses digital authentication and encryption for software packages, visit the SecureApt section on the Ubuntu help web site (https://help.ubuntu.com/community/SecureApt).*

Preparing to Install

If you are going to erase everything on your computer's hard disk and install Ubuntu, you don't have to make preparations for your install in advance. If you want to keep any data from your hard disk, back up that data before proceeding. To keep existing data on your hard disk and add Ubuntu, you may need to resize existing disk partitions and repartition your disk. See Chapter 7 for information on disk resizing and partitioning commands.

Choosing Installation Options

After booting from the Standard Install CD, you will be presented with a menu of options as shown in Table 2-1.

Table 2-1: Boot Options When Installing Ubuntu (Standard CD)

Boot Option	Description
Start or Install Ubuntu	Begin the installation process immediately.
Start Ubuntu in safe graphics mode	Boot your system from CD without using your hard drive if you need to fix something, or want to perform maintenance on drive partitions.
Install with driver update CD	Ubuntu will interrupt the install process to allow you to insert a special driver CD before continuing with the rest of the install.
Check CD for defects	Test the CD for problems, reading the CD to find problems now instead of in the middle of the install.
Memory test	If you suspect there are problems with your RAM, Ubuntu allows you to run Memtest86 (www.memtest.org/) to stress test your RAM to look for errors.
Boot from first hard disk	If you've accidentally booted with the CD-ROM in the drive, simply pick this menu item to boot from your first hard drive.

The alternate install CD has neither safe graphics mode nor the driver update CD option. Instead it offers the menu items in Table 2-2.

19

Table 2-2: Boot Options When Installing Ubuntu (Alternate CD)

Boot Option	Description
Install in text mode	Install using text mode when a VGA subsystem is unavailable or not desired.
Text mode install for manufacturers	Install Ubuntu with an oem (original equipment manufacturer) user account that is used to customize the system. After running a command to remove the oem login, the system is then triggered to ask the user to create an account on the next boot.
Install a command-line system	Install a Ubuntu system with just the basics (servers, firewalls, gateways, low resource systems)

You can find out more about the Ubuntu install methods on the Ubuntu wiki at `https://wiki.ubuntu.com/Testing/InstallMethods`.

Answering Installation Questions

The most common question after booting from an Ubuntu CD is, what next? Most Ubuntu downloads are live CD images. That is, you can run Ubuntu from the CD without installation on your hard disk. When Ubuntu starts up, the next step is to try it out. If you decide to install Ubuntu, click on the Install icon on the desktop. This launches the Ubuntu installation program.

Most of the screens you see during Ubuntu installation are quite intuitive. Table 2-3 offers a quick review of those screens, along with tips where you might need some help.

Table 2-3: Ubuntu Installation Screen Summary

Install Screen	Description
Install welcome	Select your language.
Where are you?	Select your location for a time zone.
Keyboard layout	Select the keyboard layout you want to use.
Prepare disk space	Select Guided partitioning if you want Ubuntu to guess how to layout the disk. Select Manual if you want to determine the partitions yourself. (Note that you will need the Alternate install CD to work with LVM.)
Migrate Documents and Settings	This will save your important information (and users) from Windows and migrate it into Ubuntu.

Table 2-3: Ubuntu Installation Screen Summary (*continued*)

Install Screen	Description
Who are you?	Enter a user name, login name, password, and computer name.
Ready to install.	Select the Advanced button if you want to configure boot loader options and participate in a survey. Click Install to complete the rest of the install process.

If you've booted into the Ubiquity installer desktop for maintenance reasons, you have six terminal sessions available via the Ctrl+Alt+F# combination (F1 through F6) if you just need a shell prompt. Also, as the install progresses, Ctrl+Alt+F8 will show any messages or errors encountered during this process. Use Ctrl+Alt+F7 to return to the Ubiquity desktop session.

Working with Debian Software Packages

If you prefer to use a GUI tool for installing software, the Synaptic Package Manager is available from the desktop or an ssh session using the -X ssh parameter to tunnel X11 (see Chapter 13). The aptitude utility provides a nice curses (text-based) front end to APT when run with no arguments. A front end for the dpkg utility, dselect (www.debian .org/doc/manuals/dselect-beginner), is also available on most Debian system, but can be difficult to learn to operate.

To learn more about the Debian package formats and different package tools, consult the Debian Programmers Manual (www.debian.org/doc/manuals/programmer) and the Debian FAQ (www.debian.org/doc/FAQ/ch-pkg_basics.en.html).

Ubuntu uses the Debian package format (an ar archive, actually), which is a standard method for packaging software for Debian-based systems. By gathering software components in separate Debian packages (.deb extension) the software can not only carry a self-contained archive of the software, it can also hold lots of information about the contents of the package. This metadata can include software descriptions, dependencies, computer architecture, vendor, size, licensing, and other information.

When a basic Ubuntu system is installed, you can add, remove, and otherwise manage .deb files to suit how you use that system. Ubuntu, Kubuntu, Xubuntu, Edubuntu, and most other Debian-based systems will use .deb files to install the bulk of the software on the system. The aptitude tool should work very well for most day-to-day software needs; however, many other tools for managing these packages exist, and you may need to use some of them occasionally.

❑ **APT** — Use APT to download and install packages from online repositories. The APT commands (apt-get, apt-cache, and so on) can be used to install packages locally. However, it's normally used for working with online software.

❑ **dpkg** — Use dpkg to work with .deb files from CD-ROM or other disk storage. The dpkg command has options for configuring, installing, and obtaining information on system software.

❑ **aptitude** — Use aptitude at the command line for working with online repositories. The aptitude tool is recommended as the first choice because it will automatically take care of some of the tasks you must do manually when working with dpkg or APT.

This chapter includes sections on each of these utilities, outlining the most appropriate circumstances for using each tool.

> **NOTE** *For more information on these package tools, visit the APT HOWTO* (www.debian.org/doc/manuals/apt-howto/ch-basico.en.html#s-dpkg-scanpackages) *or consult the man pages for APT and dpkg.*

Ubuntu (and the other *buntu offerings) are installed from a single CD-ROM or DVD. After installing, you can run the apt-cache stats command to report on the total number of packages available:

```
$ apt-cache stats
Total package names : 27748 (1110k)
  Normal packages: 21182
...
```

As you can see, from a bare-bones stock Ubuntu install, there are well over 20,000 pieces of software available. The Debian community is very careful to include only software that is appropriate for redistribution. The Debian Tutorial at www.debian .org/doc/manuals/debian-tutorial/ch-introduction.html points out:

> Although Debian believes in free software, there are cases where people want or need to put proprietary software on their machine. Whenever possible Debian will support this; though proprietary software is not included in the main distribution, it is sometimes available on the ftp site in the non-free directory, and there are a growing number of packages whose sole job is to install proprietary software we are not allowed to distribute ourselves.

The Canonical group holds Ubuntu to similar standards (www.ubuntu.com/ community/ubuntustory/licensing), offering software in four categories: main, restricted, universe, and multiverse (www.ubuntu.com/community/ ubuntustory/components):

❑ **main** — Contains software which is freely distributable and supported by the Ubuntu team. Much of this software is installed when you install Ubuntu.

❑ **restricted** — Contains software that is common to many Linux systems, supported by the Ubuntu team, but may not be under a completely free license.

❏ **universe** — Contains a snapshot of nearly every piece of open source software available in the Linux world and available under licenses which may not be as free as the others. Software in this component is not guaranteed for security fixes or support.

❏ **multiverse** — Contains software which does not meet the *free* concept of software as it applies to the Ubuntu *main* component license policy. Software in this component is not supported in any way and it's up to you to determine licensing validity.

You can find more information on Ubuntu software components on the Ubuntu web site at www.ubuntu.com/community/ubuntustory/components.

Working with Software Packages

The following sections describe the basics of package management, explaining what goes on behind the scenes and how to install packages. Learning this forms a necessary first step prior to moving on to other tools such as aptitude.

The dpkg command is very powerful for installing single deb packages, but will not sift through and install dependencies that are needed by different pieces of software, nor does it care about software repositories, such as the Ubuntu components mentioned above. APT, on the other hand, will resolve and install dependencies and consult the configured repositories, but is not used to install .deb files lying on a hard drive or other local disk.

Handling Locale Error Messages

If you are working at the command line with Ubuntu (Feisty Fawn), you may see a locale error messages like one of these while trying to install packages:

```
perl: warning: Setting locale failed.
perl: warning: Please check that your locale settings:
locale: Cannot set LC_CTYPE to default locale: No such file or directory
```

This seems to be a problem related to the installed language settings, or something with internationalized encoding in general. One workaround you can use to keep things satisfied is to export the LC_ALL environment variable and set it the same as your LANG setting.

```
$ export LC_ALL="$LANG"
```

There are several other possible workarounds on the help sites, but this one will be the easiest to undo in case the cure causes more problems than the condition. It should also work regardless of what language you speak. Note that you will have to run this command every time you open a local or ssh shell. You can automate this task by placing the command in your ~/.bashrc file.

Several other Linux distributions also use packaging systems similar to APT. Red Hat–based/derived distributions (including CentOS, Fedora, and Mandriva) have tools such as yum, rpm, urpmi, and smart to manage software. Although these tools are quite different from the ones Ubuntu uses, the ideas are similar; a configuration file is set up to tell the packaging tool where online to find the latest software packages. The packaging tool then works in conjunction with an installer to get the software on the system.

This system of having an online package fetcher (so to speak) and a back-end packaging tool is a very powerful combination to resolve dependency issues, digitally authenticate software integrity, easily keep a system up to date, and allow distribution maintainers to distribute changes simply and on a large scale.

Enabling More Repositories for apt

In previous releases of Ubuntu, the multiverse and universe repositories were not enabled by default. These repositories now come enabled by default with Ubuntu, so doing updates and searching for software will turn up many more options. One concern you may have, however, is that support, licensing, and patches may not be available for the universe and multiverse repositories. This could be a problem if you are considering an installation where you need to adhere to certain policies and procedures.

To disable the universe or muliverse repositories, open the file /etc/apt/sources .list in a text editor and comment out the lines which have multiverse or universe components enabled. You may want to initial the comments to make note of what you commented out, as shown by the #cn in the following examples:

```
#cn deb http://us.archive.ubuntu.com/ubuntu/ feisty universe
#cn deb-src http://us.archive.ubuntu.com/ubuntu/ feisty universe
#cn deb http://us.archive.ubuntu.com/ubuntu/ feisty multiverse
#cn deb-src http://us.archive.ubuntu.com/ubuntu/ feisty multiverse
#cn deb http://security.ubuntu.com/ubuntu feisty-security universe
#cn deb-src http://security.ubuntu.com/ubuntu feisty-security universe
#cn deb http://security.ubuntu.com/ubuntu feisty-security multiverse
#cn deb-src http://security.ubuntu.com/ubuntu feisty-security multiverse
```

Likewise, if you want to add extra repositories that may be offered by individuals or companies, you can do so by adding a line to the /etc/apt/sources.list file. To edit this file, you must have root permissions:

```
$ sudo vi /etc/apt/sources.list
```

Insert a line starting with deb (for pre-built packages) or deb-src (for source packages), then the URL for the repository, along with the distribution (such as feisty above), and the component descriptions (universe in the examples). Typically, you'll describe components as contrib for contributed (that is, not from the Ubuntu project) and free or non-free. Normally, you should receive all this information from the site that offers the repository.

If you do add other third-party repositories, be sure to look into the authenticity of the entity offering the software before modifying your Linux system. Although it's not a big problem with Linux these days, it is easy to add broken or malicious software to your system if you do not exercise care and reasonable caution.

Only use software from well-known sources, and always have a means to verify software you download prior to installing. For more information on software repositories, see the Debian Repository HOWTO (`www.debian.org/doc/manuals/repository-howto/repository-howto`).

An example from the HOWTO document follows:

```
deb ftp://sunsite.cnlab-switch.ch/mirror/debian/ unstable main contrib non-free
```

Managing Software with APT

Although dpkg and APT work in conjunction with each other, most of the time, APT will suffice for any software you need to install, download, upgrade, check, or search for on any Debian system. Table 2-4 shows how to perform different tasks using the apt commands. For a quick command line reference of apt capabilities, use the –h option on the command line.

> **NOTE** *The aptitude utility is preferred over APT; however, in the interest of fundamentals, we will cover APT first.*

Table 2-4: Some Common Uses of the Advanced Package Tool

APT Command	What It Does
`sudo apt-get update`	Consults `/etc/apt/sources.list` and updates the database of available packages. Be sure to run this command whenever `sources.list` is changed.
`apt-cache search <keyword>`	Case-insensitive search of the package database for the keyword given. The package names and descriptions are returned where that keyword is found.
`sudo apt-get install <package>`	Download and install the given package name as found in the package database. Starting with APT version 0.6, this command will automatically verify package authenticity for gpg keys it knows about (`http://wiki.debian.org/SecureApt`).

Continued

Table 2-4: Some Common Uses of the Advanced Package Tool
(*continued*)

APT Command	What It Does
`sudo apt-get -d install <package>`	Download the package only, placing it in `/var/cache/apt/archives`.
`apt-cache show <package>`	Display information about the software from the named package.
`sudo apt-get upgrade`	Check updates for all installed packages and then prompt to download and install them.
`sudo apt-get dist-upgrade`	Updates the entire system to a new release, even if it means removing packages. *Note:* This is not the preferred method for updating a system.
`sudo apt-get autoclean`	Can be run anytime to delete partially downloaded packages, or packages no longer installed.
`sudo apt-get clean`	Removes all cached packages from `/var/cache/apt/archives` to free up disk space.
`sudo apt-get --purge remove <package>`	Remove the named package and all its configuration files. Remove the `--purge` keyword to keep config files.
`sudo apt-get -f install`	Do a sanity check for broken packages. This tries to fix any "unmet dependency" messages.
`apt-config -V`	Print version information of installed APT utilities.
`sudo apt-key list`	List gpg keys that APT knows about.
`apt-cache stats`	Print statistics on all packages installed.
`apt-cache depends`	Print dependencies for a package (whether it's installed or not).
`apt-cache pkgnames`	List all packages installed on the system.

As an example, we will install the Google Picasa program (http://picasa.google.com/), which is software Google has made available for free as a means for managing and sharing digital photos. In this example, we will install from a third-party software repository, and use some of the APT utilities to verify, query, and install the software.

Adding an APT Repository and Third-Party Signature Key

To get started using the Google repository, bring up the /etc/apt/sources.list file in a text editor (nano, vi) via sudo:

```
$ sudo vi /etc/apt/sources.list
```

Then add the following two lines to the bottom of the sources.list file:

```
# cn - added for google software
deb http://dl.google.com/linux/deb/ stable non-free
```

You also need to **download the Google signing key for authenticating the Google packages** by way of a digital signature. This digital key could be downloaded using wget and placing the downloaded file in the /tmp/ directory for importing as a second step.

```
$ wget https://dl-ssl.google.com/linux/linux_signing_key.pub -O /tmp/key.pub
--08:26:46--  https://dl-ssl.google.com/linux/linux_signing_key.pub
`/tmp/key.pub'
...
```

The wget command (described in Chapter 12) downloads a file from the Google site and places it into /tmp/key.pub. The crucial part here is that this is the public encryption key used to verify the packages downloaded from the Google site.

Then import the key into APT using the apt-key command:

```
$ sudo apt-key add /tmp/key.pub
Password:
OK
```

Check the APT security keys to make sure the Google digital signature was imported correctly (some output omitted):

```
$ sudo apt-key list
...
uid                 Google, Inc. Linux Package Signing Key
<linux-packages-keymaster@google.com>
sub    2048g/C07CB649 2007-03-08
```

Next, **update the APT package cache to refresh the new repository.** This is done using `sudo` and running `apt-get update`. Make sure to check for the Google repository as it scrolls by:

```
$ sudo apt-get update
Get:1 http://dl.google.com stable Release.gpg [189B]
Ign http://dl.google.com stable/non-free Translation-en_US
Get:2 http://dl.google.com stable Release [1026B]
...
```

Finding Packages with APT

Now that a new repository is set up, you can **query for new software** you can add:

```
$ apt-cache search picasa
picasa - Picasa is software that helps you instantly find, edit and share all
the pictures on your PC.
```

You can also **ask APT to show info** about this Picasa package:

```
$ apt-cache show picasa
Package: picasa
Version: 2.2.2820-5
...
```

Just how much extra software will Picasa require to be updated? **Check for dependencies** with the following:

```
$ apt-cache depends picasa
picasa
  Depends: libc6
```

Installing Packages with APT

You can now **install, using sudo, any available software authored by Google** for Ubuntu, using APT or another package tool. This shows Picasa being installed using APT:

```
$ sudo apt-get install picasa
Reading package lists... Done
Building dependency tree
Reading state information... Done
The following NEW packages will be installed:
  picasa
0 upgraded, 1 newly installed, 0 to remove and 115 not upgraded.
Need to get 21.7MB of archives.
After unpacking 82.3MB of additional disk space will be used.
Get:1 http://dl.google.com stable/non-free picasa 2.2.2820-5 [21.7MB]
Fetched 21.7MB in 1m3s (340kB/s)
Selecting previously deselected package picasa.
(Reading database ... 88015 files and directories currently installed.)
Unpacking picasa (from .../picasa_2.2.2820-5_i386.deb) ...
Setting up picasa (2.2.2820-5) ...
```

You can now run the Picasa program by typing `picasa` on the command line, or selecting it from the Applications ⇨ Graphics menu on the Ubuntu desktop.

Upgrading Packages with APT

Over time, packages change, and new versions add neat new features and fix problems. You can use APT to upgrade your system to new versions following a two-step process.

First, **check for updates** to the packages your Ubuntu system knows about using the `update` option to `apt-get`:

```
$ sudo apt-get update
```

This command searches the repositories for new versions of packages available for downloading and updates the list of packages and versions cached on your Ubuntu system.

Second, upgrade the packages on your Ubuntu system by using the `upgrade` option to `apt-get`.

```
$ sudo apt-get upgrade
```

You should always update the package list prior to upgrading packages, so it is a good idea to always run these commands together. Separate the commands with a semicolon to tell the shell to run them both, one after the other:

```
$ sudo apt-get update; sudo apt-get upgrade
Get:1 http://dl.google.com stable Release.gpg [189B]
...
The following packages will be upgraded:
  app-install-data app-install-data-commercial apport apport-gtk bind9-host
capplets-data dbus dbus-1-utils
...
112 upgraded, 0 newly installed, 0 to remove and 3 not upgraded.
Need to get 140MB of archives.
After unpacking 3891kB of additional disk space will be used.
Do you want to continue [Y/n]? n
```

Upgrading a Single Package with APT

Upgrading a single system package on Ubuntu is pretty straightforward using `apt-get install <package>`. You need to run this command with `sudo` to gain root permissions. The old version is automatically updated to the newest one available.

> **NOTE** *It may seem counterintuitive, but the* `upgrade` *option to* `apt-get` *upgrades all packages. The* `install` *option installs a new package or installs an upgrade to one or more specific packages.*

First, **check the version of the currently installed application** (in this example, the minicom application, an application for communicating over serial lines). Like most commands, the minicom program supports an option to display its current version number:

```
$ minicom --version
minicom version 2.1 (compiled Nov  5 2005)
...
```

Now use APT to install the latest version of the minicom package from the repositories. APT tells us we are upgrading a package:

```
$ sudo apt-get install minicom
...
The following packages will be upgraded:
  minicom
```

Now ask minicom for its version again and you can see it has indeed been upgraded:

```
$ minicom --version
minicom version 2.2 (compiled Mar  7 2007)
...
```

Removing Packages with APT

You can **remove a package** from your Ubuntu system by giving apt-get the remove option. You will be prompted to confirm before actually removing the software:

```
$ sudo apt-get remove picasa
Reading package lists... Done
Building dependency tree
Reading state information... Done
The following packages will be REMOVED:
  picasa
0 upgraded, 0 newly installed, 1 to remove and 115 not upgraded.
Need to get 0B of archives.
After unpacking 82.3MB disk space will be freed.
Do you want to continue [Y/n]? n
```

Cleaning Up Packages with APT

After your initial installation of an Ubuntu release, Ubuntu keeps downloaded packages cached in /var/cache/apt/ to speed up downloading if you ever need them again. This can eventually use up a lot of disk space. You can remove this package cache, but you will need to download a removed package again at a later date if it is needed for dependencies. Clean up the cache by giving apt-get the clean option. We show how this works by first running the Linux find command on the /var/cache/apt/ directory to show the packages currently cached:

```
$ find /var/cache/apt/ -name \*.deb
/var/cache/apt/archives/picasa_2.2.2820-5_i386.deb
/var/cache/apt/archives/minicom_2.2-4build1_i386.deb
```

Now clean up all the packages cached in the APT cache directory, and then verify that they are removed by running the find command again:

```
$ sudo apt-get clean
$ find /var/cache/apt/ -name \*.deb
```

The directory is empty now.

> **NOTE** *If you've run the –h option with* apt-get, *you may have noticed that the Ubuntu version of APT has Super Cow Powers. You can find out more about these Powers by asking* apt-get *to* moo.

Managing Software with dpkg

The dpkg utility works at a layer lower than the APT utilities do. APT uses dpkg behind the scenes to manage software on your Ubuntu system. APT and dpkg work similar to the way yum and rpm do on Red Hat–based Linux distributions. Usually, APT will have enough functionality to get you through just about anything, but there are times when dpkg will be needed, such as finding out which package is associated with a given file on your system. Table 2-5 shows some common dpkg commands and operations.

> **NOTE** dpkg *uses the* –D *flag to signify debugging information to be printed while performing various operations. If you want more information than the default output, try* –D1 *with some of the* dpkg *commands. A section in the* dpkg *man page lists output levels for use with the* –D *flag.*

Table 2-5: Some Common Uses of the dpkg Utility

dpkg Command	What It Does
dpkg -c <.deb file>	Lists files which are installed by the .deb file given (.deb file must be path/filename).
dpkg -I <.deb file>	Lists information about the .deb given file.
dpkg -p <package>	Lists information about the package.
dkpg -S <filename>	Lists the packages where the given file name is found. This can be a path, or just the name of a file.

Continued

Table 2-5: Some Common Uses of the dpkg Utility (*continued*)

dpkg Command	What It Does
dpkg -l	Lists installed packages. This will also take options for more specific info.
dpkg -L <*package*>	Lists all the files which have been installed from package (package must have been previously installed).
dpkg -s <*package*>	Lists the status of the given package.
sudo dpkg -i <.deb file>	Installs the given .deb file.
sudo dpkg -r <*package*>	Removes the given package from the system, but leaves files behind.
sudo dpkg -P <*package*>	Removes package and config files of given package.
sudo dpkg -x <.deb file> <*directory*>	Extracts the files contained in the .deb file to a destination directory. Note that this will reset permissions on the target directory.

Using the dpkg command, any user can query the package database. To use the command to install or remove software from your system, you must have root privileges.

Installing a Package with dpkg

The dpkg command focuses just on packages, while apt-get will take care of the messy details of finding out which repository hosts a package and downloading from there. For simplicity, the following example uses apt-get to download a package and then dpkg to install it, just to provide a flavor of the underlying dpkg command.

First, download the .deb file using apt-get. The -d option in the command is for *download only*. This command downloads but does not install the minicom package.

```
$ sudo apt-get -d install minicom
...
Fetched 168kB in 1s (131kB/s)
Download complete and in download only mode
```

This gets you a .deb file to install. The command downloads the package to the /var/cache/apt/archives directory.

Second, install the .deb file using the command dpkg -i (for *install*).

```
$ sudo dpkg -i /var/cache/apt/archives/minicom_2.2-4build1_i386.deb
Selecting previously deselected package minicom.
(Reading database ... 89127 files and directories currently installed.)
Unpacking minicom (from .../minicom_2.2-4build1_i386.deb) ...
Setting up minicom (2.2-4build1) ...
```

Removing a Package with dpkg

To remove an installed package with dpkg, use the -r option as follows:

```
$ sudo dpkg -r minicom
(Reading database ... 89182 files and directories currently installed.)
Removing minicom ...
```

If you want to remove the package and its config files all at once, or remove the config files after removing the package, use the following:

```
$ sudo dpkg -P minicom
(Reading database ... 89126 files and directories currently installed.)
Removing minicom ...
Purging configuration files for minicom ...
```

Extracting Files from a .deb File with dpkg

Debian and Ubuntu packages come bundled into single files, .deb files. Each .deb file contains one or more files that make up the package itself, such as a pre-built command, support files, documentation, and perhaps the source code. So, a .deb file is basically an archive of files that you want to install to your computer, plus some header and control information that identifies the software (descriptions, checksums, build information, and so on). You can extract a lot of this information on a package with the dpkg command. This example extracts the files from the .deb file residing in the current directory for the rsync package to a directory under /tmp:

```
$ mkdir /tmp/rsync_contents
$ sudo dpkg -x rsync_2.6.9-3ubuntu1.1_i386.deb /tmp/rsync_contents
$ ls /tmp/rsync_contents/
etc  usr
```

You can replace the file rsync_2.6.9-3ubuntu1.1_i386.deb in the above command with any .deb file you download.

Querying Information about .deb Packages

The following example shows how to query installed packages for a package named rsync and display version information about that package:

```
$ dpkg -p rsync
...
Version: 2.6.9-3ubuntu1.1
```

Use the -I option to get information about a .deb file in the present directory:

```
$ dpkg -I rsync_2.6.9-3ubuntu1.1_i386.deb
new debian package, version 2.0.
...
```

To page through a list of all packages installed on your system, type the following:

```
$ dpkg -l | less
...
ii  acpi              0.09-1              displays information on ACPI devices
...
```

Or to just see a listing of a specific package use the –l option with a package name:

```
$ dpkg -l rsync
...
ii  rsync            2.6.9-3ubuntu1     fast remote file copy program (like rcp)
```

Check a file on your system to see what package the file belongs to, if any:

```
$ dpkg -S /usr/bin/rsync
rsync: /usr/bin/rsync
```

Now that you know how to select the package(s) you want to query, let's get a little more information out of them. This example lists standard details about an installed package:

```
$ dpkg -s rsync
Package: rsync
Status: install ok installed
Priority: optional
Section: net
Installed-Size: 500
...
```

This lists the content of a .deb file in the local directory:

```
$ dpkg -c rsync_2.6.9-3ubuntu1.1_i386.deb
drwxr-xr-x root/root            0 2007-08-17 20:48 ./
drwxr-xr-x root/root            0 2007-08-17 20:48 ./usr/
drwxr-xr-x root/root            0 2007-08-17 20:48 ./usr/bin/
-rwxr-xr-x root/root       294864 2007-08-17 20:48 ./usr/bin/rsync
drwxr-xr-x root/root            0 2007-08-17 20:48 ./usr/share/
drwxr-xr-x root/root            0 2007-08-17 20:48 ./usr/share/doc/
...
```

This example extracts the control scripts inside a .deb file on disk to a destination directory. Use care when extracting as this command will reset the permissions on the target directory to 0755. (The 55 means that users other than you will have limited permissions on /tmp, and most applications assume they have wide open permissions to /tmp.) For this example, we create the directory /tmp/my_$RANDOM (my_ and a random number) to work in:

```
$ sudo dpkg -e rsync_2.6.9-3ubuntu1.1_i386.deb /tmp/my_$RANDOM
$ ls -lart /tmp/my_25445/
total 28
-rwxr-xr-x 1 root root  491 Aug 17 20:47 prerm
-rwxr-xr-x 1 root root  110 Aug 17 20:47 postrm
-rwxr-xr-x 1 root root  523 Aug 17 20:47 postinst
-rw-r--r-- 1 root root   37 Aug 17 20:48 conffiles
-rw-r--r-- 1 root root  926 Aug 17 20:48 control
drwxr-xr-x 2 root root 4096 Aug 17 20:48 .
```

To **extract all the non-control files** contained in the .deb file to a directory, use the -x option as follows (again, be aware that the directory permissions on the target directory will be reset to 0755):

```
$ sudo dpkg -x minicom_2.2-4build1_i386.deb /tmp/dx_$RANDOM
$ ls -lart /tmp/dx_4921/
total 16
drwxr-xr-x  4 root root 4096 Mar  7 09:10 usr
drwxr-xr-x  3 root root 4096 Mar  7 09:10 etc
drwxr-xr-x  4 root root 4096 Mar  7 09:10 .
drwxrwxrwt 11 root root 4096 Sep  1 08:19 ..
...
```

To **see the installed files a package is using on the system,** use the -L option:

```
$ dpkg -L minicom
/.
/usr
/usr/share
/usr/share/man
/usr/share/man/man1
/usr/share/man/man1/minicom.1.gz
/usr/share/man/man1/xminicom.1.gz
/usr/share/man/man1/ascii-xfr.1.gz
...
```

If the package is not removed completely, you may see some configuration files left over:

```
$ dpkg -L minicom
/etc
/etc/minicom
/etc/minicom/minicom.users
```

These examples cover some of the basic uses for dpkg, but by no means is this an exhaustive list. Other available options include those for reconfiguring packages (dpkg-reconfigure), telling dpkg what packages to ignore (dpkg hold), and setting selection states. Check the dpkg man page for more information.

Managing Software with aptitude

The dpkg and APT tools have been around for a long time and work well, but there are many nuances to both tools that can require a fair amount of understanding to use correctly. The aptitude tool tries to make things easier by automating some of the important package operations (like running apt-get update before upgrading or installing) while allowing enough flexibility to be useful. For these reasons, we recommend the use of aptitude at the command line whenever possible.

The aptitude program aims to be both a curses application and command line tool. It is the command line usage we will focus on in this section. Table 2-6 shows a breakdown of ways to manage software packages with aptitude. Note that most of the options are similar to those of the apt-get command.

> **NOTE** *For more information on navigating the curses interface of aptitude, or other details, visit the Aptitude Survival Guide* (https://help.ubuntu.com/community/AptitudeSurvivalGuide), *or the Aptitude User's Manual* (http://people.debian.org/~dburrows/aptitude-doc/en/), *or run* man aptitude *at the command line.*

Table 2-6: Some Common aptitude Functionality

aptitude Command	What It Does
sudo aptitude	Starts the curses interface. Use Ctrl+t to access the menu and the q key to quit.
aptitude help	Lists help for aptitude usage.
aptitude search <keyword>	Lists packages matching the given keyword.
sudo aptitude update	Updates the available package indexes from the APT sources.
sudo aptitude upgrade	Upgrades all packages in use to their latest versions.
aptitude show <package>	Lists information about the given package, installed or not.
sudo aptitude download <package>	Downloads the given package, but does not install it.
sudo aptitude clean	Removes all downloaded .deb files from the /var/cache/apt/archives directory.

Table 2-6: Some Common aptitude Functionality (*continued*)

aptitude Command	What It Does
sudo aptitude autoclean	Removes all outdated .deb files from the /var/cache/apt/archives directory. This maintains a current cache without filling up the disk.
sudo aptitude install e>	Installs the given package to the system. *Note:* There are several options for selecting specific versions and using wildcards.
sudo aptitude remov age>	Removes the given package from the system.
sudo aptitude dis e	Upgrades all packages to their most recent versions, removing or installing packages as necessary. The upgrade option is advised over dist-upgrade.

Updating ᴀ̶ pgrading Packages with aptiᵗ̶

By default, apt̶ always perform an apt-get update before installing or upgrading. Yo̶ vever, still issue a command to **perform only the update**:

```
$ sudo aptit̶e
Get:1 http:̶.ubuntu.com feisty-security Release.gpg [191B]
Ign http://̶ubuntu.com feisty-security/main Translation-en_US
Get:2 http̶hive.ubuntu.com feisty Release.gpg [191B]
...
```

If you w̶ rade all packages on the system, you can send along the upgrade option with a̶ is will install any new packages waiting in the repositories (in this examp̶ were no new packages on hand).

```
$ su̶ e upgrade
Read̶ ge lists... Done
Bui̶ endency tree
Re̶ e information... Done
R̶ ended state information
̶ ng package states... Done
̶ ag database... Done
̶ es will be installed, upgraded, or removed.
̶ es upgraded, 0 newly installed, 0 to remove and 0 not upgraded.
̶ get 0B of archives. After unpacking 0B will be used.
```

Querying Information about Packages with aptitude

You can search with aptitude using keywords or full package names, just as with the other package tools. Here is a search using the word *minic*, which returns the minicom package and and xfce window manager plug-in.

```
$ aptitude search minic
i   minicom                      - friendly menu driven serial communication
program
p   xfce4-minicmd-plugin         - Mini-command line plugin for the Xfce4 panel
$ aptitude show minicom
Package: minicom
State: not installed
Version: 2.2-4build1
Priority: optional
Section: comm
```

Installing Packages with aptitude

You downloaded a package using apt-get before. Here you use aptitude to do the same thing — download a package without installing it:

```
$ sudo aptitude download minicom
...
Get:1 http://us.archive.ubuntu.com feisty/main minicom 2.2-4build1 [168kB]
Fetched 1B in 0s (2B/s)
```

If you just want to install the minicom package, you can invoke aptitude like this:

```
$ sudo aptitude install minicom
...
Need to get 0B/265kB of archives. After unpacking 1401kB will be used.
Do you want to continue? [Y/n/?] n
```

If there are a series of packages you want to install, you can give aptitude a wildcard to select with. Here, we install any package containing the word *minic* (as with the aptitude search shown above). This also selects all of the dependencies for each package using what aptitude calls a *matcher*. Use the ~n matcher, prefixed to your keyword, to install all packages containing the word *minic*:

```
$ sudo aptitude install "~nminic"
...
The following NEW packages will be automatically installed:
  libxfce4mcs-client3 libxfce4mcs-manager3 libxfce4util4 libxfcegui4-4 lrzsz
xfce4-panel
```

```
The following NEW packages will be installed:
  libxfce4mcs-client3 libxfce4mcs-manager3 libxfce4util4 libxfcegui4-4 lrzsz
minicom xfce4-minicmd-plugin
  xfce4-panel
0 packages upgraded, 8 newly installed, 0 to remove and 0 not upgraded.
Need to get 702kB/967kB of archives. After unpacking 4645kB will be used.
Do you want to continue? [Y/n/?]
```

Removing Packages with aptitude

Removing packages with aptitude is as easy as installing them. Just pass along the remove option:

```
$ sudo aptitude remove minicom
...
The following packages are unused and will be REMOVED:
  lrzsz
The following packages will be REMOVED:
  minicom
0 packages upgraded, 0 newly installed, 2 to remove and 0 not upgraded.
Need to get 0B of archives. After unpacking 1401kB will be freed.
Do you want to continue? [Y/n/?]
```

Cleaning Up Packages with aptitude

As you install things with aptitude, it will always download the .deb file and place it in the directory /var/cache/apt/archives. Over time you will want to purge these files from the cache using the clean option, or at least the autoclean option to save disk space. If you look, you can see there are some files in the cache already:

```
$ ls /var/cache/apt/archives/
lock  lrzsz_0.12.21-4.1_i386.deb  minicom_2.2-4build1_i386.deb  partial
Removing these with aptitude only requires using the clean or autoclean option:
```

```
$ sudo aptitude clean
Reading package lists... Done
Building dependency tree
Reading state information... Done
Reading extended state information
Initializing package states... Done
Building tag database... Done
```

Issuing the ls command again will show that the packages are indeed gone, so if you have a slow connection and it took you a week to download the last updates, you may want to think twice about this or use the autoclean option that only removes outdated packages.

Useful Combinations of Options with aptitude

The −v option **adds verbosity to aptitude operations.** Used multiple times, you can get more than the usual information printed out as the operation executes. If you invoke aptitude with −v, it shows the md5sum of the package. This is a digital fingerprint of sorts that can be used to test if the package has been tampered with or corrupted. **Using −w will offer up even more information:**

```
$ aptitude show -vv minicom
Package: minicom
State: installed
...
Filename: pool/main/m/minicom/minicom_2.2-4build1_i386.deb
MD5sum: c408085cd37dfced2d3060b94ececd46
...
```

You can use the −s option with aptitude to tell it you want to **simulate what would happen without actually performing the operation.** This will work regardless of aptitude operation.

```
$ sudo aptitude -s install minicom
Reading package lists... Done
...
Do you want to continue? [Y/n/?] y
Would download/install/remove packages.
```

Adding the −v option along with −s gives even more output:

```
$ sudo aptitude -vs install minicom
Reading package lists... Done
...
Do you want to continue? [Y/n/?] y
Inst lrzsz (0.12.21-4.1 Ubuntu:7.04/feisty)
Inst minicom (2.2-4build1 Ubuntu:7.04/feisty)
Conf lrzsz (0.12.21-4.1 Ubuntu:7.04/feisty)
Conf minicom (2.2-4build1 Ubuntu:7.04/feisty)
```

If you **don't want to be prompted** to answer the question "Do you want to continue?" you can answer ahead of time by adding the −y option to your command:

```
$ sudo aptitude -vs -y install "~ninc"
Reading package lists... Done
Building dependency tree
Reading state information... Done
Reading extended state information
Initializing package states... Done
...
```

Be very careful with the −y option as there is no undo feature with `aptitude`.

Lastly, `aptitude` −h will return a reference of options that can be used if you need a refresher at any time. Interestingly enough, we find out that the Ubuntu version of aptitude is lacking something:

```
$ aptitude -h
aptitude 0.4.4
...
This aptitude does not have Super Cow Powers.
```

No Super Cow Powers? We are curious, so we ask `aptitude` to moo.

```
$ aptitude moo
There are no Easter Eggs in this program.
```

Easter eggs are items hidden in a program as a sort of surprise. Hmm. Maybe we can use the −v option for added verbosity.

```
$ aptitude -v moo
There really are no Easter Eggs in this program.
```

Maybe we need even more verbosity. We press aptitude for a little more information:

```
$ aptitude -vv moo
Didn't I already tell you that there are no Easter Eggs in this program?
```

We're beginning to see a pattern here. Maybe adding more verbosity will lead somewhere.

Verifying Installed Packages with debsums

There are times when you will question the behavior of a binary or package installed on the system. It may not perform correctly, or may not even start at all. Problems with corrupt packages from unstable network connections or power outages do happen. In addition, malicious users may attempt to replace powerful commands with their own versions to cause further harm. It becomes useful to check the files on the file system against the information stored in the package.

The debsums program is a utility for Ubuntu and other Debian-based systems that checks the MD5 sums of every installed package against the md5sum files found in the /var/ lib/dpkg/info directory.

Install this program with the following command:

```
$ sudo aptitude install debsums
```

Table 2-7 shows some of the most useful options for running debsums. See the man page for debsums to reveal all detailed information.

Table 2-7: Some Common debsums Options

debsum command	What It Does
debsums -a	Checks all files (including configuration files which are, by default, left out).
debsums -e	Checks config files for packages only.
debsums -c	Lists only changed files to stdout.
debsums -l	Lists files that don't have md5sum info.
debsums -s	Lists only errors; otherwise be silent.
debsums <package names>	Lists the packages you want debsums to analyze.

NOTE *For many operations, you won't need to run this utility as root (using* sudo*). Some files may not have read access by regular users, so the use of* sudo *will be required if you get a message like this:* debsums: can't open at file /etc/at.deny (Permission denied).

If you run debsums with no options, it will check every file on the system that it knows about. The output can be redirected to a file if needed for later. The file name debsums prints out will be accompanied by an OK status on the right side of the output if the md5sum checks out for the file. Other messages may be printed out, such as md5sums missing for a certain file, or the word REPLACED if the md5sum does not match. You will need to be wary of false positives. If you want to use this tool as a baseline for assessments at a later date, you will want to get everything set up the way you want and re-generate md5sums for stuff that is missing or incorrect. That way you know you have the latest info.

This command will check every file on the system against the stock md5sum files. You can see there are some missing and replaced files. You would want to verify the system does not already have problems with these files before you re-generate md5sums for everything:

```
$ debsums
/usr/bin/acpi                           OK
/usr/share/man/man1/acpi.1.gz           OK
/usr/share/doc/acpi/README              OK
/usr/share/doc/acpi/AUTHORS             OK
...
```

```
/usr/share/app-install/icons/pybliographic.png          OK
debsums: no md5sums for bsdutils
debsums: no md5sums for bzip2
debsums: no md5sums for cdrecord
...
/usr/share/locale-langpack/en_AU/LC_MESSAGES/adduser.mo      REPLACED
/usr/share/locale-langpack/en_AU/LC_MESSAGES/alsa-utils.mo   OK
...
```

If you want to save this info to a file, and to save stdout and stderr messages, **redirect both stdout and stderr streams into a file.** We also background the command with a final ampersand so we can continue working at the shell:

```
$ debsums &> /tmp/foo &
```

To **check the configuration files distributed with each package for changes,** run debsums with the –a option:

```
$ debsums -a
/usr/bin/acpi                       OK
/usr/share/man/man1/acpi.1.gz       OK
...
```

To **only check configuration files, and ignore everything else,** use the –e option. This is a good way to tell if you have inadvertently edited a config file you didn't want to. You can see some of the X configuration files have been changed.

```
$ debsums -e
...
/etc/X11/Xresources/x11-common                          OK
/etc/X11/Xsession                                       FAILED
/etc/X11/rgb.txt                                        OK
/etc/init.d/x11-common                                  OK
/etc/X11/Xsession.d/50x11-common_determine-startup      OK
/etc/X11/Xsession.d/30x11-common_xresources             OK
/etc/X11/Xsession.d/20x11-common_process-args           OK
/etc/X11/Xsession.options                               FAILED
...
```

As debsums spits out a lot of information, you may want to **see only changed files.** Issuing debsums with the –c options will do that:

```
$ debsums -c
debsums: no md5sums for at
debsums: no md5sums for base-files
debsums: no md5sums for bc
...
```

With the preceding command, you will see messages being printed for files that have no md5sum info. You can **check for files that have no md5sum info** by running `debsums` with the `-l` option:

```
$ debsums -l
at
base-files
bc
binutils
binutils-static
...
```

If you want `debsums` to show only errors, use the `-s` option to **tell debsums to be silent except for errors:**

```
$ debsums -s
debsums: no md5sums for at
debsums: no md5sums for base-files
debsums: no md5sums for bc
debsums: no md5sums for binutils
...
```

To **check a specific package**, give `debsums` a package name as an argument:

```
$ debsums coreutils
/bin/cat                              OK
/bin/chgrp                            OK
/bin/chmod                            OK
...
```

This will check only the files listed in that package's md5sum file in the `/var/lib/dpkg/info` directory, so if the package does not come with an md5sum file, you will get an error:

```
$ debsums rsync
debsums: no md5sums for rsync
```

To generate the missing md5sums data for rsync, use a combination of `dpkg`, the md5sum utility, and a little shell scripting. First, use `dpkg -L` to ask for a list of all the files `dpkg` knows about, in the rsync package. The list `dpkg` returns will have other lines of data in it besides just the file names, so we pipe that output to `grep` and filter out everything that does not start with a slash. On the second line, we have the shell test whether the line of output from `dpkg` is a directory or a file (directories start with a slash also). If it is a file, `md5sum` is run on the line of output, which at this point should just be a file name. Lastly, all output at the third line is saved into a text file with the same naming convention as the md5sum files in the `/var/lib/dpkg/info` directory.

```
$ for file in `dpkg -L rsync | grep ^/`; do
test -f "$file" && md5sum "$file";
done > /tmp/rsync.md5sums
```

What you gain from this command is an md5sum database you can burn to CD-ROM and use to check your system. If the md5sums are on CD-ROM, they cannot be deleted accidentally, or be subject to file system problems of a hard disk. If you want to check your md5sums at a later time, you can use the md5sum command with the -c option and feed it the file name of the md5sum data:

```
$ md5sum -c /tmp/rsync.md5sums
/usr/bin/rsync: OK
/usr/share/doc/rsync/examples/rsyncd.conf: OK
/usr/share/doc/rsync/README.gz: OK
/usr/share/doc/rsync/TODO.gz: OK
. . .
```

To use the rsync.md5sum file with debsums, we need to make one modification that will cause problems for md5sum, but is necessary for use with debsums, and that is removing the leading slash in the file name. We can do this in a text editor, or with a little more shell scripting:

```
$ cat /tmp/rsync.md5sums
302916114c29191cd9c8cb51d67ee60a  /usr/bin/rsync
. . .
```

To remove the leading slash in front of /usr/bin/rsync, you could use a text editor or just use the Stream Editor (sed) to do this:

```
$ sed -e 's# /# #g' /tmp/rsync.md5sums > /tmp/rsync.debsums
$ cat /tmp/rsync.debsums
302916114c29191cd9c8cb51d67ee60a  usr/bin/rsync
```

With the leading slash removed, you can now copy rsync.debsums into the /var/lib/dpkg/info directory and debsums will be able to use it:

```
$ sudo mv /tmp/rsync.debsums /var/lib/dpkg/info/rsync.md5sums
$ debsums rsync
/usr/bin/rsync                                          OK
/usr/share/doc/rsync/examples/rsyncd.conf              OK
/usr/share/doc/rsync/README.gz                         OK
. . .
```

Building deb Packages

By rebuilding the .deb file that is used to build a Debian package, you can change it to better suit the way you use the software (for example, including an md5sum file). To begin, you need to extract a .deb file that you want to modify into a working directory. You then modify the file tree and control files to suit your needs.

For example, you could download and extract the rsync package and control files into the current directory by typing the following commands (your $RANDOM directory will be different of course):

```
$ aptitude download rsync
```

Then extract the package contents and the control files from the downloaded file. Note that the $RANDOM directory is found by typing /tmp/rsync_ and pressing Tab:

```
$ sudo dpkg -x rsync_2.6.9-3ubuntu1.1_i386.deb /tmp/rsync_$RANDOM
$ sudo dpkg -e rsync_2.6.9-3ubuntu1.1_i386.deb /tmp/rsync_17197/
```

Now change to your package directory, where you extracted the .deb file to, and have a look around. You should see a directory structure that looks very similar to this:

```
$ cd /tmp/rsync_17197
$ ls -lart
-rwxr-xr-x  1 root root   491 2007-08-17 20:47 prerm
-rwxr-xr-x  1 root root   110 2007-08-17 20:47 postrm
-rwxr-xr-x  1 root root   523 2007-08-17 20:47 postinst
drwxr-xr-x  4 root root  4096 2007-08-17 20:48 usr
drwxr-xr-x  4 root root  4096 2007-08-17 20:48 etc
-rw-r--r--  1 root root    37 2007-08-17 20:48 conffiles
-rw-r--r--  1 root root   985 2007-09-02 12:02 control
drwxr-xr-x  4 root root  4096 2007-09-02 12:02 .
drwxrwxrwt 10 root root  4096 2007-09-02 13:24 ..
```

Now you have to configure the package directory to fit the formats that dpkg will want for building the .deb file. This involves creating a subdirectory named rsync_2.6.9-3cn1.1/DEBIAN and moving the install files into it. The control file itself is a specially formatted file that contains header and content fields and is parsed by the package tools to print out information about the package:

```
$ sudo mkdir -p rsync_2.6.9-3cn1.1/DEBIAN
$ sudo mv control conffiles prerm postrm postinst rsync_2.6.9-3cn1.1/DEBIAN
```

You also need to move the etc/ and usr/ directories under the rsync_2.6.9-3cn1.1 directory:

```
$ sudo mv usr etc rsync_2.6.9-3cn1.1
```

You should end up with everything filed away correctly, and all that is left is the rsync_2.6.9-3cn1.1 directory in your current directory.

Now move the md5sums file you made earlier into your DEBIAN subdirectory and rename it to md5sums. This will allow debsums to have some md5sums to check:

```
$ sudo mv /var/lib/dpkg/info/rsync.md5sums rsync_2.6.9-3cn1.1/DEBIAN/md5sums
```

Now edit the control file to modify some of the information. You certainly don't want to install your modified version of rsync with the same package info as the original. Open the control file in vi or another editor and change the Version line to reflect the one below. You will notice the word Version has a colon after it; this is the header field. The information field follows right after it. Be sure to maintain the space after the colon, and do not put any extra carriage returns or spaces in the file. It is very picky about formatting.

```
$ sudo vi rsync_2.6.9-3cn1.1/DEBIAN/control
...
Version: 2.6.9-3cn1.1
...
```

A little farther down, you can add to the Description field. This will show up in the descriptions whenever someone views the package details. Notice the space right before the words fast remote .... The space is part of the special formatting and is how dpkg tells the description text from the multiline header. Be sure to put a space in the first column if you wrap the description to the next line:

```
...
Description: Modified by CN 2007-09-02 to include md5sums.
 fast remote file copy program (like rcp)
...
```

Now build your new package using dpkg -b and the name of the control file subdirectory you created. You will get a warning about Original-Maintainer being a user-defined field. You can safely ignore the warning.

```
$ sudo dpkg -b rsync_2.6.9-3cn1.1
warning, `rsync_2.6.9-3cn1.1/DEBIAN/control' contains user-defined field
`Original-Maintainer'
dpkg-deb: building package `rsync' in `rsync_2.6.9-3cn1.1.deb'.
dpkg-deb: ignoring 1 warnings about the control file(s)
```

You now have a new .deb file and can ask dpkg to display information about it. Just run dpkg with the -I option to see the new package info:

```
$ dpkg -I rsync_2.6.9-3cn1.1.deb
 new debian package, version 2.0.
 size 1004 bytes: control archive= 712 bytes.
    970 bytes,    21 lines      control
 Package: rsync
 Version: 2.6.9-3cn1.1
...
```

You could install the new rsync package at this point. This exercise is mainly a demonstration for building a custom package, not necessarily for hacking up the system needlessly. Nonetheless, the following code shows that this package will install and act like a regular Debian package. You want debsums to work also. Notice dpkg tells you about the downgrade:

```
$ sudo dpkg -i rsync_2.6.9-3cn1.1.deb
dpkg - warning: downgrading rsync from 2.6.9-3ubuntu1 to 2.6.9-3cn1.1.
(Reading database ... 88107 files and directories currently installed.)
```

```
Preparing to replace rsync 2.6.9-3ubuntu1 (using rsync_2.6.9-3cn1.1.deb) ...
Unpacking replacement rsync ...
Setting up rsync (2.6.9-3cn1.1) ...
```

The debsums utility now has some md5sum files to test with, and anywhere your new rsync package is installed, this will be the same:

```
$ debsums rsync
/usr/bin/rsync                                      OK
/usr/share/doc/rsync/examples/rsyncd.conf          OK
/usr/share/doc/rsync/README.gz                     OK
...
```

You can also ask dpkg to list your rsync package using the -l option to confirm that the new version is installed:

```
$ dpkg -l rsync
...
ii  rsync    2.6.9-3cn1.1  Modified by CN 2007-09-02 to include md5sums.
```

> **NOTE** *You can find out more about building* .deb *files by visiting the Debian Binary Package Building HOWTO* (http://tldp.org/HOWTO/Debian-Binary-Package-Building-HOWTO). *The* dpkg-deb *man page is also a good source of info on deb package building.*

Summary

Software for Ubuntu and other Debian-based distributions is packaged in the deb format. The Ubiquity installer is used to initially install Ubuntu. From the Boot menu, you can boot into a full Ubuntu environment and install from there, or run Ubuntu from a CD-ROM. To install additional software, you can use the aptitude and APT utilities to get packages from online repositories. To install packages locally, as well as build custom Debian packages, you can use the dpkg utility. APT, aptitude, and dpkg all offer a means to query software. You can verify installed packages by using the debsums and md5sum utilities.

3

Using the Shell

The use of a shell command interpreter (usually just called a shell) dates back to the early days of the first Unix systems. Besides its obvious use of running commands, shells have many built-in features such as environment variables, aliases, and a variety of functions for programming. Although the shell used most often with Linux systems is called the Bourne Again Shell (bash), other shells are available as well (such as sh, csh, ksh, tcsh, and others). In many cases, these shells, such as sh, are really symbolic links to other shell programs, such as bash. On Ubuntu Linux, sh is a symbolic link to /bin/dash. The sh shell is important as it is called in most shell scripts as the shell to run scripts. For interactive usage, bash forms the default shell.

IN THIS CHAPTER

Accessing the shell

Using command history and completion

Assigning aliases

Gaining super user access

Writing simple shell scripts

This chapter offers information that will help you use Linux shells, in general, and the bash shell, in particular.

Terminal Windows and Shell Access

The most common way to access a shell from a Linux graphical interface is using a Terminal window. From a graphical interface, you can often access virtual terminals to get to a shell. With no graphical interface, with a text-based login you are typically dropped directly to a shell after login.

Using Terminal Windows

To open a Terminal window from GNOME (the default Ubuntu desktop), select Applications ⇨ Accessories ⇨ Terminal. This opens a gnome-terminal window, displaying a bash shell prompt. Figure 3-1 shows an example of a gnome-terminal window.

Commands shown in Figure 3-1 illustrate that the *current shell* is the bash shell (/bin/bash), the *current user* is the desktop user who launched the window (chris), and the *current directory* is that user's home directory (/home/chris). The user name (chris) and hostname (localhost) appear in the title bar.

Figure 3-1: Type shell commands into a gnome-terminal window.

The gnome-terminal window not only lets you access a shell, it also has controls for managing your shells. For example, click File ⇨ Open Tab to open another shell on a different tab, click File ⇨ Open Terminal to open a new Terminal window, or select Terminal ⇨ Set Title to set a new title in the title bar.

You can also use control key sequences to work with a Terminal window. Open a shell on a new tab by typing Shift+Ctrl+t, open a new Terminal window with Shift+Ctrl+n, close a tab with Shift+Ctrl+w, and close a Terminal window with Shift+Ctrl+q. Highlight text and copy it with Shift+Ctrl+c, then paste it in the same or different window with Shift+Ctrl+v or by clicking the center button on your mouse.

> **NOTE** *In most applications, such as the OpenOffice.org word processor, Ctrl+c, not Shift+Ctrl+c, invokes the copy function, and Ctrl+v, not Shif+Ctrl+v, invokes the paste function. Because Ctrl+c means something special in a shell window (sending a signal to a program that normally causes it to die), the gnome-terminal window maps the expected graphical desktop functions using the Shift key as a modifier.*

Other key sequences for controlling Terminal windows include pressing F11 to show the window in *full screen mode*. Type Ctrl+Shift++ to zoom in (make text larger) or Ctrl+- (that's Ctrl and a minus sign) to zoom out (make text smaller). Switch among tabs using Ctrl+PageUp and Ctrl+PageDown (previous and next tab), or use Alt+1, Alt+2, Alt+3, and so on to go to tab one, two, or three (and so on). Type Ctrl+d to exit the shell, which closes the current tab or entire Terminal window (if it's the last tab).

The gnome-terminal window also supports profiles (select Edit ⇨ Current Profile). Some profile settings are cosmetic (*allow bold text, cursor blinks, terminal bell, colors, images,* and *transparency*). Other settings are functional. For example, by default, the terminal saves 500 scrollback lines (318 kilobytes). Some people like to be able to scroll back further and are willing to give up more memory to allow that.

If you launch gnome-terminal manually, you can add options. Here are some examples:

```
$ gnome-terminal -x alsamixer          Start terminal with alsamixer displayed
$ gnome-terminal --tab --tab --tab     Start a terminal with three open tabs
$ gnome-terminal --geometry 80x20      Start terminal 80 characters by 20 lines
$ gnome-terminal --zoom=2              Start terminal with larger font
```

Besides gnome-terminal, there are many other terminal windows you can use. Here are some examples: xterm (basic terminal emulator that comes with the X Window System), aterm (terminal emulator modeled after the Afterstep XVT VT102 emulator), and konsole (terminal emulator delivered with the KDE desktop). The Enlightenment desktop project offers the eterm terminal (which includes features such as message logs on the screen background).

Using Virtual Terminals

When Ubuntu boots in multi-user mode (runlevel 2, 3, or 5), six virtual consoles (known as *tty1* through *tty6*) are created with text-based logins. If an X Window System desktop is running, X is probably running in virtual console 7. If X isn't running, chances are you're looking at virtual console 1.

From X, you can **switch to another virtual console** with Ctrl+Alt+F1, Ctrl+Alt+F2, and so on up to 6. From a text virtual console, you can switch using Alt+F1, Alt+F2, and so on. Press Alt+F7 to return to the X GUI. Each console allows you to log in using different user accounts. Switching to look at another console doesn't affect running processes in any of them. When you switch to virtual terminal one through six, you see a login prompt similar to the following:

```
Ubuntu 7.04 localhost tty2

localhost login:
```

Separate getty processes manage each virtual terminal. Type this command to see what getty processes look like before you log in to any virtual terminals:

```
$ ps awx | grep -v grep | grep getty
  4366 tty4     Ss+   0:00 /sbin/getty 38400 tty4
  4367 tty5     Ss+   0:00 /sbin/getty 38400 tty5
  4372 tty2     Ss+   0:00 /sbin/getty 38400 tty2
  4373 tty3     Ss+   0:00 /sbin/getty 38400 tty3
  4374 tty1     Ss+   0:00 /sbin/getty 38400 tty1
  4375 tty6     Ss+   0:00 /sbin/getty 38400 tty6
```

After I log in on the first console, getty handles my login, and then fires up a bash shell:

```
$ ps awx | grep -v grep | grep tty
  4366 tty4     Ss+   0:00 /sbin/getty 38400 tty4
  4367 tty5     Ss+   0:00 /sbin/getty 38400 tty5
  4372 tty2     Ss    0:00 /bin/login --
  4373 tty3     Ss+   0:00 /sbin/getty 38400 tty3
  4374 tty1     Ss+   0:00 /sbin/getty 38400 tty1
  4375 tty6     Ss+   0:00 /sbin/getty 38400 tty6
  7214 tty2     S+    0:00 -bash
```

Virtual consoles are configured in the /etc/event.d directory. A script appears for each virtual console, such as tty1 for the tty1 console, tty2 for the tty2 console, and so on.

NOTE *Most other versions of Linux configure the consoles in one file,* /etc/ inittab. *The init daemon uses* /etc/inittab *as its configuration file. Ubuntu Linux, on the other hand, replaces init with a new program called upstart, which uses the* /etc/event.d *directory to hold its configuration files.*

Using the Shell

After you open a shell (whether from a text-based login or Terminal window), the shell environment is set up based on the user who started the shell. Bash shell settings for all users' shells are located in a number of files. You can make your own versions of these files to override the system settings. There are two types of files holding these settings: startup files and initialization files.

Bash runs startup files for any shell that is a login shell. These files define settings that apply across your entire login. Bash runs initialization files for shells run interactively — that is, not running a shell script.

Bash looks for startup files in /etc/profile (system-wide) or for personal settings in several dot files in the user's home directory (if they exist): .bash_profile, .bash_login, and .profile.

NOTE *Other versions of Linux store the system-wide files in* /etc/profile *and* /etc/profile.d/.

Bash looks for initialization files in /etc/bash.bashrc (system-wide) or for personal settings in .bashrc in your home directory.

NOTE *Other versions of Linux store the system-wide files in* /etc/bashrc.

When a shell is closed, any commands in the user's ~/.bash_logout file are executed. Changing settings in these files permanently changes the user's shell settings but does not affect shells that are already running. (Other shells use different configuration files.)

There are a variety of ways in which you can list and change your shell environment. One of the biggest ways is to change which user you are; in particular, to become the super user (see "Acquiring Super User Power" later in this chapter).

Using Bash History

The Bourne Again Shell (bash) is the shell used by default by most modern Linux systems and quite a few other operating systems such as Mac OS X. Built into bash, as with other shells, is a history feature that lets you review, change, and reuse commands that you have run in the past. This can prove very helpful as many Linux commands are long and complicated.

When bash starts, it reads the ~/.bash_history file and loads it into memory. This file is set by the value of $HISTFILE.

> **NOTE** *See the section "Using Environment Variables" later in this chapter for more on how to work with shell environment variables such as* $HISTFILE.

During a bash session, commands are added to history in memory. When bash exits, history in memory is written back to the .bash_history file. The **number of commands held in history during a bash session** is set by $HISTSIZE, while the **number of commands actually stored in the history file** is set by $HISTFILESIZE:

```
$ echo $HISTFILE $HISTSIZE $HISTFILESIZE
/home/fcaen/.bash_history 500 500
```

To **list the entire history**, type history. To **list a previous number of history commands**, follow history with a number. This lists the previous five commands in your history:

```
$ history 5
975  mkdir extras
976  mv *doc extras/
977  ls -CF
978  vi house.txt
979  history
```

To **move among the commands** in your history, use the up arrow and down arrow. Once a command is displayed, you can use the keyboard to **edit the current command** like any other command: left arrow, right arrow, Delete, Backspace, and so on. Here are some other ways to recall and run commands from your bash history:

```
$ !!                    Run the previous command
$ !997                  Run command number 997 from history
ls -CF
$ !997 *doc             Append *doc to command 997 from history
ls -CF *doc
$ !?CF?                 Run previous command line containing the CF string
ls -CF *doc
$ !ls                   Run the previous ls command
ls -CF *doc
$ !ls:s/CF/1            Run previous ls command, replacing CF with 1
ls -1 *doc
```

Another way to **edit the command history** is using the fc command. With fc, you open the chosen command from history using the vi editor. The edited command runs when you exit the editor. Change to a different editor by setting the FCEDIT variable (for example, FCEDIT=gedit) or on the fc command line. For example:

```
$ fc 978                Edit command number 978, then run it
$ fc                    Edit the previous command, then run it
$ fc -e /usr/bin/nano 989   Use nano to edit command 989
```

Use Ctrl+r to **search for a string in history**. For example, typing Ctrl+r followed by the string ss resulted in the following:

```
# <Ctrl+r>
(reverse-i-search)`ss': sudo /usr/bin/less /var/log/messages
```

Press Ctrl+r repeatedly to **search backwards through your history list** for other occurrences of the ss string.

> **NOTE** *By default, bash command history editing uses emacs-style commands. If you prefer the vi editor, you can use vi-style editing of your history by using the* set *command to set your editor to vi. To do that, type the following:* set -o vi.

Using Command Line Completion

You can use the Tab key to complete different types of information on the command line. Here are some examples where you type a partial name, followed by the Tab key, to **have bash try to complete the information you want** on your command line:

```
$ tracer<Tab>         Command completion: Completes to traceroute command
$ cd /home/ch<Tab>    File completion: Completes to /home/chris directory
$ cd ~jo<Tab>         User homedir completion: Completes to /home/john
$ echo $PA<Tab>       Env variable completion: Completes to $PATH
$ ping <Alt+@><Tab>   Host completion: Show hosts from /etc/hosts
@davinci.example.com  @ritchie.example.com  @thompson.example.com
@localhost            @zooey
```

Redirecting stdin and stdout

Typing a command in a shell makes it run interactively. The resulting process has two output streams: stdout for normal command output and stderr for error output. In the following example, when /tmpp isn't found, an error message goes to stderr but output from listing /tmp (which is found) goes to stdout:

```
$ ls /tmp /tmpp
ls: /tmpp: No such file or directory
/tmp/:
gconfd-fcaen  keyring-b41WuB  keyring-ItEWbz  mapping-fcaen  orbit-fcaen
```

By default, all output is directed to the screen. Use the greater-than sign (>) to **direct output to a file**. More specifically, you can direct the standard output stream (using >) or standard error stream (using 2>) to a file. Here are examples:

```
$ ls /tmp /tmmp > output.txt
ls: /tmpp: No such file or directory
```

```
$ ls /tmp /tmmp 2> errors.txt
/tmp/:
gconfd-fcaen  keyring-b41WuB  keyring-ItEWbz  mapping-fcaen  orbit-fcaen

$ ls /tmp /tmmp 2> errors.txt > output.txt

$ ls /tmp /tmmp > everything.txt 2>&1
```

In the first example, stdout is redirected to the file output.txt, while stderr is still directed to the screen. In the second example, stderr (stream 2) is directed to errors.txt whereas stdout goes to the screen. In the third example, the first two examples are combined. The last example directs both streams to the everything.txt file. **To append to a file** instead of overwriting it, use two greater-than signs:

```
$ ls /tmp >> output.txt
```

If you don't ever want to see an output stream, you can simply **direct the output stream to a special bit bucket file** (/dev/null):

```
$ ls /tmp 2> /dev/null
```

> **TIP**   *Another time you may want to redirect stderr is when you run jobs with crontab. You could redirect stderr to a mail message that goes to the crontab's owner. That way any error messages can be sent to the person running the job.*

Just as you can direct standard output from a command, you can also **direct standard input to a command**. For example, the following command e-mails the /etc/hosts file to the user named chris on the local system:

```
$ mail chris < /etc/hosts
```

Using pipes, you can **redirect output from one process to another process** rather than just files. Here is an example where the output of the ls command is piped to the sort command to have the output sorted:

```
$ ls /tmp | sort
```

In the next example, a **pipe and redirection are combined** (the stdout of the ls command is sorted and stderr is dumped to the bit bucket):

```
$ ls /tmp/ /tmmp 2> /dev/null | sort
```

Pipes can be used for tons of things:

```
$ dpkg-query -l | grep -i sql | wc -l
$ ps auwx | grep firefox
$ ps auwx | less
$ whereis -m bash | awk '{print $2}'
```

The first command line in the preceding code lists all installed packages, grabs those packages that have sql in them (regardless of case), and does a count of how many lines are left (effectively counting packages with sql in the name). The second command line displays Firefox processes taken from the long process list (assuming the Firefox web browser is running), as well as any process whose command line references firefox, such as the command issued in this example. The third command line lets you page through the process list. The last line displays the word bash: followed by the path to the bash man page, and then displays only the path to the man page (the second element on the line).

Using backticks, you can **execute one section of a command line first and feed the output of that command to the rest of the command line.** Here are examples:

```
$ dpkg-query -S `which ps`
$ ls -l `which bash`
```

The first command line in the preceding example finds the full path of the ps command and finds the package that contains that ps command. The second command line finds the full path to the bash command and does a long list (ls -l) of that command.

A more advanced and powerful way to **take the output of one command and pass it as parameters to** another is with the xargs command. For example:

```
$ ls /bin/b* | xargs dpkg-query -S
```

To display the command xargs is going to run, use the following:

```
$ ls /bin/b* | xargs -t dpkg-query -S
dpkg-query -S /bin/bash /bin/bunzip2 /bin/bzcat /bin/bzcmp /bin/bzdiff
/bin/bzegrep /bin/bzexe /bin/bzfgrep /bin/bzgrep /bin/bzip2 /bin/bzip2recover
/bin/bzless /bin/bzmore
bash: /bin/bash
bzip2: /bin/bunzip2
bzip2: /bin/bzcat
bzip2: /bin/bzcmp
bzip2: /bin/bzdiff
bzip2: /bin/bzegrep
bzip2: /bin/bzexe
bzip2: /bin/bzfgrep
bzip2: /bin/bzgrep
bzip2: /bin/bzip2
bzip2: /bin/bzip2recover
bzip2: /bin/bzless
bzip2: /bin/bzmore
```

In this example, the entire output of ls is passed to a single dpkg-query -S command. Using the -t option to xargs, a verbose output of the command line appears before the command is executed. Now let's have xargs pass each output string from ls as input to individual dpkg-query commands. We define {} as the placeholder for the string:

```
$ ls /bin/b* | xargs -t -I{} dpkg-query -S {}
dpkg-query -S /bin/bash
bash: /bin/bash
dpkg-query -S /bin/bunzip2
bzip2: /bin/bunzip2
dpkg-query -S /bin/bzcat
bzip2: /bin/bzcat
dpkg-query -S /bin/bzcmp
bzip2: /bin/bzcmp
dpkg-query -S /bin/bzdiff
bzip2: /bin/bzdiff
dpkg-query -S /bin/bzegrep
bzip2: /bin/bzegrep
dpkg-query -S /bin/bzexe
bzip2: /bin/bzexe
dpkg-query -S /bin/bzfgrep
bzip2: /bin/bzfgrep
dpkg-query -S /bin/bzgrep
bzip2: /bin/bzgrep
dpkg-query -S /bin/bzip2
bzip2: /bin/bzip2
dpkg-query -S /bin/bzip2recover
bzip2: /bin/bzip2recover
dpkg-query -S /bin/bzless
bzip2: /bin/bzless
dpkg-query -S /bin/bzmore
bzip2: /bin/bzmore
```

As you can see from the output, separate dpkg-query -S commands are run for each option passed by ls.

Using alias

Use the alias command to **set and list aliases**. Some aliases are already set in the system-wide or user-specific shell initialization files discussed previously. Here's how to **list the aliases that are currently set:**

```
$ alias
alias cp='cp -i'
alias ls='ls --color=auto'
alias mv='mv -i'
alias rm='rm -i'
```

Notice that some aliases are set simply as a way of adding options to the default behavior of a command (such as mv -i, so that the user is always prompted before moving a file).

NOTE *Ubuntu Linux ships only with the* ls *alias defined, which turns on color output when you list files. The other aliases are useful examples you may want to use, especially since they help you prevent accidental deletion of files.*

You can **define your own aliases for the current bash session** as follows:

```
$ alias la='ls -la'
```

Add that line to your ~/.bashrc file for the definition to occur for each new bash session. **Remove an alias from the current bash session** using the unalias command, as follows:

```
$ unalias la            Unalias the previously aliased la command
$ unalias -a            Unalias all aliased commands
```

Watching Commands

If you need to keep an eye on a command whose output is changing, use the watch command. For example, to keep an eye on your load average:

```
$ watch 'cat /proc/loadavg'
```

Every two seconds, watch runs the cat command again. Use Ctrl+c to quit. To change the refresh rate to 10 seconds, type the following:

```
$ watch -n 10 'ls -l'
```

To highlight the difference between screen updates, type:

```
$ watch -d 'ls -l'
```

Type Ctrl+c to exit the watch command. Note that files need to change so that differences can be highlighted.

Watching Files

You can use the watch command to watch the size of a file. For example, to watch a large ISO file named mydownload.iso as it downloads, use the following command:

```
$ watch 'ls -l mydownload.iso'
```

To watch the contents of a plain text file grow over time, you can use the tail command. For example, you can watch as messages are added to the /var/log/messages file as follows:

```
$ sudo tail -f /var/log/messages
```

Pressing Ctrl+c will exit from the tail command.

Acquiring Super User Power

When you open a shell, you are able to run commands and access files and directories based on your user/group ID and the permissions set for those components. Many system features are restricted to the *root user*, also referred to as the *super user*.

There are three main ways to acquire super user power:

❑ Log in as the root user.

❑ Temporarily become the root user with the `su` command.

❑ Run one command with root user privileges with the `sudo` command.

In most cases, you do not want to log in as the root user, as you may accidentally make changes to your system that you do not intend. Most Linux users either use the `su` command to change to the root user from a normal login or run the `sudo` command to execute a single command as the root user.

Ubuntu Linux is set up for users to run the `sudo` command. So, in most cases, to run an administrative command (such as `useradd` to add a new user), you would precede that command with the `sudo` command. For example:

```
$ sudo useradd -m joe        As root user, add a new user named joe
```

By default, Ubuntu restricts the system such that the root user cannot log in. Because of this, Ubuntu is also not set up to use the `su` command, which is normally used on other Linux systems, to change to the root user.

If you find that you need to run a series of commands as root user, you could type the following command to open a shell as the root user:

```
$ sudo bash        Open a shell as root user
#
```

If you decide that you want to add a password for the root user (allowing you to log in as the root user or use the `su` command to temporarily become root), you can also do that using the `sudo` command:

```
$ sudo passwd root        Set the root user's password
```

Most Ubuntu desktop users, however, simply use `sudo` and never set a root password.

Using the su Command

If you did decide at some point to add a password to your root user account, with a shell open as a regular user, you can use the `su` (super user) command to **become the root user**. You can also use the `su` command to switch to a different, non-root user. The following sections describe how the `su` command works.

59

Simply using su, as in the following code, doesn't give you a login shell with root's environment:

```
$ su
Password:*****
# echo $PATH
/usr/local/sbin:/usr/local/bin:/usr/sbin:/usr/bin:/sbin:/bin:/usr/games
/usr/kerberos/sbin:/usr/kerberos/bin:/usr/local/bin:/usr/bin:/bin:/usr/X11R6/bin
:/home/fcaen/bin
```

After running su, the user still has the user fcaen's PATH. To **enable the root user's environment**, use the su command with the dash option (-), as follows:

```
# exit
$ su -
Password: *****
# echo $PATH
/usr/kerberos/sbin:/usr/kerberos/bin:/usr/local/sbin:/usr/local/bin:/sbin:/bin:/
usr/sbin:/usr/bin:/root/bin
```

In most cases, use su -, unless you have a very specific reason not to. If no user is specified, su defaults to the root user. However, su can also be used **to become other users:**

```
$ su - cnegus
```

The su command can also be used to **execute a single command as a particular user:**

```
$ su -c whoami
Password: ******
root
# su -c 'less /var/log/messages'
```

Although in the second example you are logged in as a regular user, when you run whoami with su -c, it shows that you are the root user. In the directly preceding example, the quotes are required around the less command line to identify /var/log/messages as an option to less. As seen above, whoami can be useful to **determine which user you're currently running a command as:**

```
$ whoami
fcaen
```

Delegating Power with sudo

The sudo command allows very granular delegation of power to users other than the root user. The sudo facility is a great tool for granting specific escalated privileges when you have multiple users and logging everything the users do with those privileges.

Unless otherwise specified, `sudo` runs as root. Ubuntu Linux uses the `sudo` command to execute privileged commands, rather than the `su` command.

The `sudo` command is configured in `/etc/sudoers`.

> **WARNING!** *Never edit this file with your normal text editor. Instead, always use the* `visudo` *command.*

The file `/etc/sudoers` is restricted, so you need to use the `sudo` command to edit the file. For example:

```
$ sudo visudo
```

The `visudo` command launches an editor, by default the nano editor, discussed previously.

If you look at the `sudoers` file that shipped with your distribution, you'll see different empty sections delimited by comments and one active statement:

```
root    ALL=(ALL) ALL
```

This means that the user root is allowed on any hosts to run any command as any user.

Ubuntu Linux adds the following so that all users who are part of the admin group can acquire root privileges:

```
%admin ALL=(ALL) ALL
```

When you installed Ubuntu Linux, the user account you created was automatically added to this group. To allow additional users to acquire root privileges, add the following line, setting the first field to a user account on your system:

```
fcaen ALL= /usr/bin/less /var/log/messages
```

> **NOTE** *The preceding setting allows this user to run the* `less` *command with root privileges. This introduces a security issue, as the* `less` *command can allow this user to gain more information on the system by examining other system files.*

Now fcaen (or whichever user you've added) can do the following:

```
$ sudo /usr/bin/less /var/log/messages
Password:
```

After fcaen types his own password, he can page through the `/var/log/messages` file. A timestamp is set at that time as well. For the next five minutes (by default), that user can type the command line above and have it work without being prompted for the password.

Normally, though, you should add such users to the admin group and not create individual entries in the /etc/sudoers file.

Every use of sudo gets logged in /var/log/secure:

```
Feb 24 21:58:57 localhost sudo: fcaen : TTY=pts/3 ; PWD=/home/fcaen ; USER=root
; COMMAND=/usr/bin/less /var/log/messages
```

Next add this line to /etc/sudoers:

```
fcaen        server1=(chris)       /bin/ls /home/chris
```

Now fcaen can do the following:

```
$ sudo -u chris /bin/ls /home/chris
```

The sudo command just shown runs as chris and will work only on the host server1. In some organizations, the /etc/sudoers file is centrally managed and deployed to all the hosts, so it can be useful to specify sudo permissions on specific hosts.

The sudo command also allows the definition of aliases, or predefined groups of users, commands, and hosts. Check the /etc/sudoers file on your Linux system for examples of those features.

Using Environment Variables

Small chunks of information that are useful to your shell environment are stored in what are referred to as *environment variables*. By convention, environment variable names are all uppercase (although that convention is not enforced). If you use the bash shell, some environment variables are set for you from various bash start scripts covered previously.

To display all of the environment variables, in alphabetical order, that are already set for your shell, type the following:

```
$ set | less
BASH=/bin/bash
COLORS=/etc/DIR_COLORS.xterm
COLUMNS=118
DISPLAY=:0.0
HOME=/home/fcaen
HOSTNAME=einstein
...
```

The output just shown contains only a few examples of the environment variables you will see. The set command lists functions as well. The env command just lists environment variables.

You can also **set, or reset, any variables yourself.** For example, to assign the value 123 to the variable ABC (then display the contents of ABC), type the following:

```
$ ABC=123
$ echo $ABC
123
```

The variable ABC exists only in the shell it was created in. If you launch a command from that shell (ls, cat, firefox, and so on), that new process will not see the variable. Start a new bash process and test this:

```
$ bash
$ echo $ABC

$
```

You can **make variables part of the environment and inheritable by children processes** by exporting them:

```
$ export ABC=123
$ bash
$ echo $ABC
123
```

Also, you can **concatenate a string to an existing variable:**

```
$ export PATH=$PATH:/home/fcaen
```

To **list your bash's environment variables:**

```
$ env
```

When you go to create your own environment variables, avoid using names that are already commonly used by the system for environment variables. See Appendix B for a list of shell environment variables.

Creating Simple Shell Scripts

Shell scripts are good for automating repetitive shell tasks. Bash and other shells include the basic constructs found in various programming languages, such as loops, tests, case statements, and so on. The main difference is that there is only one type of variable: strings.

Editing and Running a Script

Shell scripts are simple text files. You can create them using your favorite text editor (such as vi). To run, the shell script file must be executable. For example, if you created a shell script with a file name of `myscript.sh`, you could make it executable as follows:

```
$ chmod u+x myscript.sh
```

Also, the first line of your bash scripts should always be the following:

```
#!/bin/bash
```

The # in this case starts a comment. The #! syntax acts as a comment for shells that don't understand this special syntax. The /bin/bash part tells any running shell, be it bash or another shell, which program should be used to run the script. (Since historically not all systems came with bash, you will often see /bin/sh as the command to run a script.)

As with any command, besides being executable the shell script you create must also either be in your PATH or be identified by its full or relative path when you run it. In other words, if you just try to run your script, you may get the following result:

```
$ myscript.sh
bash: myscript.sh: command not found
```

In this example, the directory containing `myscript.sh` is not included in your PATH. To correct this problem, you can edit your path, copy the script to a directory in your PATH, or enter the full or relative path to your script. Those four examples, respectively, are shown below:

```
$ mkdir ~/bin ; cp myscript.sh ~/bin/ ; PATH=$PATH:~/bin
$ cp myscript.sh /usr/local/bin
$ ./myscript.sh
$ /tmp/myscript.sh
```

Avoid putting a dot (.) into the PATH environment variable to indicate that commands can be run from the current directory. This is a technique that could result in commands with the same file name as important, well-known commands (such as `ls` or `cat`), which could be overridden if a command of the same name exists in the current directory. This can become a major security issue.

Adding Content to Your Script

Although a shell script can be a simple sequence of commands, shell scripts can also be used as you would any programming language. For example, a script can produce different results based on giving it different input. This section describes how to use compound commands, such as if/then statements, case statements, and for/while loops in your shell scripts.

The following example code assigns the string abc to the variable MYSTRING. It then tests the input to see if it equals abc and acts based on the outcome of the test. The test is between the brackets ([ ]):

```
MYSTRING=abc
if [ $MYSTRING = abc ] ; then
echo "The variable is abc"
fi
```

To **negate the test**, use ! = instead of = as shown in the following:

```
if [ $MYSTRING != abc ] ; then
echo "$MYSTRING is not abc";
fi
```

The following are examples of **testing for numbers**:

```
MYNUMBER=1
if [ $MYNUMBER -eq 1 ] ; then echo "MYNUMBER equals 1"; fi
if [ $MYNUMBER -lt 2 ] ; then echo "MYNUMBER <2"; fi
if [ $MYNUMBER -le 1 ] ; then echo "MYNUMBER <=1"; fi
if [ $MYNUMBER -gt 0 ] ; then echo "MYNUMBER >0"; fi
if [ $MYNUMBER -ge 1 ] ; then echo "MYNUMBER >=1"; fi
```

Let's look at some **tests on file names**. In this example, you can check if a file exists (-e), if it's a regular file (-f), or if it is a directory (-d). These checks are done with if/then statements. If there is no match, then the else statement is used to produce the result.

```
filename="$HOME"
if [ -e $filename ] ; then echo "$filename exists"; fi
if [ -f "$filename" ] ; then
   echo "$filename is a regular file"
elif [ -d "$filename" ] ; then
   echo "$filename is a directory"
else
   echo "I have no idea what $filename is"
fi
```

Table 3-1 shows examples of tests that you can perform on files, strings, and variables.

Table 3-1: Operators for Test Expressions

Operator	Test Being Performed
-a *file*	Check that the file exists (same as -e)
-b *file*	Check whether the file is a special block device

Continued

Table 3-1: Operators for Test Expressions (*continued*)

Operator	Test being performed
-c *file*	Check whether the file is a character special device (such as a serial device)
-d *file*	Check whether the file is a directory
-e *file*	Check whether the file exists (same as -a)
-f *file*	Check whether the file exists and is a regular file (for example, not a directory, socket, pipe, link, or device file)
-g *file*	Check whether the file has the set-group-id bit set
-h *file*	Check whether the file is a symbolic link (same as -L)
-k *file*	Check whether the file has the sticky bit set
-L *file*	Check whether the file is a symbolic link (same as -h)
-n *string*	Check whether the string length is greater than 0 bytes
-O *file*	Check whether you own the file
-p *file*	Check whether the file is a named pipe
-r *file*	Check whether the file is readable by you
-s *file*	Check whether the file exists and is larger than 0 bytes
-S *file*	Check whether the file exists and is a socket
-t *fd*	Check whether the file descriptor is connected to a terminal
-u *file*	Check whether the file has the set-user-id bit set
-w *file*	Check whether the file is writable by you
-x *file*	Check whether the file is executable by you
-z *string*	Check whether the length of the string is 0 (zero) bytes
expr1 -a *expr2*	Check whether both the first and the second expressions are true
expr1 -o *expr2*	Check whether either of the two expressions is true
file1 -nt *file2*	Check whether the first file is newer than the second file (using the modification timestamp)

Table 3-1: Operators for Test Expressions (*continued*)

Operator	Test being performed
file1 -ot *file2*	Check whether the first file is older than the second file (using the modification timestamp)
file1 -ef *file2*	Check whether the two files are associated by a link (a hard link or a symbolic link)
var1 = *var2*	Check whether the first variable is equal to the second variable
var1 -eq *var2*	Check whether the first variable is equal to the second variable
var1 -ge *var2*	Check whether the first variable is greater than or equal to the second variable
var1 -gt *var2*	Check whether the first variable is greater than the second variable
var1 -le *var2*	Check whether the first variable is less than or equal to the second variable
var1 -lt *var2*	Check whether the first variable is less than the second variable
var1 != *var2* *var1* -ne *var2*	Check whether the first variable is not equal to the second variable

Another frequently used construct is the case command. Using the case statement, you can test for different cases and take an action based on the result. Similar to a switch statement in programming languages, case statements can take the place of several nested if statements.

```
case "$VAR" in
   string1)
      { action1 };;
   string2)
      { action2 };;
   *)
      { default action } ;;
esac
```

You can find examples of case usage in the system start-up scripts (initscripts) found in the /etc/init.d/ directory. Each initscript takes actions based on what parameter was passed to it (start, stop, and so on) and the selection is done via a large case construct.

> **NOTE** *The* /etc/init.d *scripts are run by the upstart scripts in* /etc/event.d.

67

The bash shell also offers **standard loop constructs**, illustrated by a few examples that follow. In the first example, all the values of the NUMBER variable (0 through 9) appear on the `for` line:

```
for NUMBER in 0 1 2 3 4 5 6 7 8 9
do
    echo The number is $NUMBER
done
```

In the following examples, the output from the `ls` command (a list of files) provides the variables that the `for` statement acts on:

```
for FILE in `/bin/ls`; do echo $FILE; done
```

Instead of feeding the whole list of values to a `for` statement, you can increment a value and **continue through a while loop until a condition is met.** In the following example, VAR begins as 0 and the `while` loop continues to increment until the value of VAR becomes 3:

```
"VAR=0"
while [ $VAR -lt 3 ]; do
    echo $VAR
    VAR=$[$VAR+1]
done
```

Another way to get the same result as the `while` statement just shown is to use the `until` statement, as shown in the following example:

```
"VAR=0"
until [ $VAR -eq 3 ]; do echo $VAR; VAR=$[$VAR+1]; done
```

If you are just starting with shell programming, refer to the Bash Guide for Beginners (`http://tldp.org/LDP/Bash-Beginners-Guide/html/index.html`). Use that guide, along with reference material such as the bash man page, to step through many examples of good shell scripting techniques.

Summary

Despite improvements in graphical user interfaces, the shell is still the most common method for power users to work with Linux systems. The Bourne Again Shell (bash) is the most common shell used with Linux. It includes many helpful features for recalling commands (history), completing commands, assigning aliases, and redirecting output from and input to commands. You can make powerful commands of your own using simple shell scripting techniques.

4

Working with Files

Everything in a Linux file system can be viewed as a file. This includes data files, directories, devices, named pipes, links, and other types of files. Associated with each file is a set of information that determines who can access the file and how they can access it. This chapter covers many commands for exploring and working with files.

Understanding File Types

Directories and regular files are by far the file types you will use most often. However, there are several other types of files you will encounter as you use Linux. From the command line, there are many ways you can create, find, and list different types of files.

Files that provide access to the hardware components on your computer are referred to as *device files*. There are character and block devices. There are *hard links* and *soft links* you can use to make the same file accessible from different locations. Less often used directly by regular users are *named pipes* and *sockets*, which provide access points for processes to communicate with each other.

Using Regular Files

Regular files consist of data files (documents, music, images, archives, and so on) and commands (binaries and scripts). You can determine the type of a file using the `file` command. In the following example, you change to the directory containing bash shell documentation and use the file command to view some of the file types in that directory:

```
$ cd /usr/share/doc/
$ file doc-base/install-docs.html
doc-base/install-docs.html: XML 1.0 document text
$ file doc-base/copyright
doc-base/copyright: ASCII English text
$ file doc-base/doc-base.html
doc-base/doc-base.html/: directory
```

```
$ file doc/doc-base/changelog.gz
doc-base/changelog.gz: gzip compressed data, was "changelog", from Unix, last
modified: Thu Feb 22 07:29:26 2007, max compression
$ file shared-mime-info/shared-mime-info-spec.pdf
shared-mime-info/shared-mime-info-spec.pdf: PDF document, version 1.4
```

The file command that was run shows document files in the Ubuntu documentation directories of different formats. It can look inside the files and determine that a file contains text that has been compressed, PDF or PostScript that can be sent to a printer, plain text, or HTML (web page) markup. There is even a subdirectory shown, unexpected since it has an odd name for a directory (doc-base.html).

Creating regular files can be done by any application that can save its data. If you just want to **create some blank files to start with**, there are many ways to do that. Here are two examples:

```
$ touch /tmp/newfile.txt          Create a blank file
$ > /tmp/newfile2.txt             Create a blank file
```

Doing a **long list on a file is another way to determine its file type**. For example:

```
$ ls -l /tmp/newfile2.txt         List a file to see its type
-rw-r--r--  1 chris chris 0 Sep 5 14:19 newfile2
```

A dash in the first character of the 10-character permission information (-rw-r--r--) indicates that the item is a regular file. (Permissions are explained in the "Setting File/Directory Permissions" section later in this chapter.) Commands are also regular files, but are saved as executables. Here are some examples:

```
$ ls -l /usr/bin/apt-key
-rwxr-xr-x 1 root root 2230 2007-03-14 12:44 /usr/bin/apt-key
$ file /usr/bin/apt-key
/usr/bin/apt-key: Bourne shell script text executable
$ file /bin/ls
/bin/ls: ELF 32-bit LSB executable, Intel 80386, version 1 (SYSV), for GNU/Linux
2.6.0, dynamically linked (uses shared libs), stripped
```

You can see that the apropos command is executable by the x settings for owner, group, and others. By running file on apt-key, you can see that it is a shell script. That's opposed to a binary executable, such as the ls command indicated above.

Using Directories

A *directory* is a container for files and subdirectories. Directories are set up in a hierarchy from the root (/) down to multiple subdirectories, each separated by a slash (/). Directories are called *folders* when you access them from graphical file managers.

To create new directories for storing your data, you can use the mkdir command. Here are examples of using mkdir to **create directories in different ways:**

```
$ mkdir /tmp/new          Create "new" directory in /tmp
$ mkdir -p /tmp/a/b/c/new  Create parent directories as needed for "new"
$ mkdir -m 700 /tmp/new2   Create new2 with drwx - - - permissions
```

The first mkdir command simply adds the new directory to the existing /tmp directory. The second example creates directories as needed (subdirectories a, b, and c) to create the resulting new directory. The last command adds the -m option to set directory permissions as well.

You can **identify the file as a directory** because the first character in the 10-character permission string for a directory is a d:

```
$ file /tmp/new
/tmp/new: directory
$ ls -l /tmp
...
drwxr-xr-x 2 ericfj ericfj 4096 2007-09-11 07:25 new
...
```

Another thing to notice about directories is that the execute bits (x) must be on, if you want people to be able to use the directory as their current directories.

Using Symbolic and Hard Links

Instead of copying files and directories to different parts of the file system, links can be set up to access that same file from multiple locations. Linux supports both *soft links* (usually called *symbolic links*) and *hard links*.

When you try to open a *symbolic link* which points to a file or change to one that points to a directory, the command you run acts on the file or directory that is the target of that link. The target has its own set of permissions and ownership that you cannot see from the symbolic link. The symbolic link can exist on a different disk partition than the target. In fact, the symbolic link can exist, even if the target doesn't.

A *hard link*, alternatively, can only be used on files (not directories) and is basically a way of giving multiple names to the same physical file. Every physical file has at least one hard link, which is commonly thought of as the file itself. Any additional names (hard links) that point to that single physical file must be on the same partition as the original target file (in fact, one way to tell that files are hard links is that they all have the same inode number). Changing permissions, ownership, date/time stamps or content of any hard link to a file results in all others being changed as well. However, deleting one link will not remove the file; it will continue to exist until the last link to the file is deleted.

Here are some examples of using the `ln` command to **create hard and symbolic links:**

```
$ touch myfile
$ ln myfile myfile-hardlink
$ ln -s myfile myfile-symlink
$ ls -li myfile*
292007 -rw-r--r-- 3 francois francois 0 Mar 25 00:07 myfile
292007 -rw-r--r-- 3 francois francois 0 Mar 25 00:07 myfile-hardlink
292008 lrwxrwxrwx 2 francois francois 6 Mar 25 00:09 myfile-symlink
```

Note that after creating the hard and symbolic link files, we used the `ls -li` command to list the results. The `-li` option shows the inodes associated with each file. You can see that `myfile` and `myfile-hardlink` both have the inode number of `292007` (signifying the exact same file on the hard disk). The `myfile-symlink` symbolic link has a different inode number. And although the hard link simply appears as a file (-), the symbolic link is identified as a link (1) with wide-open permissions. You won't know if you can access the file the symbolic link points to until you try it or list the link target.

Using Device Files

When applications need to communicate with your computer's hardware, they direct data to *device files*. By convention, device files are stored in the /dev directory. Devices are generally divided into block devices (such as storage media) and character devices (such as serial ports and terminal devices).

> **NOTE** *Device files are often called device drivers. In Linux and Unix, the operating system treats almost everything as a file, hence the term device files.*

Each device file is associated with a major number (indicating the type of device) and minor number (indicating the instance number of the device). For example, terminal (tty) devices are represented by major character device 4, while SCSI hard disks are represented by major block device number 8. Here are **examples of device files:**

```
$ ls -l /dev/tty0 /dev/sda1   List character and block special devices
brw-rw---- 1 root disk 8, 1 2007-09-05 08:34 /dev/sda1
crw-rw---- 1 root root 4, 0 2007-09-05 08:34 /dev/tty0
```

A listing of device names and numbers allocated in Linux is available in Ubuntu in the online manual page for the MAKEDEV command. Most device files are created automatically for you at boot time. So most people never create device files manually. However, you can **create your own device file** using the mknod command. Here's an example:

```
$ sudo mknod /dev/ttyS4 c 4 68   Add device for fifth serial port
$ ls -l /dev/ttyS4               List new device file
crw-r--r-- 1 root root 4, 68 Sep  6 00:35 /dev/ttyS4
```

Using Named Pipes and Sockets

When you want to allow one process to send information to another process, you can simply pipe (|) the output from one to the input of the other. However, to provide a presence in the file system from which a process can communicate with other processes, you can create *named pipes* or *sockets*. Named pipes are typically used for interprocess communication on the local system, while sockets can be used for processes to communicate over a network.

Named pipes and sockets are often set up by applications in the /tmp directory. Here are some examples of named pipes and sockets:

```
$ ls -l /tmp/.TV-chris/tvtimefifo-local /tmp/.X11-unix/X0
prw-------  1 chris chris 0 Sep 26  2007 /tmp/.TV-chris/tvtimefifo-local
srwxrwxrwx  1 root  chris 0 Sep  4 01:30 /tmp/.X11-unix/X0
```

The first listing is a named pipe set up by the tvtime TV card player (note the p at the beginning indicating a named pipe). The second listing is a socket set up by the X GUI for interprocess communications.

To create your own named pipe, use the mkfifo command as follows:

```
$ mkfifo mypipe
$ ls -l mypipe
prw-r--r--  1 chris chris 0 Sep 26 00:57 mypipe
```

Setting File/Directory Permissions

The ability to access files, run commands, and change to a directory can be restricted with permission settings for user, group, and other users. When you do a long list (ls -l) of files and directories in Linux, the beginning 10 characters shown indicate what the item is (file, directory, block device, and so on) along with whether or not the item can be read, written, and/or executed. Figure 4-1 illustrates the meaning of those 10 characters.

Figure 4-1: Read, write, and execute permissions are set for files and directories.

To follow along with examples in this section, create a directory called /tmp/test and a file called /tmp/test/hello.txt. Then do a long listing of those two items, as follows:

```
$ mkdir /tmp/test
$ echo "some text" > /tmp/test/hello.txt
$ ls -ld /tmp/test/ /tmp/test/hello.txt
drwxr-xr-x  2 francois sales 4096 Mar 21 13:11 /tmp/test
-rw-r--r--  2 francois sales   10 Mar 21 13:11 /tmp/test/hello.txt
```

After creating the directory and file, the first character of the long listing shows /tmp/test as a directory (d) and hello.txt as a file (-). Other types of files available in Linux that would appear as the first character include character devices (c), block devices (b) or symbolic links (l), named pipes (p), and sockets (s).

The next nine characters represent the permissions set on the file and directory. The first rwx indicates that the owner (francois) has read, write, and execute permissions on the directory. Likewise, the group sales has the more restricted permissions (r-x) with no write permission. Then all other users have only read and execute permissions (r-x); the dash indicates the missing write permission. For the hello.txt file, the user has read and write permissions (rw-) and members of the group and all others have read permission (r--).

When you set out to change permissions, each permission can be represented by an octal number (where read is 4, write is 2, and execute is 1) or a letter (rwx). Generally speaking, read permission lets you view the contents of the directory, write lets you change (add or modify) the contents of the directory, and execute lets you change to (in other words, access) the directory.

If you don't like the permissions you see on files or directories you own, you can change those permissions using the chmod command.

Changing Permissions with chmod

The chmod command lets you change the access permissions of files and directories. Table 4-1 shows several chmod command lines and how access to the directory or file changes.

Table 4-1: Changing Directory and File Access Permissions

chmod command (octal or letters)	Original Permission	New Permission	Description
chmod 0700	any	drwx------	The directory's owner can read or write files in that directory as well as change to it. All other users (except root) have no access.

Table 4-1: Changing Directory and File Access Permissions (*continued*)

chmod command (octal or letters)	Original Permission	New Permission	Description
chmod 0711	any	drwx--x--x	Same as for the owner. All others can change to the directory, but not view or change files in the directory. This can be useful for server hardening, where you prevent someone from listing directory contents, but allow access to a file in the directory if someone already knows it's there.
chmod go+r	drwx------	drwxr--r--	Adding read permission to a directory may not give desired results. Without execute on, others can't view the contents of any files in that directory.
chmod 0777 chmod a=rwx	any	drwxrwxrwx	All permissions are wide open.
chmod 0000 chmod a-rwx	any	d---------	All permissions are closed. Good to protect a directory from errant changes. However, backup programs that run as non-root may fail to back up the directory's contents.
chmod 666	any	-rw-rw-rw-	Open read/write permissions completely on a file.
chmod go-rw	-rw-rw-rw-	-rw-------	Don't let anyone except the owner view, change, or delete the file.
chmod 644	any	-rw-r--r--	Only the owner can change or delete the file, but all can view it.

The first 0 in the mode line can usually be dropped (so you can use 777 instead of 0777). That placeholder has special meaning. It is an octal digit that can be used on commands (executables) to indicate that the command can run as a set-UID program (4), run as a set-GID program (2), or become a *sticky* program (1). With set-UID and set-GID, the command runs with the assigned user or group permissions (instead of running with permission of the user or group that launched the command).

> **WARNING!** *SUID should not be used on shell scripts. Here is a warning from the Linux Security HOWTO: "SUID shell scripts are a serious security risk, and for this reason the kernel will not honor them. Regardless of how secure you think the shell script is, it can be exploited to give the cracker a root shell."*

Having the sticky bit on for a directory keeps users from removing or renaming files from that directory that they don't own (/tmp is an example). Given the right permission settings, however, users can change the contents of files they don't own in a sticky bit directory. The final permission character is t instead of x on a sticky directory. A command with sticky bit on used to cause the command to stay in memory, even while not being used. This is an old Unix feature that is not supported in Linux.

The -R option is a handy feature of the chmod command. With -R, you can **recursively change permissions of all files and directories starting from a point in the file system.** Here are some examples:

```
$ sudo chmod -R 700 /tmp/test     Open permission only to owner below /tmp/test
$ sudo chmod -R 000 /tmp/test     Close all permissions below /tmp/test
$ sudo chmod -R a+rwx /tmp/test   Open all permissions to all below /tmp/test
```

Note that the -R option is inclusive of the directory you indicate. So the permissions above, for example, would change for the /tmp/test directory itself, and not just for the files and directories below that directory.

Setting the umask

Permissions given to a file or directory are assigned originally at the time that item is created. How those permissions are set is based on the user's current *umask* value. Using the umask command, you can **set the permissions given to files and directories** when you create them.

```
$ umask 0066     Make directories drwx--x--x and files -rw-------
$ umask 0077     Make directories drwx------ and files -rw-------
$ umask 0022     Make directories drwxr-xr-x and files -rw-r--r--
$ umask 0777     Make directories d--------- and files ----------
```

Changing Ownership

When you create a file or directory, your user account is assigned to that file or directory. So is your primary group. As root user, you can **change the ownership (user) and group assigned to a file to a different user and/or group** using the chown and chgrp commands. Here are some examples:

```
$ chown chris test/           Change owner to chris
$ chown chris:market test/    Change owner to chris and group to market
$ chgrp market test/          Change group to market
$ chown -R chris test/        Change all files below test/ to owner chris
```

The recursive option to chown (-R) just shown is useful if you need to change the ownership of an entire directory structure. As with chmod, using chown recursively changes permissions for the directory named, along with its contents. You might use chown recursively when a person leaves a company or stops using your web service. You can use chown -R to reassign their entire /home directory to a different user.

Related commands for changing group assignments and passwords include `newgrp` and `gpasswd`, as well as the /etc/gshadow file.

Traversing the File System

Basic commands for changing directories (cd), checking the current directory (pwd) and listing directory contents (ls) are well known to even casual shell users. So this section focuses on some less-common options to those commands, as well as other lesser-known features for moving around the file system. Here are some quick examples of cd for **moving around the file system**:

```
$ cd                    Change to your home directory
$ cd $HOME              Change to your home directory
$ cd ~                  Change to your home directory
$ cd ~francois          Change to francois' home directory
$ cd -                  Change to previous working directory
$ cd $OLDPWD            Change to previous working directory
$ cd ~/public_html      Change to public_html in your home directory
$ cd ..                 Change to parent of current directory
$ cd /usr/bin           Change to usr/bin from root directory
$ cd usr/bin            Change to usr/bin beneath current directory
```

If you want to **find out what your current directory is**, use pwd (print working directory):

```
$ pwd
/home/francois
```

Creating *symbolic links* is a way to access a file from other parts of the file system (see the section "Using Symbolic and Hard Links" earlier in the chapter for more information on symbolic and hard links). However, symbolic links can cause some confusion about how parent directories are viewed. The following commands **create a symbolic link** to the /tmp directory from your home directory and show how to tell where you are related to a linked directory:

```
$ cd $HOME
$ ln -s /tmp tmp-link
$ ls -l tmp-link
lrwxrwxrwx 1 francois francois 13 Mar 24 12:41 tmp-link -> /tmp
$ cd tmp-link/
$ pwd
/home/francois/tmp-link
$ pwd -P
/tmp
$ pwd -L
/home/francois/tmp-link
$ cd -L ..
$ pwd
/home/francois
$ cd tmp-link
```

```
$ cd -P ..
$ pwd
/
```

Using the -P and -L options to pwd and cd, you can **work with symbolically linked directories in their permanent or link locations**, respectively. For example, cd -L .. takes you up one level to your home directory, whereas cd -P .. takes you up one level above the permanent directory (/). Likewise, -P and -L options to pwd show permanent and link locations.

Bash can remember a list of working directories. Such a list can be useful if you want to return to previously visited directories. That list is organized in the form of a stack. Use pushd and popd to **add and remove directories**:

```
$ pwd
/home/francois
$ pushd /usr/share/man/
/usr/share/man ~
$ pushd /var/log/
/var/log /usr/share/man ~
$ dirs
/var/log /usr/share/man ~
$ dirs -v
 0  /var/log
 1  /usr/share/man
 2  ~
$ popd
/usr/share/man ~
$ pwd
/usr/share/man
$ popd
~
$ pwd
/home/francois
```

The dirs, pushd, and popd commands can also be used to manipulate the order of directories on the stack. For example, pushd -0 pushes the last directory on the stack to the top of the stack (making it the current directory). The pushd -2 command pushes the third directory from the bottom of the stack to the top.

Copying Files

Provided you have write permission to the target directory, copying files and directories can be done with some fairly simple commands. The standard cp command will **copy a file to a new name or the same name in a new directory**, with a new time stamp associated with the new file. Other options to cp let you retain date/time stamps, copy recursively, and prompt before overwriting. Here are some examples:

```
$ cd ; touch index.html
$ mkdir /tmp/html
```

```
$ cp -i index.html /tmp/html/
$ cp -il index.html /tmp //html
$ mkdir /tmp/back
$ cp -a /tmp /html /mp/back/
$ cp -R /tmp /html /tmp/back/
```

The above examples show ways of copying files related. In the first cp example above, if an index.html file exists in /tmp/html, you are prompted before overwriting it with the new file. In the next example, the index.html file is hard-linked to a file of the same name in the /tmp/html directory. In that case, because both hard links point to the same file, editing the file from either location will change the contents of the file in both locations. (The link can only be done if /tmp/html and your home directory are in the same file system.)

The cp -a command copies all files below the /tmp/html directory, retaining all ownership and permission settings. If, for example, /tmp/back represented a USB flash drive, that command would be a way to copy the contents of your web server to that drive. The -R option also recursively copies a directory structure, but assigns ownership to the current user and adds current date/time stamps.

The dd command is another way to **copy data**. This command is very powerful because on Linux systems, everything is a file, including hardware peripherals. Here is an example:

```
$ dd if=/dev/zero of=/tmp/mynullfile count=1
1+0 records in
1+0 records out
512 bytes (512 B) copied, 0.000308544 s, 1.7 MB/s
```

/dev/zero is a special file that generates null characters. In the example just shown, the dd command takes /dev/zero as input file and outputs to /tmp/mynullfile. The count is the number of blocks. By default, a block is 512 bytes. The result is a 512-bytes-long file full of null characters. You could use less or vi to view the contents of the file. However, a better tool to view the file would be the od (Octal Dump) command:

```
$ od -vt x1 /tmp/mynullfile        View an octal dump of a file
```

Here's another example of the dd command:

```
$ dd if=/dev/zero of=/tmp/mynullfile count=10 bs=2
10+0 records in
10+0 records out
20 bytes (20 B) copied, 0.000595714 s, 33.6 kB/s
```

This time, we set the block size to 2 bytes and copied 10 blocks (20 bytes). The following command line **clones the first partition of the primary master IDE drive** to the second partition of the primary slave IDE drive (back up all data before trying anything like this):

```
$ sudo dd if=/dev/hda1 of=/dev/hdb2
```

79

> **WARNING!** *Be very careful with this command. You normally do not want to blindly overwrite parts of your hard drives.*

The next example makes a compressed backup of the first partition of the primary master IDE drive. Typically the partition should be unmounted before a backup such as this.

```
$ sudo umount /dev/hda1
$ sudo dd if=/dev/hda1 | gzip > bootpart.gz
```

The following command copies an ISO image file from a CD or DVD to your USB flash drive (assuming the drive appears as /dev/sdb1):

```
$ sudo dd if=whatever.iso of=/dev/sdb1
```

Note that this command is making a binary copy of the bytes in the file, which may not be what you want to do.

This next example copies the Master Boot Record from the primary master IDE hard drive to a file named mymbrfile:

```
$ dd if=/dev/hda of=mymbrfile bs=512 count=1
```

If you want to make a copy of the ISO image that was burned to a CD or DVD, insert that medium into your CD/DVD drive and (assuming /dev/cdrom is associated with your computer's CD drive) type the following command:

```
$ dd if=/dev/cdrom of=whatever.iso
```

> **NOTE** *Ubuntu also creates* /dev/cdrw *and* /dev/dvd *devices files as well as* /dev/cdrom.

Changing File Attributes

Files and directories in Linux file systems all have read, write and execute permissions associated with user, group, and others. However, there are also other attributes that can be attached to files and directories that are specific to certain file system types.

Files on ext2 and ext3 file systems have special attributes that you may choose to use. You can list these attributes with the lsattr command. Most attributes are obscure and not turned on by default. Here's an example of using lsattr to see some files' attributes:

```
$ lsattr /etc/host*
------------- /etc/host.conf
------------- /etc/hosts
------------- /etc/host.allow
------------- /etc/host.deny
$ lsattr -aR /tmp/ | less          Recursively list all /tmp attributes
```

The dashes represent 13 ext2/ext3 attributes that can be set. None are on by default. Those attributes are the following: a (append only), c (compressed), d (no dump), i (immutable), j (data journalling), s (secure deletion), t (no tail-merging), u (undeletable), A (no atime updates), D (synchronous directory updates), S (synchronous updates), and T (top of directory hierarchy). You can **change these attributes** using the chattr command. Here are some examples:

```
$ sudo chattr +i whatever.iso
$ sudo chattr +A -R /home/francois/images/*
$ sudo chattr +d ubuntu-7.04-desktop.i386.iso
$ lsattr whatever.iso /home/francois/images/* ubuntu-7.04-desktop.i386.iso
----i-------- whatever.iso
-------A----- /home/francois/images/einstein.jpg
-------A----- /home/francois/images/goth.jpg
------d------ ubuntu-7.04-desktop.i386.iso
```

As shown in the preceding example, with the +i option set, the whatever.iso file becomes immutable, meaning that it can't be deleted, renamed, or changed, or have a link created to it. Here, this prevents any arbitrary changes to the file. (Not even the root user can change the file until the i attribute is gone.) You can use this to help protect system files.

The -R option in the example recursively sets the +A option, so all files in the images directory and below can't have access times (atime record) modified. Setting A attributes can save some disk I/O on laptops or flash drives. If you use the dump command to back up your ext2/ext3 file systems, the +d option can prevent selected files from being backed up. In this case, we chose to not have a large ISO image backed up.

To **remove an attribute** with chatter, use the minus sign (-). For example:

```
$ sudo chattr -i whatever.iso
```

> **NOTE** *Crackers who successfully break into a machine will often replace some system binaries (such as* ls *or* ps*) with corrupt versions and make them immutable. It's a good idea to occasionally check the attributes set for your executables (in* /bin, /usr/bin, /sbin, *and* /usr/sbin, *for example).*

Searching for Files

Ubuntu keeps a database of all the files in the file system (with a few exceptions defined in /etc/updatedb.conf) using features of the mlocate package. The locate command allows you to search that database. (On Ubuntu, the locate command is a symbolic link to the secure version of the command, slocate.) The results come back instantly, since the database is searched and not the actual file system. Before locate was available, most Linux users ran the find command to find files in the file system. Both locate and find are covered here.

Finding Files with locate

Because the database contains the name of every node in the file system, and not just commands, you can use `locate` to find commands, devices, man pages, data files, or anything else identified by a name in the file system. Here is an example:

```
$ locate e1000
/lib/modules/2.6.20-16-generic/kernel/drivers/net/e1000
/lib/modules/2.6.20-16-generic/kernel/drivers/net/e1000/e1000.ko
/lib/modules/2.6.20-15-generic/kernel/drivers/net/e1000
/lib/modules/2.6.20-15-generic/kernel/drivers/net/e1000/e1000.ko
/usr/src/linux-headers-2.6.20-16-generic/include/config/e1000
/usr/src/linux-headers-2.6.20-16-generic/include/config/e1000/napi.h
/usr/src/linux-headers-2.6.20-16-generic/include/config/e1000.h
/usr/src/linux-headers-2.6.20-15-generic/include/config/e1000
/usr/src/linux-headers-2.6.20-15-generic/include/config/e1000/napi.h
/usr/src/linux-headers-2.6.20-15-generic/include/config/e1000.h
/usr/src/linux-headers-2.6.20-15/include/config/e1000.h
/usr/src/linux-headers-2.6.20-15/drivers/net/e1000
/usr/src/linux-headers-2.6.20-15/drivers/net/e1000/Makefile
/usr/src/linux-headers-2.6.20-16/include/config/e1000.h
/usr/src/linux-headers-2.6.20-16/drivers/net/e1000
/usr/src/linux-headers-2.6.20-16/drivers/net/e1000/Makefile
```

The above example found two versions of the e1000.ko and e1000.ko kernel modules. `locate` is case sensitive unless you use the `-i` option. Here's an example:

```
$ locate -i itco_wdt
/lib/modules/2.6.20-16-generic/kernel/drivers/char/watchdog/iTCO_wdt.ko
/lib/modules/2.6.20-15-generic/kernel/drivers/char/watchdog/iTCO_wdt.ko
```

The slocate package (or mlocate on some Linux distributions) includes a cron job that runs the `updatedb` command once per day to update the locate database of files.

To update the locate database immediately, you can run the `updatedb` command manually:

```
$ sudo updatedb
```

Locating Files with find

Before the days of `locate`, the way to find files was with the `find` command. Although `locate` will come up with a file faster, `find` has many other powerful options for finding files based on attributes other than the name.

> **NOTE** *Searching the entire file system can take a long time to complete. Before searching the whole file system, consider searching a subset of the file system or excluding certain directories or remotely mounted file systems.*

This example searches the root file system (/) recursively for files named e100:

```
$ find / -name "e100*" -print
find: /usr/lib/audit: Permission denied
find: /usr/libexec/utempter: Permission denied
/sys/module/e100
/sys/bus/pci/drivers/e100
...
```

Running find as a normal user can result in long lists of Permission denied as find tries to enter a directory you do not have permissions to. You can filter out the inaccessible directories:

```
$ find / -name e100 -print 2>&1 | grep -v "Permission denied"
```

Or send all errors to the /dev/null bit bucket:

```
$ find / -name e100 -print 2> /dev/null
```

Because searches with find are case sensitive and must match the name exactly (e100 won't match e100.ko), you can use regular expressions to make your searches more inclusive. Here's an example:

```
$ find / -name 'e100*' -print
/lib/modules/2.6.20-16-generic/kernel/drivers/net/e1000
/lib/modules/2.6.20-16-generic/kernel/drivers/net/e1000/e1000.ko
/lib/modules/2.6.20-16-generic/kernel/drivers/net/e100.ko
/lib/modules/2.6.20-15-generic/kernel/drivers/net/e1000
/lib/modules/2.6.20-15-generic/kernel/drivers/net/e1000/e1000.ko
/lib/modules/2.6.20-15-generic/kernel/drivers/net/e100.ko
/usr/src/linux-headers-2.6.20-16-generic/include/config/e100.h
/usr/src/linux-headers-2.6.20-16-generic/include/config/e1000
/usr/src/linux-headers-2.6.20-16-generic/include/config/e1000.h
/usr/src/linux-headers-2.6.20-15-generic/include/config/e100.h
/usr/src/linux-headers-2.6.20-15-generic/include/config/e1000
/usr/src/linux-headers-2.6.20-15-generic/include/config/e1000.h
/usr/src/linux-headers-2.6.20-15/include/config/e100.h
/usr/src/linux-headers-2.6.20-15/include/config/e1000.h
/usr/src/linux-headers-2.6.20-15/drivers/net/e1000
/usr/src/linux-headers-2.6.20-16/include/config/e100.h
/usr/src/linux-headers-2.6.20-16/include/config/e1000.h
/usr/src/linux-headers-2.6.20-16/drivers/net/e1000
```

You can also find files based on timestamps. This command line finds files in /usr/bin/ that have been accessed in the past two minutes:

```
$ find /usr/bin/ -amin -2 -print
/usr/bin/
/usr/bin/find
```

This command line finds files that have not been accessed in /home/chris for more than 60 days:

```
$ find /home/chris/ -atime +60
```

Use the -type d option to find directories. The following command line finds all directories under /etc and redirects stderr to the bit bucket (/dev/null):

```
$ find /etc -type d -print 2> /dev/null
```

This command line finds files in /sbin with permissions that match 750:

```
$ find /sbin/ -perm 750 -print
```

(which match none in a default Ubuntu installation.)

The exec option to find is very powerful, because it lets you **act on the files found with the find command.** The following command finds all the files in /var owned by the user francois (must be a valid user) and executes the ls -1 command on each one:

```
$ find /var -user francois -exec ls -l {} \;
```

An alternative to find's exec option is xargs:

```
$ find /var -user francois -print | xargs ls -l
```

There are big differences on how the two commands just shown operate, leading to very different performance. The find -exec spawns the command ls for each result it finds. The xargs command works more efficiently by passing many results as input to a single ls command.

To **negate a search criteria,** place an exclamation point (!) before that criteria. The next example finds all the files that are not owned by the group root and are regular files, and then does an ls -1 on each:

```
$ find / ! -group root -type f -print 2> /dev/null | xargs ls -l
```

The next example finds the files in /sbin that are regular files and are not writable by others, then feeds them to an ls -1 command:

```
$ find /sbin/ -type f ! -perm /o+w -print | xargs ls -l
-rwxr-xr-x 1 root root     3056 2007-03-07 15:44 /sbin/acpi_available
-rwxr-xr-x 1 root root    43204 2007-02-18 20:18 /sbin/alsactl
```

Finding files by size is a great way to determine what is filling up your hard disks. The following command line finds all files that are greater than 10 MB (+10M), lists those files from largest to smallest (ls -1S) and directs that list to a file (/tmp/bigfiles.txt):

```
$ find / -xdev -size +10M -print | xargs ls -lS > /tmp/bigfiles.txt
```

In this example, the -xdev option prevents any mounted file systems, besides the root file system, from being searched. This is a good way to keep the find command from searching the /proc directory and any remotely mounted file systems, as well as other locally mounted file systems.

Using Other Commands to Find Files

Other commands for finding files include the whereis and which commands. Here are some examples of those commands:

```
$ whereis man
man: /usr/bin/man /usr/X11R6/bin/man /usr/bin/X11/man /usr/local/man
/usr/share/man /usr/share/man/man1/man.1.gz /usr/share/man/man7/man.7.gz
$ which ls
/bin/ls
```

The whereis command is useful because it not only finds commands, it also **finds man pages and configuration files associated with a command.** From the example of whereis for the word man, you can see the man executable, its configuration file, and the location of man pages for the man command. The which example shows where the ls executable is (/bin/ls). The which command is useful when you're looking for the actual location of an executable file in your PATH, as in this example:

```
$ dpkg-query -S `which ps`
procps: /bin/ps
```

Finding Out More About Files

Now that you know how to find files, you can get more information about those files. Using less-common options to the ls command lets you list information about a file that you won't see when you run ls without options. Commands such as file help you identify a file's type. With md5sum and sha1sum, you can verify the validity of a file.

Listing Files

Although you are probably quite familiar with the ls command, you may not be familiar with many of the useful options for ls that can help you find out a lot about the files on your system. Here are some examples of **using ls to display long lists** (-1) of files and directories:

```
$ ls -l      Files and directories in current directory
$ ls -la     Includes files/directories beginning with dot (.)
$ ls -lt     Orders files by time recently changed
$ ls -lu     Orders files by time recently accessed
$ ls -lS     Orders files by size
$ ls -li     Lists the inode associated with each file
$ ls -ln     List numeric user/group IDs, instead of names
$ ls -lh     List file sizes in human-readable form (K, M, etc.)
$ ls -lR     List files recursively, from current directory and subdirectories
```

When you list files, there are also ways to **have different types of files appear differently** in the listing:

```
$ ls -F              Add a character to indicate file type
myfile-symlink@    config/  memo.txt  pipefile|   script.sh*  xpid.socket=
$ ls --color=always  Show file types as different colors
$ ls -C              Show files listing in columns
```

In the `-F` example, the output shows several different file types. The `myfile-symlink@` indicates a symbolic link to a directory, `config/` is a regular directory, `memo.txt` is a regular file (no extra characters), `pipefile|` is a named pipe (created with `mkfifo`), `script.sh*` is an executable file, and `xpid.socket=` is a socket. The next two examples display different file types in different colors and lists output in columns, respectively.

Verifying Files

When files such as software packages and CD or DVD images are shared over the Internet, often a SHA1SUM or MD5SUM file is published with it. Those files contain checksums that can be used to make sure that the file you downloaded is exactly the one that the repository published.

The following are examples of the `md5sum` and `sha1sum` commands being used to **produce checksums of files**:

```
$ md5sum whatever.iso
d41d8cd98f00b204e9800998ecf8427e  whatever.iso
$ sha1sum whatever.iso
da39a3ee5e6b4b0d3255bfef95601890afd80709  whatever.iso
```

Which command you choose depends on whether the provider of the file you are checking distributed md5sum or sha1sum information. For example, here is what the `md5sum.txt` file for the Ubuntu Feisty distribution looked like:

```
90537599d934967f4de97ee0e7e66e6c  ./dists/feisty/main/binary-i386/Release
c53152b488a9ed521c96fdfb12a1bbba  ./dists/feisty/main/binary-i386/Packages
ba9a035c270ba6df978097ee68b8d7c6  ./dists/feisty/main/binary-i386/Packages.gz
...
```

This file lists the MD5 checksums for all files on the Ubuntu 7.04 Live CD.

With all the files listed in this `md5sum.txt` file contained in the current directory, you can **verify them all at once** using the `-c` option to `md5sum`. Here is an example:

```
$ md5sum -c md5sum.txt
./dists/feisty/main/binary-i386/Release: OK
./dists/feisty/main/binary-i386/Packages: OK
./dists/feisty/main/binary-i386/Packages.gz: OK...
```

To verify only one of the files listed in the file, you could do something like the following:

```
$ cat md5sum.txt | grep Release.gpg |md5sum -c
./dists/feisty/Release.gpg: OK
```

If you had an SHA1SUM file instead of a md5sum.txt file to check against, you could use the sha1sum command in the same way. By combining the find command described earlier in this chapter with the md5sum command, you can verify any part of your file system. For example, here's how to create an MD5 checksum for every file in the /etc directory so they can be checked later to see if any have changed:

```
$ sudo find /etc -type f -exec md5sum {}  \; > /tmp/md5.list 2> /dev/null
```

The result of the previous command line is a /tmp/md5.list file that contains a 128-bit checksum for every file in the /etc directory. Later, you could type the following command to see if any of those files have changed:

```
$ cd /etc
$ md5sum -c /tmp/md5.list | grep -v 'OK'
./hosts.allow: FAILED
md5sum: WARNING: 1 of 1668 computed checksums did NOT match
```

As you can see from the output, only one file changed (hosts.allow). So the next step is to check the changed file and see if the changes to that file were intentional.

Summary

There are dozens of commands for exploring and working with files in Linux. Commands such as chmod can change the permissions associated with a file, whereas commands that include lsattr and chattr can be used to list and change file attributes that are associated with ext2 and ext3 file system types.

To move around the file system, people use the cd command most often. However, to move repeatedly among the same directories, you can use the pushd and popd commands to work with a stack of directories.

Copying files is done with the cp command. However, the dd command can be used to copy files (such as disk images) from a device (such as a CD-ROM drive). For creating directories, you can use the mkdir command.

Instead of keeping multiple copies of a file around on the file system, you can use symbolic links and hard links to have multiple file names point to the same file or directory. Symbolic links can be anywhere in the file system, while hard links must exist on the same partition that the original file is on.

To search for files, Linux offers the locate and find commands. To verify the integrity of files you download from the Internet, you can use the md5sum and sha1sum commands.

5

Manipulating Text

With only a shell available on the first Unix systems (on which Linux was based), using those systems meant dealing primarily with commands and plain text files. Documents, program code, configuration files, e-mail, and almost anything you created or configured was represented by text files. To work with those files, early developers created many text manipulation tools.

Despite having graphical tools for working with text, most seasoned Linux users find command line tools to be more efficient and convenient. Text editors such as vi (Vim), Emacs, JOE, nano, and Pico are available with most Linux distributions. Commands such as grep, sed, and awk can be used to find, and possibly change, pieces of information within text files.

This chapter shows how to use many popular commands for working with text files in Ubuntu. It also explores some of the less common uses of text manipulation commands that you might find interesting.

Matching Text with Regular Expressions

Many of the tools for working with text enable you to use *regular expressions*, sometimes referred to as *regex*, to identify the text you are looking for based on some pattern. You can use these strings to find text within a text editor or use them with search commands to scan multiple files for the strings of text you want.

A regex search pattern can include a specific string of text (as in a word such as *Linux*) or a location (such as the end of a line or the beginning of a word). It can also be specific (find just the word *hello*) or more inclusive (find any word beginning with *h* and ending with *o*).

Appendix C includes reference information for shell metacharacters that can be used in conjunction with regular expressions to do the exact kinds of matches you are looking for. This section shows examples of using regular expressions with several different tools you encounter throughout this chapter.

Table 5-1 shows some examples using basic regular expressions to match text strings.

Many examples of regular expressions are used in examples throughout this chapter. Keep in mind that not every command that incorporates regex uses its features the same way.

Table 5-1: Matching Using Regular Expressions

Expression	Matches
a*	a, ab, abc, and aecjejich
^a	Any "a" appearing at the beginning of a line
*a$	Any "a" appearing at the end of a line
a.c	Three-character strings that begin with a and end with c
[bcf]at	bat, cat, or fat
[a-d]at	aat, bat, cat, dat, but not Aat, Bat, and so on
[A-D]at	Aat, Bat, Cat, and Dat, but not aat, bat, and so on
1[3-5]7	137, 147, and 157
\tHello	A tab character preceding the word Hello
\.[tT][xX][Tt]	.txt, .TXT, .TxT, or other case combinations

Editing Text Files

There are many text editors in the Linux/Unix world. The editor that is most common is vi, which can be found virtually on any Unix system available today. That is why knowing how to at least make minor file edits in vi is a critical skill for any Linux administrator. One day, if you find yourself in a minimalist, foreign Linux environment trying to bring a server back online, vi is the tool that will almost always be there.

On Ubuntu, make sure you have the vim-enhanced package installed. Vim (Vi IMproved) with the vim-enhanced package will provide the most up-to-date, feature-rich, and user-friendly vi editor. For more details about using vi, refer to Appendix A.

NOTE   *Ubuntu installs vim by default.*

Traditionally, the other popular Unix text editor has been Emacs and its more graphical variant, XEmacs. Emacs is a powerful multi-function tool that can also act as a mail/news reader or shell, and perform other functions. Emacs is also known for its very complex series of keyboard shortcuts that require three arms to execute properly.

In the mid-90s, Emacs was ahead of vi in terms of features. Now that Vim is widely available, both can provide all the text editing features you'll ever need. If you are not already familiar with either vi or Emacs, we recommend you start by learning vi.

There are many other command line and GUI text editors available for Linux. Text-based editors that you may find to be simpler than vi and Emacs include JED, JOE, and nano. Start any of those editors by typing its command name, optionally followed by the file name you want to edit. The following sections offer some quick descriptions of how to use each of those editors.

Using the JOE Editor

If you have used classic word processors such as WordStar that worked with text files, you might be comfortable with the JOE editor. To use JOE, install the joe package. To use the spell checker in JOE, make sure the aspell package is installed. (Ubuntu installs aspell by default.) To install JOE, run the following command:

```
$ sudo apt-get install joe
```

With JOE, instead of entering a command or text mode, you are always ready to type. To move around in the file, you can use control characters or the arrow keys. To open a text file for editing, just type **joe** and the file name or use some of the following options:

```
$ joe memo.txt                        Open memo.txt for editing
$ joe -wordwrap memo.txt              Turn on wordwrap while editing
$ joe -lmargin 5 -tab 5 memo.txt      Set left margin to 5 and tab to 5
$ joe +25 memo.txt                    Begin editing on line 25
```

To add text, just begin typing. You can use keyboard shortcuts for many functions. Use arrow keys to move the cursor left, right, up, or down. Use the Delete key to delete text under the cursor or the Backspace key to erase text to the left of the cursor. Press Enter to add a line break. Press Ctrl+k+h to see the help screen. Table 5-2 shows the most commonly used control keys for editing in JOE.

Table 5-2: Control Keys for Editing with JOE

Key Combo	Result
Cursor	
Ctrl+b	Left
Ctrl+p	Up
Ctrl+f	Right
Ctrl+n	Down
Ctrl+z	Previous word
Ctrl+x	Next word
Search	
Ctrl+k+f	Find text
Ctrl+l	Find next
Block	
Ctrl+k+b	Begin
Ctrl+k+k	End
Ctrl+k+m	Move block
Ctrl+k+c	Copy block
Ctrl+k+w	Write block to file
Ctrl+k+y	Delete block
Ctrl+k+/	Filter
Misc	
Ctrl+k+a	Center line
Ctrl+t	Options
Ctrl+r	Refresh
File	
Ctrl+k+e	Open new file to edit

Table 5-2: Control Keys for Editing with JOE (*continued*)

Key Combo	Result
File (*continued*)	
Ctrl+k+r	Insert file at cursor
Ctrl+k+d	Save
Goto	
Ctrl+u	Previous screen
Ctrl+v	Next screen
Ctrl+a	Line beginning
Ctrl+e	End of line
Ctrl+k+u	Top of file
Ctrl+k+v	End of file
Ctrl+k+l	To line number
Delete	
Ctrl+d	Delete character
Ctrl+y	Delete line
Ctrl+w	Delete word right
Ctrl+o	Delete word left
Ctrl+j	Delete line to right
Ctrl+-	Undo
Ctrl+6	Redo
Exit	
Ctrl+k+x	Save and quit
Ctrl+c	Abort
Ctrl+k+z	Shell

Continued

Table 5-2: Control Keys for Editing with JOE (*continued*)

Key Combo	Result
Spell	
Ctrl+[+n	Word
Ctrl+[+l	File

Using the Pico and nano Editors

Pico is a popular, very small text editor, distributed as part of the Pine e-mail client. Although Pico is free, it is not truly open source. Therefore, many Linux distributions, including Ubuntu, don't offer Pico. Instead, they offer an open source clone of Pico called nano (*nano's ano*ther editor). This section describes the nano editor.

NOTE *Ubuntu links the command* pico *to the program for the nano editor.*

Nano (represented by the nano command) is a compact text editor that runs from the shell, but is screen-oriented (owing to the fact that it is based on the curses library). Nano is popular with those who formerly used the Pine e-mail client because nano's editing features are the same as those used by Pine's Pico editor. On the rare occasion that you don't have the vi editor available on a Linux system (such as when installing a minimal Gentoo Linux), nano may be available. Ubuntu installs nano by default. You need the spell command, rather than aspell, to perform a spelling check within nano.

As with the JOE editor, instead of having command and typing modes, you can just begin typing. To **open a text file for editing**, just type **nano** and the file name or use some of the following options:

```
$ nano memo.txt          Open memo.txt for editing
$ nano -B memo.txt       When saving, back up previous to ~.filename
$ nano -m memo.txt       Turn on mouse to move cursor (if supported)
$ nano +83 memo.txt      Begin editing on line 83
```

The -m command-line option turns on support for a mouse. You can use the mouse to select a position in the text, and the cursor moves to that position. After the first click, though, nano uses the mouse to mark a block of text, which may not be what you are expecting.

As with JOE, to **add text**, just begin typing. Use arrow keys to move the cursor left, right, up, or down. Use the Delete key to delete text under the cursor or the Backspace key to erase text to the left of the cursor. Press Enter to add a line break. Press Ctrl+g to read help text. Table 5-3 shows the control codes for nano that are described on the help screen.

Table 5-3: Control Keys for Editing with nano

Control Code	Function Key	Description
Ctrl+g	F1	Show help text. (Press Ctrl+x to exit help.)
Ctrl+x	F2	Exit nano (or close the current file buffer).
Ctrl+o	F3	Save the current file.
Ctrl+j	F4	Justify the current text in the current paragraph.
Ctrl+r	F5	Insert a file into the current file.
Ctrl+w	F6	Search for text.
Ctrl+y	F7	Go to the previous screen.
Ctrl+v	F8	Go to the next screen.
Ctrl+k	F9	Cut (and store) the current line or marked text.
Ctrl+u	F10	Uncut (paste) the previously cut line into the file.
Ctrl+c	F11	Display the current cursor position.
Ctrl+t	F12	Start spell checking.
Ctrl+-		Go to selected line and column numbers.
Ctrl+\		Search and replace text.
Ctrl+6		Mark text, starting at the cursor (Ctrl+6 to unset mark).
Ctrl+f		Go forward one character.
Ctrl+b		Go back one character.
Ctrl+Space		Go forward one word.
Alt+Space		Go backward one word.
Ctrl+p		Go to the previous line.
Ctrl+n		Go to the next line.
Ctrl+a		Go to the beginning of the current line.
Ctrl+e		Go to the end of the current line.
Alt+(		Go to the beginning of the current paragraph.

Continued

Table 5-3: Control Keys for Editing with nano (*continued*)

Control Code	Function Key	Description
Alt+)		Go to the end of the current paragraph.
Alt+\		Go to the first line of the file.
Alt+/		Go to the last line of the file.
Alt+]		Go to the bracket matching the current bracket.
Alt+=		Scroll down one line.
Alt+-		Scroll up the line.

Graphical Text Editors

Just because you are editing text doesn't mean you have to use a text-based editor. The main advantages of using a graphical text editor is that you can use a mouse to select menus, highlight text, cut and copy text, or run special plug-ins.

You can expect to have the GNOME text editor (gedit) if your Linux system has the GNOME desktop installed. Features in gedit enable you to check spelling, list document statistics, change display fonts and colors, and print your documents. The KDE desktop also has its own KDE text editor (kedit in the kdeutils package). It includes similar features to the GNOME text editor, along with a few extras, such as the ability to send the current document with kmail or another user-configurable KDE component.

Vim itself comes with an X GUI version. It is launched with the gvim command, which is part of the vim-X11 package. If you'd like to turn GUI Vim into a more user-friendly text editor, you can download a third-party configuration called Cream from http://cream.sourceforge.net/.

NOTE   *To use gvim, you need to install an additional package, vim-gnome.*

Other text editors you can install include nedit (with features for using macros and executing shell commands and aimed at software developers) and leafpad (which is similar to the Windows Notepad text editor). The Scribes text editor (scribes) includes some advanced features for automatic correction, replacement, indentation, and word completion.

Listing, Sorting, and Changing Text

Instead of just editing a single text file, you can use a variety of Linux commands to display, search, and manipulate the contents of one or more text files at a time.

Listing Text Files

The most basic method to display the contents of a text file is with the `cat` command. The `cat` command concatenates (in other words, outputs as a string of characters) the contents of a text file to your display (by default). You can then use different shell metacharacters to **direct the contents of that file in different ways.** For example:

```
$ cat myfile.txt                        Send entire file to the screen
$ cat myfile.txt > copy.txt             Direct file contents to another file
$ cat myfile.txt >> myotherfile.txt     Append file contents to another file
$ cat -s myfile.txt                     Display consecutive blank lines as one
$ cat -n myfile.txt                     Show line numbers with output
$ cat -b myfile.txt                     Show line numbers only on non-blank lines
```

However, if your block of text is more than a few lines long, using `cat` by itself becomes impractical. That's when you need better tools to look at the beginning or the end, or page through the entire text.

To **view the top of a file,** use `head`:

```
$ head myfile.txt
$ cat myfile.txt | head
```

Both of these command lines use the `head` command to output the top 10 lines of the file. You can specify the line count as a parameter to display any number of lines from the beginning of a file. For example:

```
$ head -n 50 myfile.txt      Show the first 50 lines of a file
$ ps auwx | head -n 15       Show the first 15 lines of ps output
```

This can also be done using this obsolete (but shorter) syntax:

```
$ head -50 myfile.txt
$ ps auwx | head -15
```

You can use the `tail` command in a similar way to **view the end of a file:**

```
$ tail -n 15 myfile.txt      Display the last 15 lines in a file
$ tail -15 myfile.txt        Display the last 15 lines in a file
$ ps auwx | tail -n 15       Display the last 15 lines of ps output
```

The `tail` command can also be used to **continuously watch the end of a file** as the file is written to by another program. This is very useful for reading live log files when troubleshooting apache, sendmail, or many other system services:

```
# tail -f /var/log/messages          Watch system messages live
# tail -f /var/log/maillog           Watch mail server messages live
# tail -f /var/log/httpd/access_log  Watch web server messages live
```

Paging Through Text

When you have a large chunk of text and need to get to more than just its beginning or end, you need a tool to **page through the text**. The original Unix system pager was the more command:

```
$ ps auwx | more      Page through the output of ps (press spacebar)
$ more myfile.txt      Page through the contents of a file
```

However, more has some limitations. For example, in the line with ps above, more could not scroll up. The less command was created as a more powerful and user-friendly more. The common saying when less was introduced was: "What is less? less is more!" We recommend you no longer use more, and use less instead.

> **NOTE** *The less command has another benefit worth noting. Unlike text editors such as vi, it does not read the entire file when it starts. This results in faster start-up times when viewing large files.*

The less command can be used with the same syntax as more in the examples above:

```
$ ps auwx | less          Page through the output of ps
$ cat myfile.txt | less    Page through the contents of a file
$ less myfile.txt          Page through a text file
```

The less command enables you to **navigate** using the up and down arrow keys, PageUp, PageDown, and the spacebar. If you are using less on a file (not standard input), press v to open the current file in an editor. Which editor gets launched is determined by environment variables defined for your account. The editor is taken from the environment variable VISUAL, if defined, or EDITOR if VISUAL is not defined. If neither is defined, less invokes the JOE editor on Ubuntu.

> **NOTE** *Other versions of Linux invoke vi as the default editor in this case.*

Press Ctrl+c to interrupt that mode. As in vi, while viewing a file with less, you can **search for a string** by pressing / (forward slash) followed by the string and Enter. To search for further occurrences, press / and Enter repeatedly.

To **scroll forward and back** while using less, use the F and B keys, respectively. For example, 10f scrolls forward 10 lines and 15b scrolls back 15 lines. Type **d** to scroll down half a screen and **u** to scroll up half a screen.

Paginating Text Files with pr

The pr command provides a quick way to format a bunch of text into a form where it can be printed. This can be particularly useful if you want to print the results of some commands, without having to open up a word processor or text editor. With pr, you can format text into pages with header information such as date, time, file name, and page number. Here is an example:

```
$ dpkg-query -1 | sort | pr --column=2 | less   Paginate package list in 2 cols
```

In this example, the rpm -qa command lists all software packages installed on your system and pipes that list to the sort command, to be sorted alphabetically. Next that list is piped to the pr command, which converts the single-column list into two columns (--columns=2) and paginates it. Finally, the less command enables you to page through the text.

Instead of paging through the output, you can send the output to a file or to a printer. Here are examples of that:

```
$ dpkg-query -1 | sort | pr --column=2 > pkg.txt   Send pr output to a file
$ dpkg-query -1 | sort | pr --column=2 | lpr       Send pr output to printer
```

Other text manipulation you can do with the pr command includes double-spacing the text (-d), showing control characters (-c), or offsetting the text a certain number of spaces from the left margin (for example, -o 5 to indent five spaces from the left).

Searching for Text with grep

The grep command comes in handy when you need to perform more advanced string searches in a file. In fact, the phrase *to grep* has actually entered the computer jargon as a verb, just as *to Google* has entered the popular language. Here are examples of the grep command:

```
$ grep francois myfile.txt               Show lines containing francois
# grep 404 /var/log/httpd/access_log     Show lines containing 404
$ ps auwx | grep init                    Show init lines from ps output
$ ps auwx | grep "\[*\]"                 Show bracketed commands
$ dmesg | grep "[ ]ata\|^ata"            Show ata kernel device information
```

These command lines have some particular uses, beyond being examples of the grep command. By searching access_log for 404 you can see requests to your web server for pages that were not found (these could be someone fishing to exploit your system, or a web page you moved or forgot to create). Displaying bracketed commands that are output from the ps command is a way to see commands for which ps cannot display options. The last command checks the kernel buffer ring for any ATA device information, such as hard disks and CD-ROM drives.

The grep command can also recursively search a few or a whole lot of files at the same time. The following command recursively searches files in the /etc/httpd/conf and /etc/httpd/conf.d directories for the string VirtualHost:

```
$ grep -R VirtualHost /etc/httpd/conf*
```

Note that your system may not have any files with names starting with conf in the /etc/httpd directory, depending on what you have installed on your system. You can apply this technique to other files as well.

Add line numbers (-n) to your grep command to find the exact lines where the search terms occur:

```
$ grep -Rn VirtualHost /etc/httpd/conf*
```

To colorize the searched term in the search results, add the --color option:

```
$ grep --color -Rn VirtualHost /etc/httpd/conf*
```

By default, in a multifile search, the file name is displayed for each search result. Use the -h option to disable the display of file names. This example searches for the string sshd in the file auth.log:

```
$ grep -h sshd /var/log/auth.log
```

If you want to ignore case when you search messages, use the -i option:

```
$ grep -i selinux /var/log/messages    Search file for selinux (any case)
```

To display only the name of the file that includes the search term, add the -l option:

```
$ grep -Rl VirtualHost /etc/httpd/conf*
```

To display all lines that do *not* match the string, add the -v option:

```
$ grep -v " 200 " /var/log/httpd/access_log*    Show lines without " 200 "
```

> **NOTE** *When piping the output of* ps *into* grep, *here's a trick to prevent the* grep *process from appearing in the* grep *results:*
>
> ```
> # ps auwx | grep "[i]nit"
> ```

Checking Word Counts with wc

There are times when you need to know the number of lines that match a search string. The wc command can be used to count the lines that it receives. For example, the following command lists how many hits in an Apache log file come from a specific IP address:

```
$ grep 192.198.1.1 /var/log/httpd/access-log | wc -l
```

The wc command has other uses as well. By default, wc prints the number of lines, words, and bytes in a file:

```
$ wc /var/log/dmesg                  List counts for a single file
436  3847 27984 /var/log/dmesg
```

```
$  wc /var/log/*.log                    List single/totals for many files
   305    3764   25772 /var/log/auth.log

   780    3517   36647 /var/log/bootstrap.log

   350    4405   39042 /var/log/daemon.log

 10109   60654 669687 /var/log/dpkg.log

    71     419    4095 /var/log/fontconfig.log

  1451   19860 135252 /var/log/kern.log

     0       0       0 /var/log/lpr.log

     0       0       0 /var/log/mail.log

     0       0       0 /var/log/pycentral.log

     0       0       0 /var/log/scrollkeeper.log

   108    1610   13864 /var/log/user.log

     0       0       0 /var/log/uucp.log

    12      43     308 /var/log/wvdialconf.log

   890    6717   46110 /var/log/Xorg.0.log

 14076 100989 970777 total
```

Sorting Output with sort

It can also be useful to **sort the content of a file or the output of a command**. This can be helpful in bringing order to disorderly output. The following examples list the names of all RPM packages currently installed, grabs any with *kernel* in the name, and sorts the results in alphanumeric order (forward and reverse):

```
$ dpkg-query -1 | grep kernel | sort       Sort in alphanumeric order
$ dpkg-query -1 | grep kernel | sort -r    Sort in reverse alphanumeric order
```

The following command **sorts processes based on descending memory usage** (fourth field of ps output). The -k option specifies the key field to use for sorting. 4,4 indicates that the fourth field, and only the fourth field, is a key field.

```
$ ps auwx | sort -r -k 4,4
```

The following command line **sorts loaded kernel modules in increasing size order**. The n option tells sort to treat the second field as a number and not a string:

```
$ lsmod | sort -k 2,2n
```

Finding Text in Binaries with Strings

Sometimes you need to read the ASCII text that is inside a binary file. Occasionally, you can learn a lot about an executable that way. For those occurrences, use `strings` to extract all the human-readable ASCII text. The `strings` command is part of the binutils package, and is installed by default on Ubuntu. Here are some examples:

```
$ strings /bin/ls | grep -i libc   Find occurrences of libc in ls
$ cat /bin/ls | strings             List all ASCII text in ls
$ strings /bin/ls                   List all ASCII text in ls
```

Replacing Text with sed

Finding text within a file is sometimes the first step towards replacing text. Editing streams of text is done using the `sed` command. The `sed` command is actually a full-blown scripting language. For the examples in this chapter, we cover basic text replacement with the `sed` command.

If you are familiar with text replacement commands in vi, `sed` has some similarities. In the following example, you would replace only the first occurrence per line of *francois* with *chris*. Here, `sed` takes its input from a pipe, while sending its output to stdout (your screen):

```
$ cat myfile.txt | sed s/francois/chris/
```

Adding a `g` to the end of the substitution line, as in the following command, causes every occurrence of *francois* to be changed to *chris*. Also, in the following example, input is directed from the file `myfile.txt` and output is directed to `mynewfile.txt`:

```
$ sed s/francois/chris/g < myfile.txt > mynewfile.txt
```

The next example replaces the first occurrences of of the text `/home/bob` to `/home2/bob` from the `/etc/passwd` file. (Note that this command does not change that file, but outputs the changed text.) This is useful for the case when user accounts are migrated to a new directory (presumably on a new disk), named with much deliberation, home2. Here, we have to use quotes and backslashes to escape the forward slashes so they are not interpreted as delimiters:

```
$ sed 's/\/home\/bob/\/home2\/bob/g' < /etc/passwd
```

Although the forward slash is the `sed` command's default delimiter, you can change the delimiter to any other character of your choice. Changing the delimiter can make your life easier when the string contains slashes. For example, the previous command line that contains a path could be replaced with either of the following commands:

```
$ sed 's-/home/bob/-/home2/bob/-' < /etc/passwd
$ sed 'sD/home/bob/D/home2/bob/D' < /etc/passwd
```

In the first line shown, a dash (-) is used as the delimiter. In the second case, the letter D is the delimiter.

The `sed` command can **run multiple substitutions at once,** by preceding each one with -e. Here, in the text streaming from `myfile.txt`, all occurrences of *francois* are changed to *FRANCOIS* and occurrences of *chris* are changed to *CHRIS*:

```
$ sed -e s/francois/FRANCOIS/g -e s/chris/CHRIS/g < myfile.txt
```

You can use `sed` to **add newline characters to a stream of text.** Where `Enter` appears, press the Enter key. The > on the second line is generated by bash, not typed in.

```
$ echo aaabccc | sed 's/b/\Enter
> /'
aaa
ccc
```

The trick just shown does not work on the left side of the `sed` substitution command. When you need to substitute newline characters, it's easier to use the `tr` command.

Translating or Removing Characters with tr

The `tr` command is an easy way to **do simple character translations on the fly.** In the following example, new lines are replaced with spaces, so all the files listed from the current directory are output on one line:

```
$ ls | tr '\n' ' '          Replace newline characters with spaces
```

The `tr` command can be used to **replace one character with another,** but does not work with strings like `sed` does. The following command replaces all instances of the lowercase letter `f` with a capital `F`.

```
$ tr f F < myfile.txt        Replace every f in the file with F
```

You can also use the `tr` command to simply **delete characters.** Here are two examples:

```
$ ls | tr -d '\n'            Delete new lines (resulting in one line)
$ tr -d f < myfile.txt       Delete every letter f from the file
```

The `tr` command can do some nifty tricks when you **specify ranges of characters** to work on. Here's an example of capitalizing lowercase letters to uppercase letters:

```
$ echo chris | tr a-z A-Z    Translate chris into CHRIS
CHRIS
```

The same result can be obtained with the following syntax:

```
$ echo chris | tr '[:lower:]' '[:upper:]'    Translate chris into CHRIS
```

Checking Differences Between Two Files with diff

When you have two versions of a file, it can be useful to know the differences between the two files. For example, when upgrading a software package, you may save your old configuration file under a new file name, such as `config.old` or `config.bak`, so you preserve your configuration. When that occurs, you can use the `diff` command to discover which lines differ between your configuration and the new configuration, in order to merge the two. For example:

```
$ diff config config.old
```

You can change the output of `diff` to what is known as *unified format*. Unified format can be easier to read by human beings. It adds three lines of context before and after each block of changed lines that it reports, and then uses + and - to show the difference between the files. The following set of commands creates a file (`f1.txt`) containing a sequence of numbers (1–7), creates a file (`f2.txt`) with one of those numbers changed (using `sed`), and compares the two files using the `diff` command:

```
$ seq 1 7 > f1.txt          Send a sequence of numbers to f1.txt
$ cat f1.txt                Display contents of f1.txt
1
2
3
4
5
6
7
$ sed s/4/FOUR/ < f1.txt > f2.txt   Change 4 to FOUR and send to f2.txt
$ diff f1.txt f2.txt
4c4                         Shows line 4 was changed in file
< 4
---
> FOUR
$ diff -u f1.txt f2.txt             Display unified output of diff
--- f1.txt 2007-09-07 18:26:06.000000000 -0500
+++ f2.txt 2007-09-07 18:26:39.000000000 -0500
@@ -1,7 +1,7 @@
1
2
3
-4
+FOUR
5
6
7
```

The `diff -u` output just displayed adds information such as modification dates and times to the regular `diff` output. The `sdiff` command can be used to give you yet another view. The sdiff command can **merge the output of two** files interactively, as shown in the following output:

```
$ sdiff f1.txt f2.txt
1                                                    1
2                                                    2
3                                                    3
4                                                  | FOUR
5                                                    5
6                                                    6
7                                                    7
```

Another variation on the diff theme is vimdiff, which opens the two files side by side in Vim and outlines the differences in color. Similarly, gvimdiff opens the two files in gVim.

> **NOTE** *You need to install the vim-gnome package to run the gvim or gvimdiff program.*

The output of diff -u can be fed into the patch command. The patch command takes an old file and a diff file as input and **outputs a patched file**. Following on the example above, we use the diff command between the two files to generate a patch and then apply the patch to the first file:

```
$ diff -u f1.txt f2.txt > patchfile.txt
$ patch f1.txt < patchfile.txt
patching file f1.txt
$ cat f1.txt
1
2
3
FOUR
5
6
7
```

That is how many OSS developers (including kernel developers) distribute their code patches. The patch and diff commands can also be run on entire directory trees. However, that usage is outside the scope of this book.

Using awk and cut to Process Columns

Another massive text processing tool is the awk command. The awk command is a full-blown programming language. Although there is much more you can do with the awk command, the following examples show you a few tricks related to **extracting columns of text**:

```
$ ps auwx | awk '{print $1,$11}'          Show columns 1, 11 of ps
$ ps auwx | awk '/francois/ {print $11}'  Show francois' processes
$ ps auwx | grep francois | awk '{print $11}' Same as above
```

The first example displays the contents of the first column (user name) and eleventh column (command name) from currently running processes output from the ps command (ps auwx). The next two commands produce the same output, with one using the awk command and the other using the grep command to find all processes owned by the user named francois. In each case, when processes owned by francois are found, column 11 (command name) is displayed for each of those processes.

By default, the awk command assumes the delimiter between columns is spaces. You can specify a different delimiter with the -F option as follows:

```
$ awk -F: '{print $1,$5}' /etc/passwd    Use colon delimiter to print cols
```

You can get similar results with the cut command. As with the previous awk example, we specify a colon (:) as the column delimiter to process information from the /etc/passwd file:

```
$ cut -d: -f1,5 /etc/passwd              Use colon delimiter to print cols
```

The cut command can also be used with ranges of fields. The following command prints columns 1 thru 5 of the /etc/passwd file:

```
$ cut -d: -f1-5 /etc/passwd              Show columns 1 through 5
```

Instead of using a dash (-) to indicate a range of numbers, you can use it to print all columns from a particular column number and above. The following command displays all columns from column 5 and above from the /etc/passwd file:

```
$ cut -d: -f5- /etc/passwd               Show columns 5 and later
```

We prefer to use the awk command when columns are separated by a varying number of spaces, such as the output of the ps command. And we prefer the cut command when dealing with files delimited by commas (,) or colons (:), such as the /etc/password file.

Converting Text Files to Different Formats

Text files in the Unix world use a different end-of-line character (\n) than those used in the DOS/Windows world (\r\n). You can view these special characters in a text file with the od command:

```
$ od -c -t x1 myfile.txt
```

So they will appear properly when copied from one environment to the other, it is necessary to convert the files. Here are some examples:

```
$ unix2dos < myunixfile.txt > mydosfile.txt
$ cat mydosfile.txt | dos2unix > myunixfile.txt
```

The `unix2dos` example just shown above converts a Linux or Unix plain text file (`myunixfile.txt`) to a DOS or Windows text file (`mydosfile.txt`). The dos2unix example does the opposite by converting a DOS/Windows file to a Linux/Unix file. These commands require you to install the tofrodos package.

Summary

Linux and Unix systems traditionally use plain text files for system configuration, documentation, output from commands, and many forms of stored information. As a result, many commands have been created to search, edit, and otherwise manipulate plain text files. Even with today's GUI interfaces, the ability to manipulate plain text files is critical to becoming a power Linux user.

This chapter explores some of the most popular commands for working with plain text files in Linux. Those commands include text editors (such as vi, nano, and JOE), as well as commands that can edit streaming data (such as `sed` and `awk` commands). There are also commands for sorting text (`sort`), counting text (`wc`), and translating characters in text (`tr`).

6

Playing with Multimedia

There's no need to go to a GUI tool, if all you need to do is play a song or convert an image or audio file to a different form. There are commands for working with multimedia files (audio or images) that are quick and efficient if you find yourself working from the shell. And if you need to manipulate batches of multimedia files, the same command you use to transform one file can be added to a script to repeat the process on many files.

This chapter focuses on tools for working with audio and digital image files from the shell.

Working with Audio

There are commands available for Linux systems that can manipulate files in dozens of audio formats. Commands such as ogg123, mpg321, and play can be used to listen to audio files. There are commands for ripping songs from music CDs and encoding them to store efficiently. There are even commands to let you stream audio so anyone on your network can listen to your playlist.

Playing Music

Depending on the audio format you want to play, you can choose from several command line players for Linux. The play command (based on the sox facility, described later), can play audio files in multiple, freely available formats. You can use ogg123 to play popular open source music formats, including Ogg Vorbis, Free Lossless Audio Codec (FLAC), and Speex files. The mpg321 player, which is available via third-party RPM repositories, is popular for playing MP3 music files.

The `play` command requires the sox package. Install it with the following command:

```
$ sudo apt-get install sox
```

Type `sox -h` to **see audio formats and effects** available to use with `play`:

```
$ sox -h
    ...
Supported file formats: 8svx aif aifc aiff aiffc al alsa au auto avr cdda cdr
cvs cvsd dat dvms fssd gsm hcom ima ircam la lu maud nist nul null ogg ossdsp
prc raw s3 sb sf sl smp snd sndt sou sph sw txw u3 u4 ub ul uw vms voc vorbis
vox wav wve xa

Supported effects: allpass band bandpass bandreject bass chorus compand dcshift
deemph dither earwax echo echos equalizer fade filter flanger highpass lowpass
mcompand mixer noiseprof noisered pad pan phaser pitch polyphase repeat resample
reverb reverse silence speed stat stretch swap synth treble tremolo trim vibro
vol
```

The `play` command uses the sox code to play sounds.

Here are some examples of playing files using `play`:

```
$ play inconceivable.wav    Play WAV file (may be ripped from CD)
$ play *.wav                 Play all WAV files in directory (up to 32)
$ play hi.au vol .6          AU file, lower volume (can lower distortion)
$ play -r 14000 short.aiff   AIFF, sampling rate of 14000 hertz
```

To play Ogg Vorbis files, install the vorbis-tools package. Here are examples for playing Ogg Vorbis (www.vorbis.com/) files with `ogg123`:

```
$ ogg123 mysong.ogg                                   Play ogg file
$ ogg123 /usr/share/example-content/ubuntu\ Sax.ogg   Play example file
$ ogg123 http://vorbis.com/music/Lumme-Badloop.ogg    Play web address
$ ogg123 -z *.ogg                                     Play files in pseudo-random order
$ ogg123 /var/music/                                  Play songs in /var/music and sub dirs
$ ogg123 -@ myplaylist                                Play songs from playlist
```

A playlist is simply a list of directories or individual Ogg files to play. When a directory is listed, all Ogg files are played from that directory or any of its subdirectories. When playing multiple files, press Ctrl+c to **skip to the next song**. Press Ctrl+c twice to **quit**.

To use the `mpg321` player to play MP3 files, you need to install the mpg321 package. Here are examples for playing MP3 audio files with `mpg321`:

```
$ mpg321 yoursong.mp3        Play MP3 file
$ mpg321 -@ mp3list          Play songs from playlist of MP3s
$ cat mp3list | mpg321 -@ -  Pipe playlist to mpg321
$ mpg321 -z *.mp3            Play files in pseudo-random order
$ mpg321 -Z *.mp3            Same as -z, but repeat forever
```

An mpg321 playlist is simply a list of files. You can produce the list using a simple `ls` command and directing the output to a file. Use full paths to the files, unless you plan to use the list from a location from which relative paths make sense.

Adjusting Audio Levels

The command line audio tools you use to enable audio devices and adjust audio levels depend on the type of audio system you use. Advanced Linux Sound Architecture (ALSA) is the sound system used by most Linux systems these days. The Open Source Sound System (OSS) has been around longer and is still used on older hardware. In general, you can use `alsamixer` to adjust sound when ALSA is used and `aumix` with OSS.

ALSA is the default sound system for many Linux systems. By adding loadable modules that enable OSS device interfaces to work as well, audio applications that require the OSS device interface can work with ALSA as well. To see if **OSS modules are loaded**, such as snd-pcm-oss (emulates /dev/dsp and /dev/audio), snd-mixer-oss (emulates /dev/mixer), and snd-seq-oss (emulates /dev/sequencer), type:

```
# lsmod | grep snd
```

If the modules are loaded, you can use `alsamixer` to adjust audio levels for OSS sound applications. **Start alsamixer** as follows:

```
$ alsamixer               Show alsamixer screen with playback view
$ alsamixer -V playback   Show only playback channels (default)
$ alsamixer -V all        Show with playback and capture views
$ alsamixer -c 1          Use alsamixer on second (1) sound card
```

Volume bars appear for each volume channel. Move right and left arrow keys to highlight different channels (Master, PCM, Headphone, and so on). Use the up and down arrow keys to raise and lower the volume on each channel. With a channel highlighted, press m to **mute or unmute** that channel. Press the spacebar on a highlighted input channel (Mic, Line, and so on) to **assign the channel as the capture channel** (to record audio input). To **quit alsamixer**, press Alt+q or the Esc key. Press Tab to cycle through settings for Playback, Capture, and All.

The `aumix` audio mixing application (for which you need to install the aumix package) can operate in screen-oriented or plain command mode. In plain text you use options to **change or display settings**. Here are examples of `aumix` command lines:

```
$ aumix -q                  Show left/right volume and type for all channels
$ aumix -l q -m q           List current settings for line and mic only
$ aumix -v 80 -m 0          Set volume to 70% and microphone to 0
$ aumix -m 80 -m R -m q     Set mic to 80%, set it to record, list mic
$ aumix                     With no options, aumix runs screen-oriented
```

When run screen-oriented, `aumix` displays all available audio channels. In screen-oriented mode, **use keys to highlight and change displayed audio settings**. Use PageUp,

PageDown, and the up arrow and down arrow keys to select channels. Use the right or left arrow key to increase or decrease volume. Type m to mute the current channel. Press the spacebar to select the current channel as the recording device. If a mouse is available, you can use it to select volume levels, balance levels, or the current recording channel.

Ripping CD Music

To be able to play your personal music collection from Linux, you can use tools such as cdparanoia to rip tracks from music CDs to WAV files on your hard disk. The ripped files can then be encoded to save disk space, using tools such as oggenc (Ogg Vorbis), flac (FLAC), or lame (MP3).

> **NOTE** *There are some excellent graphical tools for ripping and encoding CDs, such as* grip *and* sound-juicer. *Because they are CDDB-enabled, those tools can also use information about the music on the CD to name the output files (artist, album, song, and so on). This section, however, describes how to use some of the underlying commands to rip and encode CD music manually.*

Using cdparanoia, you can check that your CD drive is capable of ripping Compact Disc Digital Audio (CDDA) CDs, retrieve audio tracks from your CD drive, and copy them to hard disk. Start by inserting a music CD in your drive and typing the following:

```
$ cdparanoia -vsQ
    . . .
Checking /dev/cdrom for cdrom...
Checking for SCSI emulation...
Checking for MMC style command set...
Verifying CDDA command set...
    . . .
Table of contents (audio tracks only):
track        length                begin        copy pre ch
===========================================================
   1.    18295 [04:03.70]        0 [00:00.00]    no   no  2
   2.    16872 [03:44.72]    18295 [04:03.70]    no   no  2
    . . .
  11.    17908 [03:58.58]   174587 [38:47.62]    no   no  2
  12.    17342 [03:51.17]   192495 [42:46.45]    no   no  2
TOTAL  209837 [46:37.62]    (audio only)
```

The snipped output shows cdparanoia checking the capabilities of /dev/cdrom, looking for SCSI emulations and MMC command set support, and verifying that the drive can handle CDDA information. Finally, it prints information about each track. Here are examples of cdparanoia command lines for ripping a CD to a hard drive:

```
$ cdparanoia -B              Rip tracks as WAV files by track name
$ cdparanoia -B -- "5-7"     Rip tracks 5-7 into separate files
$ cdparanoia -- "3-8" abc.wav   Rip tracks 3-8 to one file (abc.wav)
```

```
$ cdparanoia -- "1:[40]-"        Rip tracks 1 from 40 secs in to end of the CD
$ cdparanoia -f -- "3"           Rip track 3 and save to AIFF format
$ cdparanoia -a -- "5"           Rip track 5 and save to AIFC format
$ cdparanoia -w -- "1" my.wav    Rip track 1 and name it my.wav
```

Encoding Music

After a music file is ripped from CD, encoding that file to save disk space is usually the next step. Popular encoders include oggenc, flac, and lame, for encoding to Ogg Vorbis, FLAC, and MP3 formats, respectively.

With oggenc, you can start with audio files or streams in WAV, AIFF, FLAC, or raw format and convert them to Ogg Vorbis format. Although Ogg Vorbis is a lossy format, the default encoding from WAV files still produces very good quality audio and can result in a file that's about one-tenth the size. Here are some examples of oggenc:

```
$ oggenc ab.wav                  Encodes WAV to Ogg (ab.ogg)
$ oggenc ab.flac -o new.ogg      Encodes FLAC to Ogg (new.ogg)
$ oggenc ab.wav -q 9             Raises encoding quality to 9
```

By default, the quality (-q) of the oggenc output is set to 3. You can **set the quality** to any number from -1 to 10 (including fractions such as 5.5).

```
$ oggenc NewSong.wav -o NewSong.ogg \
    -a Bernstein -G Classical       \
    -d 06/15/1972 -t "Simple Song"  \
    -l "Bernsteins Mass"            \
    -c info="From Kennedy Center"
```

The command just shown converts MySong.wav to MySong.ogg. The artist name is Bernstein and the music type is Classical. The date is June 15, 1972, the song title is Simple Song and the album name is Bernsteins Mass. A comment is From Kennedy Center. The backslashes aren't needed if you just keep typing the whole command on one line. However, if you do add backslashes, make sure there are no spaces after the backslash.

The preceding example adds information to the header of the resulting Ogg file. You can **see the header information**, with other information about the file, using ogginfo:

```
$ ogginfo NewSong.ogg
Processing file "NewSong.ogg"...
    ...
Channels: 2
Rate: 44100
Nominal bitrate: 112.000000 kb/s
User comments section follows...
        info=From Kennedy Center
        title=Simple Song
```

```
          artist=Bernstein
          genre=Classical
          date=06/15/1972
          album=Bernsteins Mass
Vorbis stream 1:
          Total data length: 3039484 bytes
          Playback length: 3m:25.240s
          Average bitrate: 118.475307 kb/s
Logical stream 1 ended
```

Here you can see that comments were added during encoding. The -c option was used to set an arbitrary field (in this case, info) with some value to the header. Besides the comments information, you can see that this file has two channels and was recorded at a 44100 bitrate. You can also see the data length, playback time, and average bitrate.

The flac command is an encoder similar to oggenc, except that the WAV, AIFF, RAW, FLAC, or Ogg file is encoded to a FLAC file. Because flac is a free *lossless* audio codec, it is a popular encoding method for those who want to save some space, but still want top-quality audio output. Using default values, our encoding from WAV to FLAC resulted in files one-half the size, as opposed to one-tenth the size with oggenc. Install the flac package to use the flac command. Here is an example of the flac command:

$ **flac now.wav**	*Encodes WAV to FLAC (now.flac)*
$ **sox now.wav now.aiff**	*Encodes WAV to AIFF (now.aiff)*
$ **flac now.aiff -o now2.flac**	*Encodes AIFF to FLAC (now.flac)*
$ **flac -8 top.wav -o top.flac**	*Raises compression level to 8*

The compression level is set to -5 by default. A range from -0 to -8 can be used, with the highest number giving the greatest compression and the lower number giving faster compression time. To **convert files to MP3 format** using the lame command, you must first install the lame package. Here are some examples of the lame command to encode from WAV and AIFF files:

$ **lame in.wav**	*Encodes WAV to MP3 (in.wav.mp3)*
$ **lame in.wav --preset standard**	*Encodes to MP3 with std presets*
$ **lame tune.aiff -o tune.mp3**	*Encodes AIFF to MP3 (tune.mp3)*
$ **lame -h -b 64 -m m in.wav out.mp3**	*High quality, 64-bit, mono mode*
$ **lame -q 0 in.wav -o abcHQ.mp3**	*Encodes with quality set to 0*

With lame, you can set the quality from 0 to 9 (5 is the default). Setting the quality to 0 uses the best encoding algorithms, while setting it to 9 disables most algorithms (but the encoding process moves much faster). As with oggenc, you can **add tag information to your MP3 file** that can be used later when you play back the file. Here's an example:

```
$ lame NewSong.wav NewSong.mp3     \
    --ta Bernstein --tg Classical \
    --ty 1972 --tt "Simple Song"  \
    --tl "Bernsteins Mass"        \
    --tc "From Kennedy Center"
```

Like the wav-to-ogg example shown earlier in this chapter, the command just shown converts MySong.wav to MySong.mp3. As before, the artist name is Bernstein and the music type is Classical. The year is 1972, the song title is Simple Song, and the album name is Bernsteins Mass. A comment is From Kennedy Center. The backslashes aren't needed if you just keep typing the whole command on one line. However, if you do add backslashes, make sure there are no spaces after the backslash.

The tag information appears on the screen in graphical MP3 players (such as Rhythmbox and Totem, when they have been enabled to play MP3 format). You can also see tag information when you use command line players, such as the following mpg321 example:

```
$ mpg123 NewSong.mp3
High Performance MPEG 1.0/2.0/2.5 Audio Player for Layer 1, 2, and 3.
   . . .
Title  : Simple Song            Artist: Bernstein
Album  : Bernsteins Mass        Year  : 1972
Comment: From Kennedy Center    Genre : Classical

Playing MPEG stream from NewSong.mp3 ...
MPEG 1.0 layer III, 128 kbit/s, 44100 Hz joint-stereo
```

Streaming Music

If your music is on one machine, but you're working from another machine, **setting up a streaming music server** is a quick way to broadcast your music so it can be picked up from one or more computers on your network. The icecast streaming media server and ices audio source client can be installed in Ubuntu by typing:

```
$ sudo apt-get install icecast2  ices2
```

Here's a quick and dirty procedure for setting up icecast and ices to stream your music. Perform this task on the computer that contains the music you want to serve:

1. Edit the /etc/icecast2/icecast.xml file to change all passwords listed. Search for hackme to find the current passwords. You probably want different user and administrative passwords, especially if you allow others to stream music to the server. Remember the passwords you set for later. You may want to change other settings in this file as well, such as hostname:

```
$ sudo vi /etc/icecast2/icecast.xml
```

2. If you have a firewall, check that TCP port 8000 is accessible.

3. Start the icecast2 server as root user by typing the following (the server will actually run as the icecast2 user), and verify with the netstat command:

```
$ sudo /etc/init.d/icecast2 start
$ sudo netstat -topnavel | grep 8000
tcp       0      0 0.0.0.0:8000        0.0.0.0:*              LISTEN
111       35790      21494/icecast     off (0.00/0/0)
```

115

4. Create the directories needed by the ices2 program, which provides the playlist and music to the icecast2 server. Run the following commands:

```
$ sudo mkdir /var/log/ices
$ sudo mkdir /etc/ices2
$ sudo mkdir /etc/ices2/music
```

5. Create a playlist using any text edit or by directing a listing of your music to a file. For example, if all your Ogg music files are in /var/music subdirectories, type the following:

```
$ find /var/music -name *.ogg > playlist.txt
```

6. The playlist.txt file must contain full paths to every music file, and the files must be accessible to the icecast2 server. Then, copy the playlist file to the /etc/ices2 directory:

```
$ sudo cp playlist.txt /etc/ices2
```

With the playlist file created, use any text editor to remove or add files or directories to make your playlist as you would like it. (If you want some files to try out for your playlist, download some from http://vorbis.com/music.)

7. As root user, edit the /etc/ices2/ices-playlist.xml file so it will play from your playlist and feed that music to your running icecast2 server. Start with the example configuration file and then edit it. Run the following commands:

```
$ sudo cp /usr/share/doc/ices2/examples/ices-playlist.xml /etc/ices2
$ sudo vi /etc/ices2/ices-playlist.xml
```

8. In particular, you want to modify the metadata, input, and instance modules (be sure to change /etc/ices2/playlist.txt to the path where you put your playlist.txt file):

```
<metadata>
    <name>My Music Server</name>
    <genre>Different music styles</genre>
    <description>Mix of my personal music</description>
</metadata>
<input>
    <module>playlist</module>
    <param name="type">basic</param>
    <param name="file">/etc/ices2/playlist.txt</param>
    <!-- random play -->
    <param name="random">1</param>
          . . .
</input>
<instance>
    <hostname>localhost</hostname>
    <port>8000</port>
    <password>MIcePw</password>
    <mount>/mymusic.ogg</mount>
          . . .
</instance>
```

Of the values just shown (in bold), the most critical are the location of your playlist and the information about the instance of your icecast2 server. The password must match the source password you added to your /etc/icecast2/icecast.xml file.

9. Launch the ices audio feed by typing the following:

```
$ sudo ices2 /etc/ices2/ices-playlist.xml &
```

10. Test that you can play music from the local computer as follows:

```
$ ogg123 http://localhost:8000/mymusic.ogg
```

11. If that test works, try playing the icecast2 stream from another computer on your network by replacing localhost with the server's IP address or hostname.

12. If there are problems, check /var/log/icecast2 and /var/log/ices log files. Recheck your passwords and locations of configuration files.

13. When you are done, just kill the icecast2 service:

```
$ sudo /etc/init.d/icecast2 stop
```

When the icecast and ices servers are running, you should have access to that streaming music from any computer that can access your server computer. Use any music player that can play from an HTTP address (ogg123, Rhythmbox, XMMS, and so on). Windows music players that can support the type of content you are serving should work as well.

NOTE   *If you want to skip a song, type this from the server:* killall -HUP ices.

Converting Audio Files

The sox utility is an extremely versatile tool for working with audio files in different freely available formats. Here are a few examples of things you can do with sox:

The following command **concatenates two WAV files to a single output file:**

```
$ sox head.wav tail.wav output.wav
```

This command **mixes two WAV files:**

```
$ soxmix sound1.wav sound2.wav output.wav
```

To use sox to **display information about a file,** use the stat effect as follows:

```
$ sox sound1.wav -e stat
Samples read:           208512
Length (seconds):       9.456327
Scaled by:           2147483647.0
Maximum amplitude:      0.200592
Minimum amplitude:     -0.224701
Midline amplitude:     -0.012054
```

```
Mean      norm:           0.030373
Mean      amplitude:      0.000054
RMS       amplitude:      0.040391
Maximum delta:            0.060852
Minimum delta:            0.000000
Mean      delta:          0.006643
RMS       delta:          0.009028
Rough     frequency:           784
Volume adjustment:          4.450
```

Use `trim` to **delete seconds of sound** from an audio file. For example:

```
$ sox sound1.wav output.wav trim 4       Trim 4 seconds from start
$ sox sound1.wav output.wav trim 2 6     Keep from 2-6 seconds of file
```

The first example deletes the first 4 seconds from `sound1.wav` and writes the results to `output.wav`. The second example takes `sound1.wav`, keeps the section between second 2 and second 6 and deletes the rest, and writes to `output.wav`.

Transforming Images

With directories full of digital images, the ability to manipulate images from the command line can be a huge time saver. The ImageMagick package (use `apt-get install imagemagick` to install the package on Ubuntu) comes with some very useful tools for transforming your digital images into forms you can work with. This section shows some commands for manipulating digital images, and provides examples of simple scripts for making those changes in batches.

Getting Information about Images

To **get information about an image**, use the `identify` command, as follows:

```
$ identify p2090142.jpg
p2090142.jpg JPEG 2048x1536+0+0 DirectClass 8-bit 402.037kb
$ identify -verbose p2090142.jpg | less
  Standard deviation: 61.1665 (0.239869)
  Colors: 205713
  Rendering intent: Undefined
  Resolution: 72x72
  Units: PixelsPerInch
  Filesize: 402.037kb
  Interlace: None
  Background color: white
  Border color: rgb(223,223,223)
  Matte color: grey74
  Transparent color: black
  Page geometry: 2048x1536+0+0
  Compression: JPEG
  Quality: 44
    ...
```

The first command in the preceding example displays basic information about the image (its file name, format, geometry, its class, channel depth, and file size). The second command shows every bit of information it can extract from the image. In addition to the information you see in the example, the verbose output also shows creation times, the type of camera used, aperture value, and ISO speed rating.

Converting Images

The convert command is a Swiss Army knife of file converters. Here are some ways to manipulate images using the convert command. The following examples convert image files from one format to another:

```
$ convert tree.jpg tree.png      Convert a JPEG to a PNG file
$ convert icon.gif icon.bmp      Convert a GIF to a BMP file
$ convert photo.tiff photo.pcx   Convert a TIFF to a PCX file
```

Image types that convert supports include .jpg, .bmp, .pcx, .gif, .png, .tiff, .xpm, and .xwd. Here are examples of convert being used to resize images:

```
$ convert -resize 1024x768 hat.jpg hat-sm.jpg
$ convert -sample 50%x50% dog.jpg dog-half.jpg
```

The first example creates an image (hat-sm.jpg) that is 1024 × 768 pixels. The second example reduced the image dog.jpg in half (50%x50%) and saves it as dog-half.jpg.

You can rotate images from 0 to 360 degrees. Here are examples:

```
$ convert -rotate 270 sky.jpg sky-final.jpg      Rotate image 270 degrees
$ convert -rotate 90 house.jpg house-final.jpg   Rotate image 90 degrees
```

You can add text to an image using the -draw option:

```
$ convert -fill black -pointsize 60 -font helvetica    \
    -draw 'text 10,80 "Copyright NegusNet Inc."'    \
    p10.jpg p10-cp.jpg
```

The previous example adds copyright information to an image, using 60 point black Helvetica font to write text on the image. The text is placed 10 points in and 80 points down from the upper left corner. The new image name is p10-cp.jpg, to indicate that the new image had copyright information added.

Here are some interesting ways to create thumbnails with the convert command:

```
$ convert -thumbnail 120x120 a.jpg a-a.png
$ convert -thumbnail 120x120 -border 8 a.jpg a-b.png
$ convert -thumbnail 120x120 -border 8 -rotate 8 a.jpg a-c.png
```

All three examples create a 120 × 120–pixel thumbnail. The second adds the -border option to put a border around the thumbnail, so it looks like a Polaroid picture. The last example rotates the image. Figure 6-1 shows the results of these three examples.

a-a.png
3.3 MB

a-b.png
23.1 KB

a-c.png
29.1 KB

Figure 6-1: Use convert to create a thumbnail, add borders, and rotate images.

Besides the things you can do to make images useful and manageable, there are also ways of making your images fun and even weird. Here are some examples:

```
$ convert -sepia-tone 75% house.jpg oldhouse.png
$ convert -charcoal 5 house.jpg char-house.png
$ convert -colorize 175 house.jpg color-house.png
```

The -sepia-tone option gives the image an Old West sort of look. The -charcoal option makes the image look as if the picture was hand-drawn using charcoal. By using the -colorize option, every pixel in the image is modified using the colorize number provided (175 in this case). Figure 6-2 shows the original house picture in the upper-left corner, the Sepia Tone in the upper-right, the charcoal in the lower left, and the colorized house in the lower right.

If you are looking for one more example of weird image conversions, try swirling your image. For example:

```
$ convert -swirl 300 photo.pcx weird.pcx
```

Converting Images in Batches

Most of the image conversions described in this chapter can be done quite easily using a graphical image manipulation tool such The GIMP. However, where the convert commands we described can really shine are when you use them in scripts. So, instead of resizing, rotating, writing on, or colorizing a single file, you can do any (or all) of those things to a whole directory of files.

You may want to create thumbnails for your duck decoy collection images. Or perhaps you want to reduce all your wedding photos so they can play well on a digital photo frame. You might even want to add copyright information to every image in a directory before you share them on the Web. All these things can be done quite easily with the convert commands already described and some simple shell scripts.

Figure 6-2: Start with a normal image and sepia-tone, charcoal, and colorize it.

Here's an example of a script you can run to **resize an entire directory of photos** to 1024×768 pixels to play on a digital photo frame:

```
$ cd $HOME/myimages
$ mkdir small
$ for pic in `ls *.png`
do
    echo "converting $pic"
    convert -resize 1024x768 $pic small/sm-$pic
done
```

Before running the script, this procedure changes to the $HOME/myimages directory (which happens to contain a set of high-resolution images). Then it creates a subdirectory to hold the reduced images called small. The script itself starts with a for loop that lists each file ending in .png in the current directory (you might need to make that .jpg or other image suffix). Then, each file is resized to 1024×768 and copied to the small directory, with sm- added to each file name.

Using that same basic script, you can use any of the `convert` command lines shown earlier, or make up your own to suit your needs. You might be able to convert a whole directory of images in a few minutes that would have taken you hours of clicking in the GUI.

Summary

The shell can provide a quick and efficient venue for working with your audio and digital image files. This chapter describes ways of playing, ripping, encoding, converting, and streaming audio files from the command line. As for digital images, we provide many examples of using the `convert` command for resizing, rotating, converting, writing on, and otherwise manipulating those images.

7

Administering File Systems

File systems provide the structures in which files, directories, devices, and other elements of the system are accessed from Linux. Linux supports many different types of file systems (ext3, VFAT, ISO9660, NTFS, and so on) as well as many different types of media on which file systems can exist (hard disks, CDs, USB flash drives, ZIP drives, and so on).

Creating and managing disk partitions and the file systems on those partitions are among the most critical jobs in administering a Linux system. That's because if you mess up your file system, you might very well lose the critical data stored on your computer's hard disk or removable media.

This chapter contains commands for partitioning storage media, creating file systems, mounting and unmounting partitions, and checking file systems for errors and disk space.

Understanding File System Basics

Even though there are a lot of different file system types available in Linux, there are not many that you need to set up a basic Linux system. For a basic Linux system, your computer hard disk may contain only three partitions: a swap partition (used to handle the overflow of information in RAM), a boot partition that contains the boot loader and kernel, and a root file system partition. The boot and root file system partitions are usually an ext3 file system type.

The ext3 file system type is based on the ext2 file system type, adding a feature called *journaling* to its predecessor. Journaling can improve data integrity and recovery, especially after unclean system shutdowns. Time-consuming file system checks are avoided during the next reboot after an unclean shutdown, because the changes that occurred since the most recent write to disk are saved and ready to be restored.

Most of the examples in this chapter use ext3 files systems to illustrate how a file system is created and managed. However, there are times when you might want to use other file system types. Table 7-1 lists different file system types and describes when you might want to use them.

Table 7-1: File System Types Supported in Linux

File System Type	Description
ext3	Most commonly used file system with Linux. Contains journaling features for safer data and fast reboots after unintended shutdowns.
ext2	Predecessor of ext3, but doesn't contain journaling.
iso9660	Evolved from the High Sierra file system (which was the original standard used on CD-ROM). May contain Rock Ridge extensions to allow iso9660 file systems to support long file names and other information (file permissions, ownership, and links).
Jffs2	Journaling Flash File System version 2 (JFFS2) that is designed for efficient operations on USB flash drives. Successor to JFFS.
jfs	JFS file system that IBM used for OS/2 Warp. Tuned for large file systems and high-performance environments.
msdos	MS-DOS file system. Can be used to mount older MS-DOS file systems, such as those on old floppy disks.
ntfs	Microsoft New Technology File System (NTFS). Useful when file systems need to share files with newer Windows systems (as with dual booting or removable drives).
reiserfs	Journaling file system that used to be used by default on some SUSE, Slackware, and other Linux systems. Reiserfs is not well-supported in Ubuntu.
squashfs	Compressed, read-only file system used on many Linux live CDs.
swap	Used on swap partitions to hold data temporarily when RAM is not currently available.
ufs	Popular file system on Solaris and SunOS operating systems from Sun Microsystems.

Table 7-1: File System Types Supported in Linux (*continued*)

File System Type	Description
vfat	Extended FAT (VFAT) file system. Useful when file systems need to share files with older Windows systems (as with dual booting or removable drives).
xfs	Journaling file system for high-performance environments. Can scale up to systems that include multiple terabytes of data that transfer data at multiple gigabytes per second.

Besides the file system types listed in the table, there are also what are referred to as network *shared* file systems. Locally, a network shared file system may be an ext3, ntfs, or other normal file system type. However, all or part of those file systems can be shared with network protocols such as Samba (smbfs or cifs file system type), NFS (nfs), and NetWare (ncpfs).

Many available file system types are either not useful for creating new file systems or not fully supported in every version of Linux. For example, file system types such as minix (for Minix systems), befs (for BeOS systems), and affs (for Amiga systems) are mostly useful if you need to mount and access old backup media from those systems. Even popular file systems may not be fully supported. For example, reiserfs file systems isn't fully supported, as of this writing, by the Kubuntu variant of Ubuntu.

Creating and Managing File Systems

Ubuntu gives you the option of either having the installer create a default partitioning and file system scheme or letting you set that all up manually when you first install Linux. The installer lets you choose to erase the entire hard disk, erase only Linux partitions, or only use free disk space to set up the partitions. To take the manual approach instead, you must choose to create a custom layout.

With the manual approach, the disk-partitioning tool (formerly called Disk Druid) lets you divide the hard disk into partitions as you choose. Later, there are a lot of command-line utilities you can use to change and work with your disk partitions and the file systems created on those partitions.

Partitioning Hard Disks

Historically, PC hard drives have used a 32-bit PC-BIOS partition table with a Master Boot Record (MBR). This limits partition sizes to 2TB and only allows four primary partitions per drive. The use of extended partitions is a way to overcome the four primary partition limit. In order to overcome the 2TB limit, PC-BIOS partition tables are being replaced with GPT (GUID Partition Tables).

The old standard command for working with disk partitions is `fdisk`. Because `fdisk` cannot work with GPT partitions, however, it is slowly being deprecated. A more powerful and actively supported tool is the `parted` command.

> **NOTE** *If you prefer to use graphical tools for partitioning, resizing, and otherwise manipulating your hard disk, you can try* gparted *or* qtparted *partitioning tools. The command names and package names are the same for those two tools, neither of which is installed by default.*

Changing Disk Partitions with fdisk

The `fdisk` command is a useful Linux tool for listing and changing disk partitions. Keep in mind that modifying or deleting partitions can cause valuable data to be removed, so be sure of your changes before writing them to disk. To use the `fdisk` command to list information about the partitions on your hard disk, type the following command as root user:

```
$ sudo fdisk -l                    List disk partitions for every disk
Disk /dev/sda: 82.3 GB, 82348277760 bytes
255 heads, 63 sectors/track, 10011 cylinders
Units = cylinders of 16065 * 512 = 8225280 bytes

   Device Boot    Start       End    Blocks   Id  System
/dev/sda1    *        1        13    104391   83  Linux
/dev/sda2            14      9881  79264710   83  Linux
/dev/sda3          9882     10011   1044225   82  Linux swap
```

This example is for an 80GB hard disk that is divided into three partitions. The first (`/dev/sda1`) is a small `/boot` partition that is configured as a Linux ext3 file system (`Id 83`). Note the asterisk (*), indicating that the first partition is bootable. The next partition is assigned to the root file system and is also ext3. The final partition is `Linux swap`.

> **NOTE** *Since version 2.6.20 of the Linux kernel, both IDE and SCSI disks use device names* /dev/sd?, *where the* ? *is replaced by a letter (a, b, or c, and so on). In older versions of Ubuntu, only SCSI disks and USB flash drives used the* /dev/sd? *names. IDE hard drives used* /dev/hd? *instead.*

If multiple disks are present, `fdisk -l` will list them all unless you indicate the specific disk you want:

```
$ sudo fdisk -l /dev/sdb        List disk partitions for a specific disk
```

To work with a specific disk with the `fdisk` command, simply indicate the disk you want with no other options:

```
$ sudo fdisk /dev/sda            Start interactive fdisk session with disk 1
Command (m for help): m          Type m to list help text as shown
Command action
   a    toggle a bootable flag
```

```
b    edit bsd disklabel
c    toggle the dos compatibility flag
d    delete a partition
l    list known partition types
m    print this menu
n    add a new partition
o    create a new empty DOS partition table
p    print the partition table
q    quit without saving changes
s    create a new empty Sun disklabel
t    change a partition's system id
u    change display/entry units
v    verify the partition table
w    write table to disk and exit
x    extra functionality (experts only)
Command (m for help):
```

With the prompt displayed, you can use any of the commands shown to work with your hard disk. In particular, you can use p (to print the same listing as fdisk -1), n (to create a new partition), d (to delete an existing partition), l (to list known file system types), or t (to change the file system type for a partition). The following examples show some of those fdisk commands in action:

`Command (m for help): `**d**	*Ask to delete a partition*
`Partition number (1-4): `**4**	*Type partition number to delete*
`Command (m for help): `**n**	*Create a new disk partition*
`First cylinder (1-4983, default 1): `**1**	*Select start (or Enter)*
`Last cylinder ... (default 4983): `**4983**	*Select end (or Enter)*
`Command (m for help): `**a**	*Make a partition bootable*
`Partition number (1-3): `**1**	*Type bootable partition number*
`Command (m for help): `**t**	*Select a file system type*
`Partition number (1-3): `**3**	*Select partition to change*
`Hex code (type L to list codes): `**82**	*Assign partition as swap*

Unless you tell it otherwise, fdisk assumes the new partition is a Linux ext3 partition (83). You could have typed L to see the same listing of file system types and hex codes produced from the l command. As noted above, 82 can assign the partition as swap. Other Linux partitions that may interest you include Linux extended (85), Linux LVM (8e), Linux software raid (fd), and EFI/GTP (ee).

For Windows partitions, you can assign a partition as HPFS/NTFS (7), Windows 95 FAT32 (b), FAT 16 (6), or Windows 95 FAT32 LBA (c). Other Unix-type file systems include Minix (be or bf), BSD/OS (e4), FreeBSD (ee), OpenBSD (ef), NeXTSTEP (f0), Darwin UFS (f1), and NetBSD (f4). Any of these file system types might be useful if you have old backup media from those file systems you want to restore.

So far, you have not made any permanent changes to your partition table. If you are now *very sure* that your new settings are correct, type w to write those changes to the partition table. To abandon your changes (or quit after writing your changes), type q to quit your fdisk session.

Copying Partition Tables with sfdisk

To backup or replicate a disk's partition table, use `sfdisk`:

```
$ sudo sfdisk -d /dev/sda > sda-table        Back up partition table to file
$ sudo sfdisk /dev/sda < sda-table           Restore partition table from file
$ sudo sfdisk -d /dev/sda | sfdisk /dev/sdb  Copy partition table from disk to disk
```

Changing Disk Partitions with parted

As with `fdisk`, `parted` can be used to list or change disk partitions. However, `parted` has a few other useful features as well. Here's how to list partitions for a given disk, /dev/sda, with parted:

```
$ sudo parted /dev/sda print
Model: ATA FUJITSU MPG3409A (scsi)
Disk /dev/sda: 41.0GB
Sector size (logical/physical): 512B/512B
Partition Table: msdos

Number  Start   End     Size    Type     File system  Flags
1       32.3kB  206MB   206MB   primary  ext3         boot
2       206MB   39.5GB  39.3GB  primary  ext3
3       39.5GB  41.0GB  1536MB  primary  linux-swap
```

This listing shows you if you have a classic msdos disk label (partition table), or a gpt one. In this case, the partition table is msdos.

To run parted interactively, type `parted` followed by the name of the storage device you want to work with (such as /dev/sda). Or, if you have only one storage device, simply type `parted`:

```
$ sudo parted
GNU Parted 1.7.1
Using /dev/sda
Welcome to GNU Parted! Type 'help' to view a list of commands.
(parted)
```

To use `parted` interactively, either type whole commands or start with a few letters and use the Tab key to complete the command (as you would in the bash shell). And if you're really efficient, you can just type enough letters to allow `parted` to guess your input, as you would with Cisco IOS: p for print, mkl for mklabel, and so on.

> **WARNING!** Unlike `fdisk`, `parted` *immediately incorporates changes you make to your partitions, without explicitly writing the changes to disk. So don't just assume you can back out of any changes by simply quitting* `parted`.

With each command in a `parted` session, you also have the option to enter the command with all the arguments (for example, `mkpart logical ext3 10.7GB 17.0GB`) or just enter the command (`mkpart`) and `parted` will guide you interactively:

```
(parted) mkpart                          Create a new partition
Partition type?  [logical]? primary
File system type?  [ext2]? ext3
Start? 17GB
End? 24GB
```

Avoid using `mkpartfs`. It cannot create ext3 partitions properly. Instead, `mkpart` an ext3 partition (as shown) and format it later outside of `parted` with the `mkfs.ext3` command. In general, `parted` support for ext3 file systems is lacking. **Resizing common Linux partitions** can be useful if you need to make space for a new partition. Here is an example:

```
(parted) resize 2                        Resize a partition
Start? [1.2GB] 1.2GB
End? [24GB] 10GB
```

> **WARNING!** *Unless you're using LVM, this will typically destroy your file system.*

To **resize NTFS partitions,** you can use the `ntfsresize` command. In Ubuntu, that command comes with the ntfsprogs package. That package also comes with commands for creating (`mkfs.ntfs`), fixing (`ntfsfix`), and getting information about (`ntfsinfo`) NTFS partitions.

Working with File System Labels

The term *label*, in regards to disk partitions, can refer to two different things. A *disk label* can be used as another name for a partition table, as seen in `parted` output. A *partition label* can also be the name of an individual partition. To **see a partition's label,** use the `e2label` command:

```
$ sudo e2label /dev/sda2
/home
```

To **set the label on a partition:**

```
$ sudo e2label /dev/sda2 mypartition
```

Bear in mind that `/etc/fstab` sometimes uses the partition label to mount the partition as in the following example. Changing this label may render the system unbootable.

```
LABEL=/boot          /boot          ext3     defaults      1 2
```

To **find a partition when you know only the label,** type the following:

```
$ sudo findfs LABEL=mypartition
/dev/sda2
```

Formatting a File System

With your disk partitions in place, you can build a file system of your choice on each partition. Most Linux systems come with the commands needed to make and check file systems that are commonly used in Linux. Commands for **formatting and checking file systems** are `mkfs` and `fsck`, respectively.

The `mkfs` command serves as the front end for many different commands aimed at formatting particular file system types, such as `mkfs.ext2`, `mkfs.ext3`, `mkfs.cramfs`, `mkfs.msdos`, `mkfs.ntfs`, and `mkfs.vfat`. By adding packages that support other file systems, additional `mkfs` commands are available to seamlessly work with `mkfs`. These include `mkfs.bfs`, `mkfs.minix`, `mkfs.xfs`, and `mkfs.xiafs`. Use each command directly (as in `mkfs.vfat /dev/sdb1`) or via the `mkfs` command (as in `mkfs -t vfat /dev/sdb1`).

Creating a File System on a Hard Disk Partition

Basic software packages you need in Ubuntu to do file system creation and checking include util-linux (includes `mkfs` and other general utilities) and e2fsprogs (ext2/ext3-specific tools). Specific `mkfs` commands for different file system types are included in ntfsprogs (ntfs), dosfstools (msdos and vfat), xfsprogs (xfs), jfsutils (jfs), mtd-utils (jffs and jffs2), and reiserfs-utils (reiserfs). The basic tools get installed with Ubuntu.

Here are examples of the **mkfs command to create file systems** (be sure to add `-t` option first):

```
$ sudo mkfs -t ext3 /dev/sdb1        Create ext3 file system on sba1
$ sudo mkfs -t ext3 -v -c /dev/sdb1  More verbose and scan for bad blocks
$ sudo mkfs.ext3 -c /dev/sdb1        Same result as previous command
```

If you would like to add a partition label to the new partition, use the `-L` option:

```
$ sudo mkfs.ext3 -c -L mypartition /dev/sdb1   Add mypartition label
```

Creating a Virtual File System

If you want to try out different file system types or simply make a file system that is more portable (in other words, not tied to a physical disk), you can create a *virtual file system*. A virtual file system is one that sits within a file on an existing file system. You can format it as any file system type you like, move it around, and use it from different computers.

Virtual file systems are useful for such things as creating live CDs or running dedicated virtual operating systems. In the example that follows, you create a blank 500MB disk image file, format it as a file system, and then mount it to access data on the file system:

```
$ dd if=/dev/zero of=mydisk count=2048000     Create zero-filled 1GB file
$ du -sh mydisk                                Check virtual file system size
1001M  mydisk
$ mkfs -t ext3 mydisk                          Create files system on mydisk
mydisk is not a block special device
Continue (y/n): y
$ sudo mkdir /mnt/image                        Create a mount point
$ sudo mount -o loop mydisk /mnt/image         Mount mydisk on /mnt/image
```

In this procedure, the dd command creates an empty disk image file of 2048000 blocks (about 1GB). The mkfs command can create any file system type you choose (ext3 is done here). Because the file is not a block special device, as is the case when formatting disk partitions, mkfs will warn you before starting to make the file system. The only other trick, after creating the mount point, is to indicate that you are mounting the file (mydisk) as a loop device (-o loop). Note that the mount command is the only command shown above that requires root privilege.

When the virtual file system is mounted, in this example under /mnt/image, you can access it as you would any file system. When you are done with the file system, leave it and unmount it:

```
$ sudo cd /mnt/image         Change to the mount point
$ sudo mkdir test            Create a directory on the file system
$ sudo cp /etc/hosts .       Copy a file to the file system
$ cd                         Leave the file system
$ sudo umount /mnt/image     Unmount the file system
```

With the virtual file system unmounted, you could move it to another system or burn it to a CD to use a file system in another location. If you don't want the file system any more, simply delete the file.

Viewing and Changing File System Attributes

Using the tune2fs or dumpe2fs commands, you can view attributes of ext2 and ext3 file systems. The tune2fs command can also be used to change file system attributes. Use the swapfs command to create a swap partition. Here are examples (both commands produce the same output):

```
$ sudo tune2fs -l /dev/sda1      View tunable file system attributes
$ sudo dumpe2fs -h /dev/sda1     Same as tune2fs output
dumpe2fs 1.39 (29-May-2006)
Filesystem volume name:   /
Last mounted on:          <not available>
Filesystem UUID:          f5f261d3-3879-41d6-8245-f2153b003204
```

131

```
Filesystem magic number:   0xEF53
Filesystem revision #:     1 (dynamic)
Filesystem features:       has_journal ext_attr resize_inode dir_index filetype
    needs_recovery sparse_super large_file
Default mount options:     user_xattr acl
Filesystem state:          clean
Errors behavior:           Continue
Filesystem OS type:        Linux
Inode count:               7914368
Block count:               7907988
Reserved block count:      395399
Free blocks:               5916863
Free inodes:               7752077
First block:               0
Block size:                4096
Fragment size:             4096
Reserved GDT blocks:       1022
Blocks per group:          32768
Fragments per group:       32768
Inodes per group:          32704
Inode blocks per group:    1022
Filesystem created:        Fri Jun 15 12:13:17 2007
Last mount time:           Tue Jul 24 06:47:35 2007
Last write time:           Tue Jul 24 06:47:35 2007
Mount count:               2
Maximum mount count:       29
Last checked:              Fri Jun 15 12:13:17 2007
Check interval:            0 (<none>)
Reserved blocks uid:       0 (user root)
Reserved blocks gid:       0 (group root)
First inode:               11
Inode size:     128
Journal inode:             8
First orphan inode:        988413
Default directory hash:    tea
Directory Hash Seed:       4137d20d-b398-467b-a47a-a9110416b393
Journal backup:            inode blocks
Journal size:              128M
```

The output shows a lot of information about the file system. For example, if you have a file system that needs to create many small files (such as a news server), you can check that you don't run out of inodes. Setting the Maximum mount count ensures that the file system is checked for errors after it has been mounted the selected number of times. You can also find dates and times for when a file system was created, last mounted, and last written to.

To change settings on an existing ext2 or ext3 file system, you can use the tune2fs command. The following command changes the number of mounts before a forced file system check:

```
$ sudo tune2fs -c 31 /dev/sda1        Sets # of mounts before check is forced
tune2fs 1.39 (29-May-2006)
Setting maximal mount count to 31
```

If you'd like to switch to forced **file system checks based on time interval** rather than number of mounts, disable mount-count checking by setting it to negative 1 (-1):

```
$ sudo tune2fs -c -1 /dev/sda1
tune2fs 1.39 (29-May-2006)
Setting maximal mount count to -1
```

Use the -i option to **enable time-dependent checking.** Here are some examples:

```
$ sudo tune2fs -i 10 /dev/sda1      Check after 10 days
$ sudo tune2fs -i 1d /dev/sda1      Check after 1 day
$ sudo tune2fs -i 3w /dev/sda1      Check after 3 weeks
$ sudo tune2fs -i 6m /dev/sda1      Check after 6 months
$ sudo tune2fs -i 0 /dev/sda1       Disable time-dependent checking
```

Be sure you always have either mount-count or time-dependent checking turned on.

Use the -j option to **turn an ext2 file system into ext3** (by adding a journal):

```
$ sudo tune2fs -j /dev/sda1         Add journaling to change ext2 to ext3
```

Creating and Using Swap Partitions

Swap partitions are needed in Linux systems to hold data that overflows from your system's RAM. If you didn't create a swap partition when you installed Linux, you can create it later using the mkswap command. You can **create your swap partition** either on a regular disk partition or in a file formatted as a swap partition. Here are some examples:

```
$ sudo mkswap /dev/sda1        Format sda1 as a swap partition
Setting up swapspace version 1, size = 205594 kB
```

To **check your swap area for bad blocks,** use the -c option to mkswap:

```
$ sudo mkswap -c /dev/sda1
```

If you don't have a spare partition, you can **create a swap area within a file:**

```
$ sudo dd if=/dev/zero of=/tmp/swapfile count=65536
65536+0 records in
65536+0 records out
33554432 bytes (34 MB) copied, 1.56578 s, 21.4 MB/s
$ sudo chmod 600 /tmp/swapfile
$ sudo mkswap /tmp/swapfile
Setting up swapspace version 1, size = 67104 kB
```

The dd command above creates a 32MB file named swapfile. The chmod command locks down the permissions on the file, to avoid getting a warning from the swapon command down the road. The mkswap command formats the /tmp/swapfile file to be a swap partition.

After you have created a swap partition or swap file, you need to tell the system to use the swap area you made using the swapon command. This is similar to what happens at boot time. Here are examples:

```
$ sudo swapon /dev/sda1          Turn swap on for /dev/sda1 partition
$ sudo swapon -v /dev/sda1       Increase verbosity as swap is turned on
swapon on /dev/sda1
$ sudo swapon -v /tmp/swapfile   Turn swap on for the /tmp/swapfile file
swapon on /tmp/swapfile
```

You can also use the swapon command to see a list of your swaps files and partitions:

```
$ swapon -s            View all swap files and partitions that are on
Filename              Type        Size      Used     Priority
/dev/sda5             partition   1020088   142764   -1
/tmp/swapfile         file        65528     0        -6
```

To turn off a swap area, you can use the swapoff command:

```
$ sudo swapoff -v /tmp/swapfile
swapoff on /tmp/swapfile
```

Swap areas are prioritized. The kernel will swap first to areas of high priorities, and then go down the list. Areas of the same priority get striped between. You can specify the priority of your swap area as you enable it using the -p option:

```
$ sudo swapon -v -p 1 /dev/sda1      Assign top swap priority to sda1
```

Mounting and Unmounting File Systems

Before you can use a regular, non-swap file system, you need to attach it to a directory in your computer's file system tree by *mounting* it. Your root file system (/) and other file systems you use on an ongoing basis are typically mounted automatically based on entries in your /etc/fstab file. Other file systems can be mounted manually as they are needed using the mount command.

Mounting File Systems from the fstab File

When you first install Linux, the /etc/fstab file is usually set up automatically to contain information about your root file systems and other file systems. Those file systems can then be set to mount at boot time or be ready to mount manually (with mount points and other options ready to use when a manual mount is done).

Here is an example of a /etc/fstab file:

```
/dev/VolGroup00/LogVol00    /           ext3    defaults    1 1
LABEL=/boot                 /boot       ext3    defaults    1 2
```

134

tmpfs	/dev/shm	tmpfs	defaults	0 0
devpts	/dev/pts	devpts	gid=5,mode=620	0 0
sysfs	/sys	sysfs	defaults	0 0
proc	/proc	proc	defaults	0 0
/dev/VolGroup00/LogVol01	swap	swap	defaults	0 0
/dev/sda1	/mnt/windows	vfat	noauto	0 0

> **NOTE** *For clarity, the UUID listing for each hard disk file system was removed in the above example. For each file system, you'll normally see an entry like the following,* UUID=da2dbc48-862e-4fbe-9529-a88b57b15bac, *prior to the file system.*

All the file systems are mounted automatically, except for /dev/sda1 (as indicated by the noauto option). The root (/) and swap hard disk partitions are configured as logical volume management (LVM) volumes. LVM volumes can make it easier to move or join physical partitions, while still retaining the volume ID. Pseudo file systems (not associated with a partition) include devpts (an interface to pty pseudo terminals), sysfs (information from 2.6 kernel), and proc (kernel information implemented prior to 2.6 kernel). The /dev/sda1 disk partition was added manually in this example to mount the Windows partition located on that device.

The /etc/fstab file no longer typically holds information about removable media. That's because the Hardware Abstraction Layer (HAL) facility automatically detects removable media and mounts those media in appropriate mount points in the /media directory (based on such things as volume ID on the media).

Table 7-2 describes each field in the /etc/fstab file.

Table 7-2: Fields in the /etc/fstab File

Field	Description
1	**The device name representing the file system.** Originally, this contained the device name of the partition to mount (such as /dev/sda1). It can now also contain a LABEL or universally unique identifier (UUID), instead of a device name.
2	**The mount point in the file system.** The file system contains all data from the mount point down the directory tree structure, unless another file system is mounted at some point beneath it.
3	**The file system type.** See Table 7-1 for a list of many common file system types.
4	**The mount command options.** Examples of mount options include noauto (to prevent the file system from mounting at boot time) and ro (to mount the file system read-only). To let any user mount a file system, you could add the user or owner option to this field. Commas must separate options. See the mount command manual page (under the -o option) for information on other supported options.

Continued

Table 7-2: Fields in the /etc/fstab File (*continued*)

Field	Description
5	**Dump file system?** This field is only significant if you run backups with dump. A number 1 signifies that the file system needs to be dumped. A zero means that it doesn't.
6	**File system check?** The number in this field indicates whether or not the file system needs to be checked with fsck. A zero indicates that the file system should not be checked. A number 1 means that the file system needs to be checked first (this is used for the root file system). A number 2 assumes that the file system can be checked at any point after the root file system is checked.

You can create your own entries for any hard disk or removable media partitions you want in the /etc/fstab file. Remote file systems (NFS, Samba, and others) can also contain entries in the /etc/fstab file to automatically mount those file systems at boot time or later by hand.

Mounting File Systems with the mount Command

The mount command is used to view mounted file systems, as well as mount any local (hard disk, USB drive, CD, DVD, and so on) or remote (NFS, Samba, and so on) file systems. Here is an example of the mount command for listing mounted file systems:

```
$ mount                          List mounted remote and local file systems
/dev/sda7 on / type ext3 (rw)
proc on /proc type proc (rw)
sysfs on /sys type sysfs (rw)
devpts on /dev/pts type devpts (rw,gid=5,mode=620)
/dev/sda6 on /mnt/debian type ext3 (rw)
/dev/sda3 on /mnt/slackware type ext3 (rw)
tmpfs on /dev/shm type tmpfs (rw)
none on /proc/sys/fs/binfmt_misc type binfmt_misc (rw)
sunrpc on /var/lib/nfs/rpc_pipefs type rpc_pipefs (rw)
```

Use the -t option to list only mounts of a specific file system type:

```
$ mount -t ext3                  List mounted ext3 file systems
/dev/sda7 on / type ext3 (rw)
/dev/sda6 on /mnt/debian type ext3 (rw)
/dev/sda3 on /mnt/slackware type ext3 (rw)
```

To display partition labels with mount information, use the -l option:

```
$ mount -t ext3 -l               List mounted ext3 file systems and labels
/dev/sda7 on / type ext3 (rw) [/123]
/dev/sda6 on /mnt/debian type ext3 (rw) [/mnt/debian]
/dev/sda3 on /mnt/slackware type ext3 (rw) [/mnt/slackware]
```

136

Here is a simple mount command to mount the /dev/sda1 device on an existing directory named /mnt/mymount/:

```
$ sudo mount /dev/sda1 /mnt/mymount/        Mount a local file system
$ sudo mount -v /dev/sda1 /mnt/mymount/   Mount file system, more verbose
mount: you didn't specify a filesystem type for /dev/sda1
I will try type ext3
/dev/sda1 on /mnt/mymount type ext3 (rw)
```

In the examples above, the mount command will either look for an entry for /dev/sda1 in the /etc/fstab file or try to guess the type of file system.

Use -t to explicitly indicate the type of file system to mount:

```
$ sudo mount -v -t ext3 /dev/sda1 /mnt/mymount/   Mount an ext3 file system
/dev/sda1 on /mnt/mymount type ext3 (rw)
```

You can also display the label/name of the partition that is mounted:

```
$ sudo mount -vl -t ext3 /dev/sda1 /mnt/mymount/   Mount file system/show label
```

If you're mounting something that is listed in your fstab file already, you only need to specify one item: mount point or device. For example, with the following fstab entry

```
/dev/sda1        /mnt/mymount        ext3     defaults      1 2
```

you can do either of the following to mount the file system:

```
$ sudo mount -v /dev/sda1        Mount file system with device name only
/dev/sda1 on /mnt/mymount type ext3 (rw)
$ sudo mount -v /mnt/mymount/   Mount file system with mount point only
/dev/sda1 on /mnt/mymount type ext3 (rw)
```

You can specify mount options by adding -o and a comma-separated list of options. They are the same options you can add to field 4 of the /etc/fstab file. By default, partitions are mounted with read/write access. You can explicitly indicate to mount a file system as read/write (rw) or read-only (ro):

```
$ sudo mount -v -t ext3 -o rw /dev/sda1 /mnt/mymount/   Mount read/write
/dev/sda1 on /mnt/mymount type ext3 (rw)
$ sudo mount -v -t ext3 -o ro /dev/sda1 /mnt/mymount/   Mount read-only
/dev/sda1 on /mnt/mymount type ext3 (ro)
```

A few other useful mount options you can use include:

❑ noatime — Does not update the access time on files. Good on file systems with a lot of I/O, such as mail spools and logs.

❑ noexec — Prevents execution of binaries located on this file system. Can be used to increase security, for example for /tmp in environments with untrusted users.

137

❏ remount — Change options on a mounted file system. With `remount`, you can unmount the file system and remount it with the new options in a single command. In this example, we change a previous read/write mount to read-only:

```
$ sudo mount -v -o remount,ro /dev/sda1
/dev/sda1 on /mnt/mymount type ext3 (ro)
```

❏ --bind — Mount an existing file system to another location in the tree. Assuming /dev/sda1 is already mounted on /mnt/mymount, type the following:

```
$ sudo mount --bind -v /mnt/mymount/ /tmp/mydir/
/mnt/mymount on /tmp/mydir type none (rw,bind)
```

Now the same file system is accessible from two locations. The new mount point has the same mount options as the original.

❏ --move — Move a file system from one mount point to another. Assuming /dev/sda1 is already mounted on /mnt/mymount, this moves the file system to /tmp/mydir:

```
$ sudo mount -v --move /mnt/mymount/ /tmp/mydir/
/mnt/mymount on /tmp/mydir type none (rw)
```

Just like you can swap to a file, you can create a file system in a file and then mount it in what is called a *loopback* mount. Creating and mounting such a file is described in the "Creating a Virtual File System" section earlier in this chapter. A common situation where you might want to **mount a file in loopback** is after downloading a Linux install CD or LiveCD. By mounting that CD image in loopback, you can view its contents or copy files from that image to your hard disk.

In the following example, the `mount` command is allowed to automatically pick an existing loopback device when mounting a CD image file (file system type iso9660). The command output shows /dev/loop0 was selected:

```
$ sudo mount -v -t iso9660 -o loop /tmp/myimage.iso /mnt/mymount/
mount: going to use the loop device /dev/loop0
/tmp/myimage.iso on /mnt/mymount type ext3 (rw,loop=/dev/loop0)
```

In the following example, we downloaded a Linux USB flash drive boot image called diskboot.img to /tmp. Here is an example of how to **mount the boot image**:

```
$ sudo mount -v -o loop /tmp/diskboot.img /mnt/mymount
mount: going to use the loop device /dev/loop0
mount: you didn't specify a filesystem type for /dev/loop0
       I will try type vfat
/tmp/diskboot.img on /mnt/mymount type vfat (rw,loop=/dev/loop0)
```

To **see the status of the loopback devices**, use the `losetup` command:

```
$ sudo losetup /dev/loop0                    List mounted loopback devices
/dev/loop0: [0807]:1009045 (/tmp/diskboot.img)
```

If a loopback mount gets stuck and you have problems during unmount, try detaching it as follows:

```
$ sudo losetup -d /dev/loop1     Force unmount of a mounted loopback device
```

> **NOTE** *The* mount *command can also be used to attach to NFS, or Samba/Windows CIFS shares. See Chapter 12 for information on mounting those remote file system types.*

Unmounting File Systems with umount

To **unmount a file system**, use the umount command. You can umount the file system using the device name or the mount point. You're better off umounting with the mount point, to avoid the confusion when using bind mounts (one device, multiple mount points). Here is an example of each, with verbosity on:

```
$ sudo umount -v /dev/sda1       Unmount by device name
/dev/sda1 umounted
$ sudo umount -v /mnt/mymount/    Unmount by mount point
/tmp/diskboot.img umounted
```

If the device is busy, the unmount will fail. A common reason for an unmount to fail is that you have a shell open with the current directory of a directory inside the mount:

```
$ sudo umount -v /mnt/mymount/
umount: /mnt/mymount: device is busy
umount: /mnt/mymount: device is busy
```

Sometimes, it's not obvious what makes the device busy. You can use lsof to list open files, then **search that list for the mount point** that interests you:

```
$ sudo lsof | grep mymount       Find open files on mymount partition
bash   9341  francois  cwd   DIR  8,1  1024   2 /mnt/mymount
```

You can see that a bash process run by francois with a PID of 9341 is preventing the mymount partition from being unmounted.

Another option when a file system is busy is to **perform a lazy unmount**:

```
$ sudo umount -vl /mnt/mymount/       Perform a lazy unmount
```

A *lazy unmount* unmounts the file system from the tree now, but waits for the device to no longer be busy before cleaning up everything. Unmounts of removable media can also be done with eject. This **unmounts a CD and ejects the CD** from the drive:

```
$ sudo eject /dev/cdrom       Unmount and eject a CD
```

Checking File Systems

In Linux, instead of just having the scandisk utility you have in Windows, you can scan a physical device for bad blocks at a physical level with the `badblocks` command and scan a file system for errors at the logical level with the `fsck` command. Here's how to scan for bad blocks:

```
$ sudo badblocks /dev/sda1          Physically scan hard disk for bad blocks
$ sudo badblocks -v /dev/sda1       Add verbosity to hard disk scan
Checking blocks 0 to 200781
Checking for bad blocks (read-only test): done
Pass completed, 0 bad blocks found.
```

By default, `badblock` does a safe read-only test of the blocks. You can also perform a non-destructive read/write test. This is the slowest test, but the best one you can perform without destroying the data on the device. Add `-s` to see the ongoing progress:

```
$ sudo badblocks -vsn /dev/sda1        Check bad blocks, non-destructive
Checking for bad blocks in non-destructive read-write mode
From block 0 to 200781
Testing with random pattern: Pass completed, 0 bad blocks found.
```

The following command performs a faster, *destructive* read-write test:

> **WARNING!**   *This will erase all the data on the partition.*

```
$ sudo badblocks -vsw /dev/sda1        Check bad blocks, destructive
Checking for bad blocks in read-write mode
From block 0 to 200781
Testing with pattern 0xaa: done
Reading and comparing: done
Testing with pattern 0x55: done
Reading and comparing: done
Testing with pattern 0xff: done
Reading and comparing: done
Testing with pattern 0x00: done
Reading and comparing: done
Pass completed, 0 bad blocks found.
```

You can perform multiple badblocks passes; for example, this command line can be used to burn in a drive and screen for hard drive infant mortality:

```
$ sudo badblocks -vswp 2 /dev/sda1
```

Like the `mkfs` command, the `fsck` command is just a front end to file-system–specific utilities. You can check an ext3 file system by simply adding the device name of the disk partition you want to check to the `fsck` command:

```
$ sudo fsck /dev/sda1
fsck 1.39 (29-May-2006)
e2fsck 1.39 (29-May-2006)
```

```
mypart has gone 18 days without being checked, check forced.
Pass 1: Checking inodes, blocks, and sizes
Pass 2: Checking directory structure
Pass 3: Checking directory connectivity
Pass 4: Checking reference counts
Pass 5: Checking group summary information
mypart: 11/50200 files (9.1% non-contiguous), 12002/200780 blocks
```

You can **add other options to fsck,** such as -T (to not display the useless fsck version number) and -V (to be more verbose about what fsck actually does):

```
$ sudo fsck -TV /dev/sda1          Check file system (verbose and no version)
[/sbin/fsck.ext3 (1) -- /dev/sda1] fsck.ext3 /dev/sda1
e2fsck 1.39 (29-May-2006)
mypart: clean, 11/50200 files, 12002/200780 blocks
```

For any problem that fsck encounters, it will ask you if you want to repair it:

```
$ sudo fsck -TV /dev/sda1          Prompting to correct problems encountered
[/sbin/fsck.ext3 (1) -- /mnt/mymount] fsck.ext3 /dev/sda1
e2fsck 1.39 (29-May-2006)
Couldn't find ext2 superblock, trying backup blocks...
Resize inode not valid.  Recreate<y>? y
```

Unless you have a very in-depth knowledge of file systems, you're better off answering yes. This can be done automatically with the -y option:

```
$ sudo fsck -TVy /dev/sda1
[/sbin/fsck.ext3 (1) -- /mnt/mymount] fsck.ext3 -y /dev/sda1
e2fsck 1.39 (29-May-2006)
Couldn't find ext2 superblock, trying backup blocks...
Resize inode not valid.  Recreate? yes
mypart was not cleanly unmounted, check forced.
Pass 1: Checking inodes, blocks, and sizes
Pass 2: Checking directory structure
Pass 3: Checking directory connectivity
Pass 4: Checking reference counts
Pass 5: Checking group summary information
Free blocks count wrong for group #0 (3552, counted=3553).
Fix? yes
Free blocks count wrong (188777, counted=188778).
Fix? yes

mypart: ***** FILE SYSTEM WAS MODIFIED *****
mypart: 11/50200 files (0.0% non-contiguous), 12002/200780 blocks
```

Checking RAID Disks

Redundant Array of Independent Drives (RAID) disks let you duplicate or distribute data across multiple hard drives. Using RAID can improve reliability and performance of your storage media. The mdadm command, which is part of the mdadm package, can be used to **check softraid devices** on your computer. Here's an example:

```
$ sudo mdadm -Q /dev/md1
/dev/md1: 1498.13MiB raid1 2 devices, 0 spares.
       Use mdadm --detail for more detail.
/dev/md1: No md super block found, not an md component.
```

The message on the last line simply means that /dev/md1 is not a member of a RAID array. That is normal, since md1 is the array itself. Similarly, if you query a member of a RAID array, your output will look like this:

```
$ sudo mdadm -Q /dev/sdb3
/dev/sdb3: is not an md array
/dev/sdb3: device 1 in 4 device active raid6 md0.  Use mdadm --examine for more
detail.
```

To obtain more detailed output, add the --detail option:

```
$ sudo mdadm -Q --detail /dev/md1
/dev/md1:
          Version : 00.90.01
    Creation Time : Fri Dec  8 16:32:12 2006
       Raid Level : raid1
       Array Size : 1534080 (1498.38 MiB 1570.90 MB)
      Device Size : 1534080 (1498.38 MiB 1570.90 MB)
     Raid Devices : 2
    Total Devices : 2
  Preferred Minor : 1
      Persistence : Superblock is persistent

      Update Time : Sun Jun 17 02:06:01 2007
            State : clean
   Active Devices : 2
  Working Devices : 2
   Failed Devices : 0
    Spare Devices : 0

             UUID : 49c564cc:2d3c9a14:d93ce1c9:070663ca
           Events : 0.42

    Number   Major   Minor   RaidDevice State
       0       3       2        0       active sync   /dev/hda2
       1       3      66        1       active sync   /dev/hdb2
```

The mdadm command can also be used to manage your softraid devices. For more info, run the following:

```
$ sudo mdadm --manage -help
$ man mdadm
```

> **NOTE** *If you use 3ware/AMCC hardware RAID controllers, which are our favorite for SATA RAID, make sure you install 3ware Disk Manager (3dm2), which is available in rpm form from ATrpms.net. The 3dm2 utility provides a monitoring daemon and a web GUI.*

Make sure that you have a RAID disk prior to installing the mdadm package. When you install mdadm, the installation program will attempt to configure your RAID drives as part of the installation. Furthermore, should you uninstall mdadm, it will likely leave behind a `mdadm.conf` file in `/etc/mdadm`. The presence of this file can cause compatibility issues with the lvm2 package, described later.

Finding Out About File System Use

Running out of disk space can be annoying on your desktop system and potentially a disaster on your servers. To determine how much disk space is available and how much is currently in use, you can use the `df` command. To check how much space particular files and directories are consuming, use the `du` command.

The `df` command provides **utilization summaries of your mounted file systems**. Using the `-h` option, you can have the data (which is shown in bytes by default) converted to megabytes (`M`) and gigabytes (`G`), to make that output more human-readable:

```
$ df -h           Display space on file systems in human-readable form
Filesystem          Size    Used    Avail Use%   Mounted on
/dev/sda2           7.6G    3.4G    3.9G   47%    /
/dev/sda1           99M     14M     80M    15%    /boot
tmpfs               501M    0       501M   0%     /dev/shm
/dev/sda5           352G    197G    137G   59%    /home
//thompson/chris    9204796 5722608 3007068 66%   /mnt/mymount
```

Because ext file systems have only so many inodes created at `mkfs` time, if you have lots of small files, you can possibly run out of inodes before you run out of actual space. To **check inode utilization,** use the `-i` option:

```
$ df -hi
Filesystem          Inodes  IUsed   IFree IUse% Mounted on
/dev/sda2           2.0M    108K    1.9M  6% /
```

If you have network mounts (such as Samba or NFS), these will show up too in your df output. To **limit df output to local file systems,** type the following:

```
$ df -hl           Display disk space only for local file systems
```

To **add the file system type** to the listing, use the `-T` option:

```
$ df -hT           Add file system type information to listing
Filesystem    Type   Size  Used Avail Use% Mounted on
/dev/sda7     ext3   8.8G  5.5G  2.9G  66% /
```

To check for disk space usage for particular files or directories in a file system, use the du command. The following command was run as the user named francois:

```
$ du -h /home/          Show disk space usage for /home directory
du: `/home/chris': Permission denied
4.0K    /home/francois/Mail
52K     /home/francois
64K     /home/
```

The output shows that access to another home directory's disk use (in this case /home/chris) was denied for security reasons. So the next examples show how to avoid permission issues and get totals that are correct by using the root user account. This is clearly visible when you use -s to summarize:

```
$ du -sh /home     Regular user is denied space totals to others' homes
du: `/home/chris': Permission denied
du: `/home/horatio199': Permission denied
64K     /home
# du -sh /home     You can display summary disk use as root user
1.6G    /home
```

You can specify multiple directories with the -c option and total them up:

```
$ sudo du -sch /home /var     Show directory and total summaries
1.6G    /home
111M    /var
1.7G    total
```

You can exclude files that match a pattern from being counted using the exclude option. In the following example, disk image files (ending with the .iso suffix) are not used in totaling the disk space used:

```
$ sudo du -sh --exclude='*.iso' /home/chris     Exclude ISO images from totals
588M    /home/chris
```

You can specify what depth in the tree you want to summarize. Set --max-depth to a number larger than the 1 value shown, to dig deeper into disk space usage:

```
$ sudo du -h --max-depth=1 /home     Provide disk space use, to one level deep
1.6G    /home/chris
52K     /home/francois
1.6G    /home
$ sudo du -h --max-depth=2 /home     Dig two-levels deep for disk space use
  ...
4.0K    /home/francois/Mail
52K     ·/home/francois
1.6G    /home
```

Logical Volume Manager (LVM)

Logical Volume Manager is a feature designed to help you cope with the changing needs for disk space on your Linux systems. With your hard disks configured as LVM volumes, you have tremendous flexibility in growing, shrinking, and moving the storage space on your systems as your needs change. LVM also allows for snapshots, a feature typically found on expensive enterprise SANs, or Storage-Area Networks.

Ubuntu incorporates LVM2 into its releases and uses it to define how disk partitions are allocated when you first install Ubuntu. Using LVM2, you define and manage volume groups (vg), logical volumes (lv), and physical volumes (pv). Each logical volume and physical volume is divided up into logical extents and physical extents, respectively.

The basic business of using LVM is to create the volume groups and logical volumes you need, then assign the extents (small chunks of disk space) to those areas where they are needed. Unlike older disk partitioning schemes, where you might have to back up your data, change your partitioning, then return data to the resized partitions, you can simply add unused extents where they are needed.

To use LVM, you need to install the lvm2 package.

LVM comes with a set of commands that can be used to work with LVM volumes. Step through the procedure in the following section to learn about many of those LVM commands.

> **WARNING!** *To avoid messing up the hard disks your computer relies on as you learn LVM, we recommend you try the following examples on some non-critical storage device. For example, we used an inexpensive 32MB USB flash drive (on* /dev/sdb) *to run the commands shown in this section.*

Creating LVM Volumes

To begin, use the fdisk command to **create physical partitions for the storage device** on which you want to create logical partitions. Here we have a 32MB USB flash drive, located on device /dev/sdb:

```
$ sudo fdisk /dev/sdb          Start command to manage disk partitions
Command (m for help): p        Print current partitions (none exist)

Disk /dev/sdb: 32 MB, 32112128 bytes
1 heads, 62 sectors/track, 1011 cylinders
Units = cylinders of 62 * 512 = 31744 bytes

   Device Boot     Start        End      Blocks   Id  System
```

```
Command (m for help): n          Create a new partition
Command action
   e   extended
   p   primary partition (1-4)
p                                Make it a primary partition
Partition number (1-4): 1        Assigned to partition 1
First cylinder (2-1011, default 2): Enter
Using default value 2
Last cylinder or +size or +sizeM or +sizeK (2-1011, default 1011): Enter
Using default value 1011


Command (m for help): t          Assign a partition type
Selected partition 1
Hex code (type L to list codes): 8E   Indicate 8E (LVM partition)
Changed system type of partition 1 to 8e (Linux LVM)
Command (m for help): p          Type p to see the new partition
Disk /dev/sdb: 32 MB, 32112128 bytes
1 heads, 62 sectors/track, 1011 cylinders
Units = cylinders of 62 * 512 = 31744 bytes
Device Boot      Start       End      Blocks   Id  System
/dev/sdb1        2          1011      31310    8e  Linux LVM
```

Before proceeding, make sure you have made the correct changes to the correct partition! If everything looks correct, write the new partition table, as follows:

```
Command (m for help): w
The partition table has been altered!
Calling ioctl() to re-read partition table.
Syncing disks.
```

Back at the shell prompt, use the sfdisk command to see the partitioning on the drive:

```
$ sudo sfdisk -l /dev/sdb        View the LVM partitions

Disk /dev/sdb: 1011 cylinders, 1 heads, 62 sectors/track
Units = cylinders of 31744 bytes, blocks of 1024 bytes, counting from 0

   Device Boot Start     End   #cyls    #blocks   Id  System
/dev/sdb1           1    1010    1010      31310   8e  Linux LVM
/dev/sdb2           0       -       0          0    0  Empty
/dev/sdb3           0       -       0          0    0  Empty
/dev/sdb4           0       -       0          0    0  Empty
```

Next, make /dev/sdb1 a new LVM physical volume and use the pvs command to view information about physical LVM volumes:

```
$ sudo pvcreate /dev/sdb1             Make sdb1 an LVM physical volume
  Physical volume "/dev/sdb1" successfully created
$ sudo pvs                            View physical LVM partitions
  PV         VG     Fmt  Attr PSize  PFree
  /dev/sdb1  vgusb  lvm2 a-   28.00M 20.00M
```

Then use `vgcreate` to create the `vgusb` volume group and list the active current volume groups:

```
$ sudo vgcreate vgusb /dev/sdb1          Create vgusb volume group
  Volume group "vgusb" successfully created
$ sudo vgs                               View current volume groups
  VG      #PV #LV #SN Attr   VSize  VFree
  vgusb    1   0   0 wz--n- 28.00M 28.00M
```

Use `lvcreate` to create a new LVM partition of 10M from the `vgusb` volume group. Then use `lvs` to see the logical volume and `vgs` to see that the amount of free space has changed:

```
$ sudo lvcreate --size 10M --name lvm_u1 vgusb
  Rounding up size to full physical extent 12.00 MB
  Logical volume "lvm_u1" created
$ sudo lvs                    View the logical volume information
  LV        VG     Attr   LSize  Origin Snap% Move Log Copy%
  lvm_u1    vgusb  -wi-a- 12.00M
$ sudo vgs                    See that you still have 16M free
  VG      #PV #LV #SN Attr   VSize  VFree
  vgusb    1   1   0 wz--n- 28.00M 16.00M
```

To create an ext3 file system on the lvm partition, use the `mkfs.ext3` command as follows:

```
$ sudo mkfs.ext3 /dev/mapper/vgusb-lvm_u1
mke2fs 1.38 (30-Jun-2005)
Filesystem label=
OS type: Linux
Block size=1024 (log=0)
Fragment size=1024 (log=0)
3072 inodes, 12288 blocks
614 blocks (5.00%) reserved for the super user
First data block=1
Maximum filesystem blocks=12582912
2 block groups
8192 blocks per group, 8192 fragments per group
1536 inodes per group
Superblock backups stored on blocks:
        8193

Writing inode tables: done
Creating journal (1024 blocks): done
Writing superblocks and filesystem accounting information: done

This filesystem will be automatically checked every 35 mounts or
180 days, whichever comes first.  Use tune2fs -c or -i to override.
```

The ext3 file system has now been created and the LVM volume is ready to use.

Using LVM Volumes

To use the new volume just created, represented by /dev/mapper/vgusb-lvm_u1, create a mount point (/mnt/u1) and mount the volume. Then use df to check the available space:

```
$ sudo mkdir /mnt/u1                                        Create mount point
$ sudo mount -t ext3 /dev/mapper/vgusb-lvm_u1 /mnt/u1    Mount volume
$ df -m /mnt/u1                                             Check disk space
Filesystem          1M-blocks      Used Available Use% Mounted on
/dev/mapper/vgusb-lvm_u1
                         12          2         10  11% /mnt/u1
```

At this point, the file system contains only the lost+found directory:

```
$ ls /mnt/u1
lost+found
```

Copy a large file to the new file system. For example, choose one of the kernel files from the /boot directory and copy it to /mnt/u1:

```
$ cp /boot/vmlinuz-* /mnt/u1/           Copy a large file to /mnt/u1
$ df -m /mnt/u1                          See that 4MB is used on /mnt/u1
Filesystem          1M-blocks      Used Available Use% Mounted on
/dev/mapper/vgusb-lvm_u1
                         12          4          9  27% /mnt/u1
```

Run md5sum on the file you copied and save the resulting checksum for later. For example:

```
$ md5sum /mnt/u1/vmlinuz-2.6.20-1.2316.fc5        Check md5sum
8d0dc0347d36ebd3f6f2b49047e1f525  /mnt/u1/vmlinuz-2.6.20-1.2316.fc5
```

Growing the LVM Volume

Say that you are running out of space and you want to add more space to your LVM volume. To do that, unmount the volume and use the lvresize command. After that, you must also check the file system with e2fsck and run resize2fs to resize the ext3 file system on that volume:

```
$ sudo umount /mnt/u1                              Unmount volume
$ sudo lvresize --size 16M /dev/vgusb/lvm_u1       Resize volume
  Extending logical volume lvm_u1 to 16.00 MB
  Logical volume lvm_u1 successfully resized
$ sudo e2fsck -f /dev/vgusb/lvm_u1
e2fsck 1.40 (12-Jul-2007)
Pass 1: Checking inodes, blocks, and sizes
Pass 2: Checking directory structure
Pass 3: Checking directory connectivity
Pass 4: Checking reference counts
Pass 5: Checking group summary information
```

```
/dev/vgusb/lvm_u1: 12/3072 files (25.0% non-contiguous), 3379/12288 blocks
$ sudo resize2fs /dev/vgusb/lvm_u1 16M          Resize file system
resize2fs 1.38 (30-Jun-2005)
Resizing the filesystem on /dev/vgusb/lvm_u1 to 16384 (1k) blocks.
The filesystem on /dev/vgusb/lvm_u1 is now 16384 blocks long.
```

In the example just shown, the volume and the file system are both resized to 16MB. Next, mount the volume again and check the disk space and the md5sum you created earlier:

```
$ sudo mount -t ext3 /dev/mapper/vgusb-lvm_u1 /mnt/u1   Remount volume
$ df -m /mnt/u1                                         See 4MB of 16MB used
Filesystem              1M-blocks     Used Available Use% Mounted on
/dev/mapper/vgusb-lvm_u1
                              16         4        13  20% /mnt/u1
$ md5sum /mnt/u1/vmlinuz-2.6.20-1.2316.fc5              Recheck md5sum
8d0dc0347d36ebd3f6f2b49047e1f525  /mnt/u1/vmlinuz-2.6.20-1.2316.fc5
```

The newly mounted volume is now 16MB instead of 10MB in size.

Shrinking an LVM Volume

You can also use the lvresize command if you want to take unneeded space from an existing LVM volume. As before, unmount the volume before resizing it and run e2fsck (to check the file system) and resize2fs (to resize it to the smaller size):

```
$ sudo umount /mnt/u1
$ sudo e2fsck -f /dev/vgusb/lvm_u1
fsck 1.38 (30-Jun-2005)
e2fsck 1.38 (30-Jun-2005)
The filesystem size (according to the superblock) is 16384 blocks
The physical size of the device is 8192 blocks
Pass 1: Checking inodes, blocks, and sizes
...
/dev/vgusb/lvm_u1: 12/3072 files (8.3% non-contiguous,3531/16384 blocks
$ sudo resize2fs /dev/vgusb/lvm_u1 12M                  Resize file system
resize2fs 1.38 (30-Jun-2005)
Resizing the filesystem on /dev/vgusb/lvm_u1 to 12288 (1k) blocks.
The filesystem on /dev/vgusb/lvm_u1 is now 12288 blocks long.
$ sudo lvresize --size 12M /dev/vgusb/lvm_u1
  WARNING: Reducing active logical volume to 12.00 MB
  THIS MAY DESTROY YOUR DATA (filesystem etc.)
Do you really want to reduce lvm_u1? [y/n]: y
  Reducing logical volume lvm_u1 to 8.00 MB
  Logical volume lvm_u1 successfully resized
$ sudo mount -t ext3 /dev/mapper/vgusb-lvm_u1 /mnt/u1   Remount volume
$ df -m /mnt/u1                                         See 4MB of 12MB used
Filesystem              1M-blocks     Used Available Use% Mounted on
/dev/mapper/vgusb-lvm_u1
                              12         4         9  20% /mnt/u1
```

The newly mounted volume appears now as 12MB instead of 16MB in size.

Removing LVM Logical Volumes and Groups

To **remove an LVM logical volume from a volume group,** use the `lvremove` command as follows:

```
$ sudo lvremove /dev/vgusb/lvm_u1
Do you really want to remove active logical volume "lvm_u1"? [y/n]: y
  Logical volume "lvm_u1" successfully removed
```

To remove an existing LVM volume group, use the `vgremove` command:

```
$ sudo vgremove vgusb
  Volume group "vgusb" successfully removed
```

There are many more ways to work with LVM. Refer to the LVM HOWTO for further information (`http://tldp.org/HOWTO/LVM-HOWTO/`).

Summary

Creating and managing file systems in Linux is a critical part of Linux system administration. Linux contains support for several standard Linux file system types (ext2, ext3, reiserfs, and others). It can also create and manage Windows file system types (VFAT, NTFS, and so on) as well as legacy and specialty Linux and Unix file system types (such as minix, jfs, and xfs).

You can partition hard disks with commands such as `fdisk` and `parted`. Tools for working with file systems include those that create file systems (`mkfs`), view and modify file system attributes (`tune2fs` and `dumpe2fs`), mount/unmount file systems (`mount` and `umount`), and check for problems (`badblocks` and `fsck`). To see how much space has been used in file systems, use the `df` and `du` commands.

8

Backups and Removable Media

Data backups in Linux were traditionally done by running commands to archive and compress the files to back up, then writing that backup archive to tape. Choices for archive tools, compression techniques, and backup media have grown tremendously in recent years. Tape archiving has, for many, been replaced with techniques for backing up data over the network, to other hard disks, or to CDs, DVDs, or other low-cost removable media.

This chapter details some useful tools for backing up and restoring your critical data. The first part of the chapter details how to use basic tools such as tar, gzip, and rsync for backups.

IN THIS CHAPTER

Creating backup archives with tar

Compressing backups with gzip, bzip2, and lzop

Backing up over the network with SSH

Doing network backups with rsync

Making backup ISO images with mkisofs

Burning backup images to CD or DVD with cdrecord and growisofs

Backing Up Data to Compressed Archives

If you are coming from a Windows background, you may be used to tools such as WinZip and PKZIP, which both archive and compress groups of files in one application. Linux offers separate tools for gathering groups of files into a single archive (such as tar) and compressing that archive for efficient storage (gzip, bzip2, and lzop). However, you can also do the two steps together by using additional options to the tar command.

Creating Backup Archives with tar

The tar command, which stands for *tape archiver*, dates back to early Unix systems. Although magnetic tape was the common medium that tar wrote to originally, today tar is most often used to create an archive file that can be distributed to a variety of media.

The fact that the `tar` command is rich in features is reflected in the dozens of options available with `tar`. The basic operations of `tar`, however, are used to create a backup archive (-c), extract files from an archive (-x), compare differences between archives (-d), and update files in an archive (-u). You can also append files to (-r or -A) or delete files from (-d) an existing archive, or list the contents of an archive (-t).

> **NOTE** *Although the `tar` command is available on nearly all Unix and Linux systems, it behaves differently on many systems. For example, Solaris does not support -z to manage tar archives compressed in gzip format. The `Star` (ess-tar) command supports access control lists (ACLs) and file flags (for extended permissions used by Samba).*

As part of the process of creating a tar archive, you can add options that compress the resulting archive. For example, add -j to compress the archive in bzip2 format or -z to compress in gzip format. By convention, regular tar files end in `.tar`, while compressed tar files end in `.tar.bz2` (compressed with bzip2) or `.tar.gz` (compressed with gzip). If you compress a file manually with `lzop` (see www.lzop.org), the compressed tar file should end in `.tar.lzo`.

Besides being used for backups, tar files are popular ways to distribute source code and binaries from software projects. That's because you can expect every Linux and Unix-like system to contain the tools you need to work with tar files.

> **NOTE** *One quirk of working with the `tar` command comes from the fact that tar was created before there were standards regarding how options are entered. Although you can prefix `tar` options with a dash, it isn't always necessary. So you might see a command that begins `tar xvf` with no dashes to indicate the options.*

A classic example for using the `tar` command might combine old-style options and pipes for compressing the output; for example:

```
$ tar c *.txt | gzip -c > myfiles.tar.gz Make archive, zip it and output
```

The example just shown illustrates a two-step process you might find in documentation for old Unix systems. The `tar` command creates (c) an archive from all `.txt` files in the current directory. The output is piped to the `gzip` command and output to stdout (-c), and then redirected to the `myfiles.tar.gz` file. Note that `tar` is one of the few commands which don't require that options be preceded by a dash (-).

New tar versions, on modern Linux systems, can **create the archive and compress the output** in one step:

```
$ tar czf myfiles.tar.gz *.txt    Create gzipped tar file of .txt files
$ tar czvf myfiles.tar.gz *.txt   Be more verbose creating archive
textfile1.txt
textfile2.txt
```

In the examples just shown, note that the new archive name (myfiles.tar.gz) must immediately follow the f option to tar (which indicates the name of the archive). Otherwise the output from tar will be directed to stdout (in other words, your screen). The z option says to do gzip compression, and v produces verbose descriptions of processing.

When you want to **return the files to a file system** (unzipping and untarring), you can also do that as either a one-step or two-step process, using the tar command and optionally the gunzip command:

```
$ gunzip -c myfiles.tar.gz | tar x          Unzips and untars archive
```

Or try the following command line instead:

```
$ gunzip myfiles.tar.gz ; tar xf myfiles.tar   Unzips then untars archive
```

To do that same procedure in one step, you could use the following command:

```
$ tar xzvf myfiles.tar.gz
textfile1.txt
textfile2.txt
```

The result of the previous commands is that the archived .txt files are copied from the archive to the current directory. The x option extracts the files, z uncompresses (unzips) the files, v makes the output, and f indicates that the next option is the name of the archive file (myfiles.tar.gz).

Using Compression Tools

Compression is an important aspect of working with backup files. It takes less disk space on your backup medium (CD, DVD, tape, and so on) or server to store compressed files. It also takes less time to transfer the archives to the media or download the files over a network.

While compression can save a lot of storage space and transfer times, it can significantly increase your CPU usage. You can consider using hardware compression on a tape drive (see www.amanda.org/docs/faq.html#id346016).

In the examples shown in the previous section, tar calls the gzip command. But tar can work with many compression tools. Out of the box on Ubuntu, tar will work with gzip and bzip2. A third compression utility we add to our toolbox is the lzop command, which can be used with tar in a different way. The order of these tools from fastest/least compression to slowest/most compression is: lzop, gzip, and bzip2.

If you are archiving and compressing large amounts of data, the time it takes to compress your backups can be significant. So you should be aware that, in general, bzip2

153

may take about 10 times longer than lzop and only give you twice the compression. However, with each compression command, you can choose different compression levels, to balance the need for more compression with the time that compression takes.

To use the tar command with **bzip2 compression**, use the -j option:

```
$ tar cjvf myfiles.tar.bz2 *.txt      Create archive, compress with bzip2
```

You can also **uncompress (-j) a bzip2 compressed file** as you extract files (-x) using the tar command:

```
$ tar xjvf myfiles.tar.bz2    Extract files, uncompress bzip2 compression
```

The lzop compression utility is a bit less integrated into tar. Before you can use lzop, you might need to install the lzop package. To do **lzop compression**, you need the --use-compress-program option:

```
$ sudo apt-get install lzop
$ tar --use-compress-program=lzop -cf myfiles.tar.lzo *.txt
$ tar --use-compress-program=lzop -xf myfiles.tar.lzo
```

In the previous examples, the command line reverses the old syntax of tar with a switch before the command. For normal use and in other examples, we used the modern syntax of tar with no switch.

> **NOTE** *You may encounter .rar compressed files in the RAR format. This format seems to be popular in the world of peer-to-peer networks. RAR is a proprietary format so there is no widespread compressing tool. On Ubuntu, you can install the unrar and rar packages to get commands to work with RAR-format files.*

Compressing with gzip

As noted, you can **use any of the compression commands alone** (as opposed to within the tar command line). Here are some examples of the gzip command to create and work with gzip-compressed files:

```
$ gzip myfile               gzips myfile and renames it myfile.gz
```

The following command provides the same result, with verbose output:

```
$ gzip -v myfile            gzips myfile with verbose output
myfile: 86.0% -- replaced with myfile.gz
$ gzip -tv myfile.gz        Tests integrity of gzip file
myfile.gz:     OK
$ gzip -lv myfile.gz        Get detailed info about gzip file
method  crc   date  time    compressed   uncompressed  ratio uncompressed_name
defla 0f27d9e4 Jul 10 04:48    46785       334045       86.0%   myfile
```

Use any one of the following commands to **compress all files in a directory**:

```
$ gzip -rv mydir              Compress all files in a directory
mydir/file1: 39.1% -- replaced with mydir/file1.gz
mydir/file2: 39.5% -- replaced with mydir/file2.gz
$ gzip -1 myfile        Fastest compression time, least compression
$ gzip -9 myfile        Slowest compression time, most compression
```

Add a dash before a number from 1 to 9 to set the compression level. As illustrated above, -1 is the fastest (least) and -9 is the slowest (most) compression. The default for gzip is level 6. The lzop command has fewer levels: 1, 3 (default), 7, 8, and 9. Compression levels for bzip2 behave differently.

To **uncompress a gzipped file**, you can use the gunzip command. Use either of the following examples:

```
$ gunzip -v myfile.gz          Unzips myfile.gz and renames it myfile
myfile.gz:       86.0% -- replaced with myfile
$ gzip -dv myfile.gz           Same as previous command line
```

Although the examples just shown refer to zipping regular files, the same options can be used to compress tar archives.

Compressing with bzip2

The **bzip2 command** is considered to provide the highest compression among the compression tools described in this chapter. Here are some examples of bzip2:

```
$ bzip2 myfile             Compresses file and renames it myfile.bz2
$ bzip2 -v myfile          Same as previous command, but more verbose
  myfile:  9.529:1, 0.840 bits/byte, 89.51% saved, 334045 in, 35056 out.
$ bunzip2 myfile.bz2       Uncompresses file and renames it myfile
$ bzip2 -d myfile.bz2      Same as previous command
$ bunzip2 -v myfile.bz2    Same as previous command, but more verbose
  myfile.bz2: done
```

Compressing with lzop

The lzop command behaves differently from gzip and bzip2. The lzop command is best in cases where compression speed is more important than the resulting compression ratio. When lzop compresses the contents of a file, it leaves the original file intact (unless you use -U), but creates a new file with a .lzo suffix. Use either of the following examples of the **lzop command to compress a file called myfile**:

```
$ lzop -v myfile               Leave myfile, create compressed myfile.lzo
compressing myfile into myfile.lzo
$ lzop -U myfile               Remove myfile, create compressed myfile.lzo
```

With myfile.lzo created, choose any of the following commands to **test, list, or uncompress** the file:

```
$ lzop -t myfile.lzo          Test the compressed file's integrity
$ lzop --info myfile.lzo      List internal header for each file
$ lzop -l myfile.lzo          List compression info for each file
method   compressed  uncompr. ratio uncompressed_name
LZO1X-1     59008       99468  59.3% myfile
$ lzop --ls myfile.lzo        Show contents of compressed file as ls -l
$ cat myfile | lzop > x.lzo   Compress standin and direct to stdout
$ lzop -dv myfile.lzo         Leave myfile.lzo, make uncompressed myfile
```

Unlike gzip and bzip2, lzop has no related command for unlzopping. Always just use the -d option to `lzop` to uncompress a file. If fed a list of file and directory names, the `lzop` command will compress all files and ignore directories. The original file name, permission modes, and timestamps are used on the compressed file as were used on the original file.

Listing, Joining, and Adding Files to tar Archives

So far, all we've done with `tar` is create and unpack archives. There are also options for listing the contents of archives, joining archives, adding files to an existing archive, and deleting files from an archive.

To **list an archive's contents**, use the -t option:

```
$ tar tvf myfiles.tar              List files from uncompressed archive
-rw-r--r-- root/root     9584 2007-07-05 11:20:33 textfile1.txt
-rw-r--r-- root/root     9584 2007-07-09 10:23:44 textfile2.txt
$ tar tzvf myfiles.tgz             List files from gzip compressed archive
```

If the archive were a tar archive compressed with lzop and named `myfile.tar.lzo`, you could **list that tar/lzo file's contents** as follows:

```
$ tar --use-compress-program=lzop -tf myfiles.tar.lzo   List lzo archives
```

To **concatenate one tar file to another**, use the -A option. The following command results in the contents of `archive2.tar` being added to the `archive1.tar` archive:

```
$ tar -Af archive1.tar archive2.tar
```

Use the -r option to **add one or more files to an existing archive**. In the following example, `myfile` is added to the `archive.tar` archive file:

```
$ tar rvf archive.tar myfile     Add a file to a tar archive
```

You can use wildcards to **match multiple files to add** to your archive:

```
$ tar rvf archive.tar *.txt      Add multiple files to a tar archive
```

Deleting Files from tar Archives

If you have a tar archive file on your hard disk, you can delete files from that archive. Note that you can't use this technique to delete files from tar output on magnetic tape. Here is an example of **deleting files from a tar archive**:

```
$ tar --delete file1.txt -f myfile.tar    Delete file1.txt from myfile.tar
```

Backing Up Over Networks

After you have backed up your files and gathered them into a tar archive, what do you do with that archive? The primary reason for having a backup is in case something happens (such as a hard disk crash) where you need to restore files from that backup. Methods you can employ to keep those backups safe include:

❑ **Copying backups to removable media** such as tape, CD, or DVD (as described later in this chapter)

❑ **Copying them to another machine over a network**

Fast and reliable networks, inexpensive high-capacity hard disks, and the security that comes with moving your data off-site have all made network backups a popular practice. For an individual backing up personal data or a small office, combining a few simple commands may be all you need to create efficient and secure backups. This approach represents a direct application of the Unix philosophy: joining together simple programs that do one thing to get a more complex job done.

Although just about any command that can copy files over a network can be used to move your backup data to a remote machine, some utilities are especially good for the job. Using OpenSSH tools such as ssh and scp, you can set up secure password-less transfers of backup archives and encrypted transmissions of those archives.

Tools such as the rsync command can save resources by backing up only files (or parts of files) that have changed since the previous backup. With tools such as unison, you can back up files over a network from Windows, as well as Linux systems.

The following sections describe some of these techniques for backing up your data to other machines over a network.

> **NOTE** *A similar tool that might interest you is the* rsnapshot *command (*yum
> install rsnapshot*). The* rsnapshot *command (*www.rsnapshot.org/*)
> can work with* rsync *to make configurable hourly, daily, weekly, or monthly snapshots of a file system. It uses hard links to keep a snapshot of a file system, which it can then sync with changed files.*
>
> *Install this tool with the following commands:*
>
> ```
> $ sudo apt-get install rsnapshot
> $ sudo apt-get install sshfs
> ```

Backing Up tar Archives Over ssh

OpenSSH (www.openssh.org/) provides tools to securely do remote login, remote execution, and remote file copy over network interfaces. By setting up two machines to share encryption keys, you can transfer files between those machines without entering passwords for each transmission. That fact lets you create scripts to back up your data from an SSH client to an SSH server, without any manual intervention.

From a central Linux system, you can **gather backups from multiple client machines** using OpenSSH commands. The following example runs the tar command on a remote site (to archive and compress the files), pipes the tar stream to standard output, and uses the ssh command to catch the backup locally (over ssh) with tar:

```
$ mkdir mybackup ; cd mybackup
$ ssh francois@server1 'tar cf - myfile*' | tar xvf -
francois@server1's password: ******
myfile1
myfile2
```

In the example just shown, all files beginning with myfile are copied from the home directory of francois on server1 and placed in the current directory. Note that the left side of the pipe creates the archive and the right side expands the files from the archive to the current directory. (Keep in mind that ssh will overwrite local files if they exist, which is why we created an empty directory in the example.)

To reverse the process and **copy files from the local system to the remote system,** we run a local tar command first. This time, however, we add a cd command to put the files in the directory of our choice on the remote machine:

```
$ tar cf - myfile* | ssh francois@server1 \
        'cd /home/francois/myfolder; tar xvf -'
francois@server1's password: ******
myfile1
myfile2
```

In this next example, we're not going to untar the files on the receiving end, but instead **write the results to tgz files:**

```
$ ssh francois@server1 'tar czf - myfile*' | cat > myfiles.tgz
$ tar cvzf - myfile* | ssh francois@server1 'cat > myfiles.tgz'
```

The first example takes all files beginning with myfile from the francois user's home directory on server1, tars and compresses those files, and directs those compressed files to the myfiles.tgz file on the local system. The second example does the reverse by taking all files beginning with myfile in the local directory and sending them to a myfiles.tgz file on the remote system.

The examples just shown are good for copying files over the network. Besides providing compression they also enable you to use any `tar` features you choose, such as incremental backup features.

Backing Up Files with rsync

A more feature-rich command for doing backups is `rsync`. What makes `rsync` so unique is the `rsync` algorithm, which compares the local and remote files one small block at a time using checksums, and only transfers the blocks that are different. This algorithm is so efficient that it has been reused in many backup products.

The `rsync` command can work either on top of a remote shell (ssh), or by running an `rsyncd` daemon on the server end. The following example uses `rsync` over ssh to mirror a directory:

```
$ rsync -avz --delete chris@server1:/home/chris/pics/ chrispics/
```

The command just shown is intended to mirror the remote directory structure (/home/chris/pics/) on the local system. The -a says to run in archive mode (recursively copying all files from the remote directory), the -z option compresses the files, and -v makes the output verbose. The --delete tells `rsync` to delete any files on the local system that no longer exist on the remote system.

For ongoing backups, you can have `rsync` do seven-day incremental backups. Here's an example:

```
# mkdir /var/backups
# rsync --delete --backup                          \
    --backup-dir=/var/backups/backup-`date +%A` \
    -avz chris@server1:/home/chris/Personal/     \
    /var/backups/current-backup/
```

When the command just shown runs, all the files from /home/chris/Personal on the remote system server1 are copied to the local directory /var/backups/current-backup. All files modified today are copied to a directory named after today's day of the week, such as /var/backups/backup-Monday. Over a week, seven directories will be created that reflect changes over each of the past seven days.

Another trick for rotated backups is to use hard links instead of multiple copies of the files. This two-step process consists of rotating the files, then running `rsync`:

```
# rm -rf /var/backups/backup-old/
# mv /var/backups/backup-current/ /var/backups/backup-old/
# rsync --delete --link-dest=/var/backups/backup-old -avz \
    chris@server1:/home/chris/Personal/ /var/backups/backup-current/
```

In the previous procedure, the existing `backup-current` directory replaces the `backup-old` directory, deleting the two-week-old full backup with last-week's full backup. When the new full backup is run with `rsync` using the `--link-dest` option, if any of the files being backed up from the remote `Personal` directory on server1 existed during the previous backup (now in `backup-old`), a hard link is created between the file in the `backup-current` directory and `backup-old` directory.

You can save a lot of space by having hard links between files in your `backup-old` and `backup-current` directory. For example, if you had a file named `file1.txt` in both directories, you could check that both were the same physical file by listing the files' inodes as follows:

```
$ ls -i /var/backups/backup*/file1.txt
260761   /var/backups/backup-current/file1.txt
260761   /var/backups/backup-old/file1.txt
```

Backing Up with unison

Although the `rsync` command is good to back up one machine to another, it assumes that the machine being backed up is the only one where the data is being modified. What if you have two machines that both modify the same file and you want to sync those files? Unison is a tool that will let you do that.

It's common for people to want to work with the same documents on their laptop and desktop systems. Those machines might even run different operating systems. Because unison is a cross-platform application, it can let you sync files that are on both Linux and Windows systems. To use unison in Ubuntu, you must install the unison package (type the `sudo apt-get install unison` command).

With unison, you can define two *roots* representing the two paths to synchronize. Those roots can be local or remote over ssh. For example:

```
$ unison /home/francois ssh://francois@server1//home/fcaen
$ unison /home/francois /mnt/backups/francois-homedir
```

> **NOTE** *Make sure you run the same version of* unison *on both machines.*

Unison contains both graphical and command-line tools for doing unison backups. It will try to run the graphical version by default. This may fail if you don't have a desktop running or if you're launching unison from within `screen`. To force unison to run in command line mode, add the `-ui text` option as follows:

```
$ unison /home/francois ssh://francois@server1//home/fcaen -ui text
Contacting server...
francois@server1's password:
Looking for changes
   Waiting for changes from server
Reconciling changes
local           server1
```

```
newfile ---->              memo.txt  [f] y
Propagating updates
   ...
```

The unison utility will then compare the two roots and for each change that occurred since last time, ask you what you want to do. In the example above, there's a new file called memo.txt on the local system. You are asked if you want to proceed with the update (in this case, copy memo.txt from the local machine to server1). Type y to do the updates.

If you trust unison, add -auto to make it take default actions without prompting you:

```
$ unison /home/francois ssh://francois@server1//home/fcaen -auto
```

For more information, see the man page for unison. In addition, you can view unison options using the -help option. You can also display and page through the unison manual using the -doc all option as shown here:

```
$ unison -help              See unison options
$ unison -doc all | less    Display unison manual
```

If you find yourself synchronizing two roots frequently, you can create a profile, which is a series of presets. In graphical mode, the default screen makes you create profiles. Profiles are stored in .prf text files in the ~/.unison/ directory. They can be as simple as the following:

```
root = /home/francois
root = ssh://francois@server1//home/fcaen
```

If this is stored in a profile called fc-home.prf, you can invoke it simply with the following command line:

```
$ unison fc-home
```

Backing Up to Removable Media

The capacity of CDs and DVDs, and the low costs of those media, has made them attractive options as computer backup media. Using tools that commonly come with Linux systems, you can gather files to back up into CD or DVD images and burn those images to the appropriate media.

Command line tools such as mkisofs (for creating CD images) and cdrecord (for burning images to CD or DVD) once provided the most popular interfaces for making backups to CD or DVD. Now there are many graphical front-ends to those tools you could also consider using. For example, GUI tools for mastering and burning CDs/DVDs include K3b (the KDE CD and DVD Kreator) and Nautilus (GNOME's file manager that offers a CD-burning feature). Other GUI tools for burning CDs include gcombust, X-CD-Roast, and graveman.

The commands for creating file system images to back up to CD or DVD, as well as to burn those images, are described in this section.

Creating Backup Images with mkisofs

Most data CDs and DVDs can be accessed on both Windows and Linux systems because they are created using the ISO9660 standard for formatting the information on those discs. Because most modern operating systems need to save more information about files and directories than the basic ISO9660 standard includes, extensions to that standard were added to contain that information.

Using the mkisofs command, you can back up the file and directory structure from any point in your Linux file system and produce an ISO9660 image. That image can include the following kinds of extensions:

❏ **System Use Sharing Protocol** (SUSP) are records identified in the Rock Ridge Interchange Protocol. SUSP records can include Unix-style attributes, such as ownership, long file names, and special files (such as character devices and symbolic links).

❏ **Joliet** directory records store longer file names in a form that makes them usable to Windows systems.

❏ **Hierarchical File System** (HFS) extensions allow the ISO image to appear as an HFS file system, which is the native file system for Macintosh computers. Likewise, Data and Resource forks can be added in different ways to be read by Macs.

When you set out to create your ISO image, consider where you will ultimately need to access the files you back up using mkisofs (Linux, Windows, or Macs). Once the image is created, it can be used in different ways, the most obvious of which is to burn the image to a CD or DVD.

Besides being useful in producing all or portions of a Linux file system to use on a portable medium, mkisofs is also useful for creating live CDs/DVDs. It does this by adding boot information to the image that can launch a Linux kernel or other operating system, bypassing the computer's hard drive.

> **NOTE** *Although you can still use the* mkisofs *command in Ubuntu,* mkisofs *is now a pointer to* genisoimage. *The* genisoimage *command was derived from* mkisofs, *which was part of the* cdrtools *package (see* http://cdrecord .berlios.de). *Development of* genisoimage *is part of the cdrkit project* (www.cdrkit.org).

Because most Linux users store their personal files in their home directories, a common way to use mkisofs to back up files is to back up everything under the /home directory. Here are some examples of using `mkisofs` to **create an ISO image from all files and directories under the** /home **directory**:

```
$ cd /tmp
$ sudo mkisofs -o home.iso /home              Create basic ISO9660 image
$ sudo mkisofs -o home2.iso -J -R /home       Add Joliet Rock Ridge extensions
$ sudo mkisofs -o home3.iso -J -R -hfs /home Also add HFS extensions
```

With the last command, you will see a warning message like the following:

```
genisoimage: Warning: no Apple/Unix files will be decoded/mapped
```

In each of the three examples above, all files and directories beneath the /home directory are added to the ISO image (home.iso). The first example has no extensions, so all file names are converted to DOS-style naming (8.3 characters). The second example uses Joliet and Rock Ridge extensions, so file names and permissions should appear as they did on the original Linux system when you open the ISO on a Linux or Windows system. The last example also makes the files on the image readable from a Mac file system.

NOTE *You can also read Rock Ridge and Joliet extensions on Mac OS X.*

You can **have multiple sources added to the image.** Here are some examples:

```
$ mkisofs -o home.iso -R -J music/ docs/ \    Multiple directories/files
         chris.pdf /var/spool/mail
$ mkisofs -o home.iso -J -R                \    Graft files on to the image
    -graft-points Pictures/=/usr/share/pixmaps/  \
    /home/chris
```

The first example above shows various files and directories being combined and placed on the root of the ISO image. The second example grafts the contents of the /var/pics directory into the /home/chris/Pictures directory. As a result, on the CD image the /Pictures directory will contain all content from the /usr/share/pixmaps directory.

Adding information into the header of the ISO image can help you identify the contents of that image later. This is especially useful if the image is being saved or distributed online, without a physical disc you can write on. Here are some examples:

```
$ mkisofs -o /tmp/home.iso -R -J           \    Add header info to ISO
    -p www.handsonhistory.com              \
    -publisher "Swan Bay Folk Art Center"  \
    -V "WebBackup"                         \
    -A "mkisofs"                           \
    -volset "1 of 4 backups, July 30, 2007" \
    /home/chris
```

In the example above, -p indicates the preparer ID, which could include a phone number, mailing address, or web site for contacting the preparer of the ISO image. With the option -publisher, you can indicate a 128-character description of the preparer (possibly the company or organization name). The -V indicates the volume ID. Volume ID is important because in many Linux systems this volume ID is used to mount the CD when it is inserted. For example, in the command line shown above, the CD would be mounted on /media/WebBackup in Ubuntu and other Linux systems. The -A option can be used to indicate the application used to create the ISO image. The -volset option can contain a string of information about a set of ISO images.

When you have created your ISO image, and before you burn it to disc, you can check the image and make sure you can access the files it contains. Here are ways to check it out:

```
$ volname home.iso              Display volume name
WebBackup
$ isoinfo -d -i home.iso        Display header information
CD-ROM is in ISO 9660 format
System id: LINUX
Volume id: WebBackup
Volume set id: All Website material on November 2, 2007
Publisher id: Swan Bay Folk Art Center
Data preparer id: www.handsonhistory.com
Application id: mkisofs
Copyright File id:
Abstract File id:
Bibliographic File id:
Volume set size is: 1
Volume set sequence number is: 1
Logical block size is: 2048
Volume size is: 23805
Joliet with UCS level 3 found
Rock Ridge signatures version 1 found
```

You can see a lot of the information entered on the mkisofs command line when the image was created. If this had been an image that was going to be published, we might also have indicated the locations on the CD of a copyright file (-copyright), abstract file (-abstract), and bibliographic file (-biblio). Provided that the header is okay, you can next try accessing files on the ISO image by mounting it:

```
$ sudo mkdir /mnt/myimage               Create a mount point
$ sudo mount -o loop home.iso /mnt/myimage    Mount the ISO in loopback
$ ls -l /mnt/myimage                    Check the ISO contents
$ sudo umount /mnt/myimage              Unmount the image when done
```

Besides checking that you can access the files and directories on the ISO, make sure that the date/time stamps, ownership, and permissions are set as you would like. That information might be useful if you need to restore the information at a later date.

Burning Backup Images with cdrecord

The `cdrecord` command is the most popular Linux command line tool for burning CD and DVD images. After you have created an ISO image (as described earlier) or obtained one otherwise (such as downloading an install CD or live CD from the Internet), `cdrecord` makes it easy to put that image on a disc.

> **NOTE** *In Ubuntu,* `cdrecord` *has been replaced with the* `wodim` *command. The* `wodim` *command was created from the* `cdrecord` *code base and still supports most of the same options. If you run* `cdrecord`, *you will actually be running* `wodim` *in this Ubuntu release. If you have problems with that utility, contact the CDRkit project* (`http://cdrkit.org`).

There is no difference in making a CD or DVD ISO image, aside from the fact that a DVD image can obviously be bigger than a CD image. Check the media you have for their capacities. A CD can typically hold 650MB, 700MB, or 800MB, whereas mini CDs can hold 50MB, 180MB, 185MB, or 193MB. Single-layer DVDs hold 4.7GB, while double-layer DVDs can hold 8.4GB.

> **NOTE** *Keep in mind, however, that CD/DVD manufacturers list their capacities based on 1000KB per 1MB, instead of 1024KB. Type* `du --si home.iso` *to list the size of your ISO, instead of* `du -sh` *as you would normally, to check if your ISO will fit on the media you have.*

Before you begin burning your image to CD or DVD, **check that your drive supports CD/DVD burning** and determine the address of the drive. Use the `--scanbus` option to `cdrecord` to do that:

```
$ cdrecord --scanbus          Shows a drive that cannot do burning
scsibus0:
        0,0,0   0) 'SAMSUNG ' 'DVD-ROM SD-616E ' 'F503' Removable CD-ROM
        0,0,0   1) *
        0,0,0   2) *
                . . .
$ cdrecord --scanbus          Shows a drive that can burn CDs or DVDs
scsibus0:
        0,0,0   0) 'LITE-ON ' 'DVDRW SOHW-1633S' 'BS0C' Removable CD-ROM
        0,0,0   1) *
        0,0,0   2) *
                . . .
```

In the two examples shown, the first indicates a CD/DVD drive that only supports reading and cannot burn CDs (DVD-ROM and CD-ROM). The second example shows a drive that can burn CDs or DVDs (DVDRW). Insert the medium you want to record on. Assuming your drive can burn the media you have, here are some simple `cdrecord` commands for **burning a CD or DVD images**:

```
$ cdrecord -dummy home.iso    Test burn without actually burning
$ cdrecord -v home.iso        Burn CD (default settings) in verbose
```

```
$ cdrecord -v speed=24 home.iso   Set specific speed
$ cdrecord -pad home.iso          Can't read track so add 15 zeroed sectors
$ cdrecord -eject home.iso        Eject CD/DVD when burn is done
$ cdrecord /dev/cdrw home.iso     Identify drive by device name (may differ)
$ cdrecord dev=0,2,0 home.iso     Identify drive by SCSI name
```

The cdrecord command can also **burn multi-session CDs/DVDs**. Here is an example:

```
$ cdrecord -multi home.iso        Start a multi-burn session
$ cdrecord -msinfo                Check the session offset for next burn
Using /dev/cdrom of unknown capabilities
0,93041
$ mkisofs -J -R -o new.iso \      Create a second ISO to burn
  -C 0,93041 /home/chris/more     Indicate start point and new data for ISO
$ cdrecord new.iso                Burn new data to existing CD
```

You can use multiple -multi burns until the CD is filled up. For the final burn, don't use -multi, so that the CD will be closed.

Making and Burning DVDs with growisofs

Using the growisofs command, you can **combine the two steps of gathering files into an ISO image (mkisofs) and burning that image to DVD (cdrecord)**. Besides saving a step, the growisofs command also offers the advantage of keeping a session open by default until you close it, so you don't need to do anything special for multi-burn sessions.

Here is an example of some growisofs commands for a **multi-burn session**:

```
$ growisofs -Z /dev/dvd -R -J /home/chris       Master and burn to DVD
$ growisofs -Z /dev/dvd -R -J /home/francois     Add to burn
$ growisofs -M /dev/dvd=/dev/zero               Close burn
```

If you want to add options when creating the ISO image, you can simply add mkisofs options to the command line. (For example, see how the -R and -J options are added in the above examples.)

If you want to **burn a DVD image using growisofs**, you can use the **-dvd-compat** option. Here's an example:

```
$ growisofs -dvd-compat -Z /dev/dvd=image.iso   Burn an ISO image to DVD
```

The -dvd-compat option can improve compatibility with different DVD drives over some multi-session DVD burning procedures.

Summary

Linux and its predecessor Unix systems handled data backups by combining commands that each handled a discrete set of features. Backups of your critical data can still be done in this way. In fact, many of the tools you can use will perform more securely and efficiently than ever before.

The tape archiver utility (`tar` command) has expanded well beyond its original job of making magnetic tape backups of data files. Because nearly every Linux and UNIX system includes `tar`, it has become a standard utility for packaging software and backing up data to compressed archives. Those archives can then be transported and stored in a variety of ways.

To move backed up data to other machines over a network, you can use remote execution features of OpenSSH tools (such as `ssh`). You can also use an excellent utility called `rsync`. With `rsync`, you can save resources by only backing up files (or parts of files) that have changed.

Inexpensive CDs and DVDs have made those media popular for doing personal and small-office backups. The `mkisofs` command can create file systems of backed up data in ISO9660 format that can be restored on a variety of systems (Linux, Windows, or Mac). Once `mkisofs` command has created an ISO image, the image can be burned to CD or DVD using the `cdrecord` or `growisofs` command.

9

Checking and Managing Running Processes

When an executable program starts up, it runs as a process that is under the management of your Linux system's process table. Linux provides all the tools you need to view and change the processes running on your system.

The ps and top commands are great for viewing information on your running processes. There are literally dozens of options to ps and top to help you view process information exactly the way you want to. The pgrep command can further help find the process you want.

There are commands such as nice and renice for raising and lowering processor priority for a process. You can move processes to run in the background (bg command) or back to the foreground (fg command).

Sending signals to a process is a way of changing its behavior or killing it altogether. Using the kill and killall commands, you can send signals to processes by PID or name, respectively. You can also send other signals to processes to do such things as reread configuration files or continue with a stopped process.

IN THIS CHAPTER

Viewing active processes with ps and top

Searching for processes with pgrep

Adjusting CPU priority with nice and renice

Moving processes to the background (bg) or foreground (fg)

Killing and signaling processes with kill and killall

Using at and batch to run commands

Scheduling commands to run repeatedly with cron

To run commands at scheduled times or so they are not tied to your shell session, you can use the at and batch commands. To run commands repetitively at set times, there are the cron and anacron facilities. Or you can drop scripts (or symbolic links to scripts) into /etc/cron.hourly (or cron.daily, cron.weekly, or cron.monthly).

Listing Active Processes

To see which processes are currently running on a system, most people use the ps and top commands. The ps command gives you a snapshot (in a simple list) of processes running at the moment. The top command offers a screen-oriented, constantly updated listing of running commands, sorted as you choose (by CPU use, memory use, UID, and so on).

Viewing Active Processes with ps

Every Linux system (as well as every system derived from Unix, such as BSD, Mac OS X, and others) includes the ps command. Over the years, however, many slightly different versions of ps have appeared, offering slightly different options. Because ps dates back to the first Unix systems, it also supports nonstandard ways of entering some options (for example, allowing you to drop the dash before an option in some cases).

The different uses of ps shown in this chapter will work on Ubuntu and most other Linux systems. Here are some examples you can run to **show processes running for the current user** (Table 9-1 contains column descriptions of ps output):

```
$ ps                    List processes of current user at current shell
 PID TTY           TIME CMD
2552 pts/0      00:00:00 bash
3438 pts/0      00:00:00 ps
$ ps -u chris           Show all chris' running processes (simple output)
PID    TTY  TIME COMMAND
2678   tty1 0:00 startx
2689   tty1 0:00 xinit
2710   tty1 0:06 gnome-session
 . . .
$ ps -u chris u         Show all chris' running processes (with CPU/MEM)
USER     PID %CPU %MEM   VSZ   RSS TTY   STAT START TIME COMMAND
chris   2678  0.0  0.0  4328   852 tty1  S+   Aug14 0:00 /bin/sh startx
chris   2689  0.0  0.1  2408   488 tty1  S+   Aug14 0:00 xinit
chris   2710  0.0  1.1 22016  5496 tty1  S    Aug14 0:06 gnome-session
 . . .
$ ps -fu chris          Show all chris' running processes (with PPID)
UID         PID  PPID  C STIME TTY         TIME CMD
chris      2678  2645  0 Aug14 tty1    00:00:00 /bin/sh /usr/X11R6/bin/startx
chris      2689  2678  0 Aug14 tty1    00:00:00 xinit /etc/X11/xinit/xinitrc
chris      2710  2689  0 Aug14 tty1    00:00:09 /usr/bin/gnome-session
 . . .
$ ps -Fu chris          Show all chris' running processes (with SZ and PSR)
UID      PID  PPID  C    SZ  RSS PSR STIME TTY        TIME CMD
chris   2678  2645  0  1082  852   0 Aug14 tty1   00:00:00 /bin/sh startx
chris   2689  2678  0   602  488   0 Aug14 tty1   00:00:00 xinit
chris   2710  2689  0  5504 5440   0 Aug14 tty1   00:00:09 gnome-session
 . . .
```

These examples illustrate some of the processes from a user running a GNOME desktop session. The first example above shows ps alone being run from a Terminal window, so you only see the processes for the current shell running in that window. Other examples let you display different information for each process (see later examples for ways of producing custom output). See Table 9-1 for descriptions of columns displayed by ps.

Here are ps examples showing output for **every process currently running on the system**:

```
$ ps -e              Show every running process
   PID TTY          TIME CMD
     1 ?        00:00:01 init
     2 ?        00:00:00 migration/0
     3 ?        00:00:00 ksoftirqd/0
   ...
$ ps -el             Show every running process, long listing
F S   UID   PID  PPID  C PRI  NI ADDR SZ WCHAN  TTY          TIME CMD
4 S     0     1     0  0  75   0 -   534 -      ?        00:00:01 init
1 S     0     2     1  0 -40   - -     0 -      ?        00:00:00 migration/0
1 S     0     3     1  0  94  19 -     0 -      ?        00:00:00 ksoftirqd/0
   ...
$ ps -ef             Show every running process, full-format listing
UID        PID  PPID  C STIME TTY          TIME CMD
root         1     0  0 Aug05 ?        00:00:01 init [5]
root         2     1  0 Aug05 ?        00:00:00 [migration/0]
root         3     1  0 Aug05 ?        00:00:00 [ksoftirqd/0]
   ...
$ ps -eF             Show every running process, extra full-format listing
UID        PID  PPID  C    SZ   RSS PSR STIME TTY          TIME CMD
root         1     0  0   534   556   0 Aug05 ?        00:00:01 init [5]
root         2     1  0     0     0   0 Aug05 ?        00:00:00 [migration/0]
root         3     1  0     0     0   0 Aug05 ?        00:00:00 [ksoftirqd/0]
   ...
$ ps ax     Show every running process, short BSD style
   PID TTY      STAT   TIME COMMAND
     1 ?        Ss     0:01 init [5]
     2 ?        S      0:00 [migration/0]
     3 ?        SN     0:00 [ksoftirqd/0]
   ...
$ ps aux     Show every running process, long BSD style
USER     PID %CPU %MEM    VSZ   RSS TTY      STAT START   TIME COMMAND
root       1  0.0  0.0   2136   556 ?        Ss   Aug05   0:01 init [5]
root       2  0.0  0.0      0     0 ?        S    Aug05   0:00 [migration/0]
root       3  0.0  0.0      0     0 ?        SN   Aug05   0:00 [ksoftirqd/0]
   ...
$ ps auwx     Show every running process, long BSD style, wide format
$ ps auwwx    Show every running process, long BSD style, unlimited width
```

Some processes start up other processes. For example, a web server (httpd daemon) will spin off multiple httpd daemons to wait for requests to your web server. You can **view the hierarchy of processes (in a tree view)** using various options with ps:

```
$ ps -ejH            Show process hierarchy with process/session IDs
   PID  PGID   SID TTY          TIME CMD
     1     1     1 ?        00:00:01 init
     2     1     1 ?        00:00:00    migration/0
```

```
  2043  2043  2043  ?      00:00:00    sshd
  2549  2549  2549  ?      00:00:00     sshd
  2551  2549  2549  ?      00:00:00      sshd
  2552  2552  2552 pts/0   00:00:00         bash
  7760  7760  7760  ?      00:00:00    httpd
  7762  7760  7760  ?      00:00:00       httpd
  7763  7760  7760  ?      00:00:00       httpd
$ ps axjf          Show process hierarchy in BSD-style output
 PPID   PID  PGID   SID TTY   TPGID STAT  UID    TIME COMMAND
    0     1     1     1 ?         -1 Ss     0   0:01 init [5]
    1     2     1     1 ?         -1 S      0   0:00 [migration/0]
    1  2043  2043  2043 ?         -1 Ss     0   0:00 /usr/sbin/sshd
 2043  2549  2549  2549 ?         -1 Ss     0   0:00 \_ sshd: chris [priv]
 2549  2551  2549  2549 ?         -1 S    500   0:00  |   \_ sshd: chris@pts
 2551  2552  2552  2552 pts/0   8398 Ss   500   0:00  |       \_ -bash
    1  7760  7760  7760 ?         -1 Ss     0   0:00 /usr/sbin/httpd
 7760  7762  7760  7760 ?         -1 S     48   0:00 \_ /usr/sbin/httpd
 7760  7763  7760  7760 ?         -1 S     48   0:00 \_ /usr/sbin/httpd
$ ps -ef --forest   Show process hierarchy in forest format
UID        PID  PPID  C STIME TTY          TIME CMD
root         1     0  0 Aug05 ?        00:00:01 init [5]
root         2     1  0 Aug05 ?        00:00:00 [migration/0]
root         3     1  0 Aug05 ?        00:00:00 [ksoftirqd/0]
root      2043     1  0 Aug05 ?        00:00:00 /usr/sbin/sshd
root      2549  2043  0 Aug16 ?        00:00:00 \_ sshd: chris [priv]
chris     2551  2549  0 Aug16 ?        00:00:00  |   \_ sshd: chris@pts/0
chris     2552  2551  0 Aug16 pts/0    00:00:00  |       \_ -bash
root      7760     1  0 18:27 ?        00:00:00 /usr/sbin/httpd
apache    7762  7760  0 18:27 ?        00:00:00 \_ /usr/sbin/httpd
apache    7763  7760  0 18:27 ?        00:00:00 \_ /usr/sbin/httpd
$ pstree           Show processes alphabetically in tree format
init-+-Xorg
     |-at-spi-registry
     |-atd
     |-auditd-+-audispd
     |        `-{auditd}
 ...
     |-sshd-+-sshd---sshd---bash---pstree
     |      |-sshd---sshd---bash---su---bash
     |      `-sshd---sshd---bash---su---bash---su---bash---vim
 ...
```

The "tree" examples just shown illustrate different ways of displaying the hierarchy of processes. The output was snipped to compare several of the same processes with different output. Note that the PPID (Parent Process ID) is the ID of the process that started each child process shown. The sshd processes show a running Secure Shell Daemon with a user logging in over the network, resulting in a bash shell (and eventually a vim editor) starting. The httpd daemon represents the Apache web server, with the parent started by the root user and child processes started as the apache user. The last example shows the pstree command, which is specifically used for displaying tree views of processes.

If you prefer personalized views of ps output, you can select exactly which columns of data to display with ps using the -o option. You can then use the --sort option to sort the output by any of those data. Table 9-1 shows available column output and the options to add to -o to have each column print with ps.

Table 9-1: Selecting and Viewing ps Column Output

Option	Column Head	Description
%cpu	%CPU	CPU utilization of process's lifetime in *00.0* format
%mem	%MEM	Percentage of process's machine's physical memory use (resident set size)
args	COMMAND	Command with all arguments
bsdstart	START	Start time of command started: *HH:MM* or *Mon Day*
bsdtime	TIME	Total (user and system) CPU time
comm	COMMAND	Command name only (no arguments shown)
cp	CP	CPU utilization in tenth-of-a-percentage
cputime	TIME	Total CPU time in [*DD-*]*HH:MM:SS* format
egid	EGID	Effective group ID of the process (as integer)
egroup	EGROUP	Effective group ID of the process (as name)
etime	ELAPSED	Time since process was started, in [[*DD-*]*HH:*]*MM:SS* format
euid	EUID	Effective user ID of the process (as integer)
euser	EUSER	Effective user ID of the process (as name)
fgid	FGID	File system access group ID (as number)
fgroup	FGROUP	File system access group ID (as name)
fname	COMMAND	First eight characters of command name
fuid	FUID	File system access user ID (as number)
fuser	FUSER	File system access user ID (as name)

Continued

Table 9-1: Selecting and Viewing ps Column Output (*continued*)

Option	Column Head	Description
lstart	STARTED	Date and time the command started
nice	NI	Nice value, from 19 (nicest) to –20 (CPU hog)
pgid	PGID	Process group ID of process
pid	PID	Process ID number of process
ppid	PPID	Parent process ID of process
psr	PSR	Processor process is assigned to (first CPU is 0)
rgid	RGID	Real group ID (as number)
rgroup	RGROUP	Real group (as name)
rss	RSS	Non-swapped physical memory (resident set size) in KB
rtprio	RTPRIO	Real-time priority
ruid	RUID	Real user ID (as number)
ruser	RUSER	Real user (as name)
s	S	One-character state display (**D**:sleep, no interrupt; **R**:running; **S**:sleep, can interrupt; **T**:stopped; **W**:paging; **X**:dead; **Z**:zombie)
sess	SESS	Session ID of session leader
sgi_p	P	Processor that process is currently running on
size	SZ	Rough amount of swap space needed if process were to swap out
start	STARTED	Time command started: *HH*:*MM*:*SS* or *Month Day*
start_time	START	Time command started: *HH*:*MM* or *MonthDay*
stat	STAT	Multi-character state: One-character "s" state plus other state characters (**<**:High priority; **N**:Low priority; **L**:Has pages locked in memory; **s**:Is session leader; **l**:Multi-threaded; **+**:in foreground process group)
sz	SZ	Size of process's core image (physical pages)

Table 9-1: Selecting and Viewing ps Column Output (*continued*)

Option	Column Head	Description
tname	TTY	Controlling tty (terminal)
user	USER	Effective user ID of process (as name)
vsize	VSZ	Process's virtual memory (1024-byte units)

Note that some values that are meant to print user names may still print numbers (UIDs) instead, if the name is too long to fit in the given space.

Using a comma-separated list of column options, you can produce your custom output. Here are some examples of **custom views of running processes**:

```
$ ps -eo ppid,user,%mem,size,vsize,comm --sort=-size     Sort by mem use
PPID USER      %MEM   SZ    VSZ COMMAND
   1 root      27.0 68176  84264 yum-updatesd
$ ps -eo ppid,user,bsdstart,bsdtime,%cpu,args --sort=-%cpu  Sort by CPU use
PPID USER       START   TIME %CPU COMMAND
   1 root       Jul 30  44:20 27.1 /usr/bin/python /usr/sbin/yum-updatesd
$ ps -eo ppid,user,nice,cputime,args --sort=-nice    Sort by low priority
PPID USER      NI    TIME COMMAND
   1 root      19 00:44:26 /usr/bin/python /usr/sbin/yum-updatesd
$ ps -eo ppid,user,stat,tname,sess,cputime,args --sort=user    Sort by user
PPID USER      STAT TTY   SESS    TIME COMMAND
   1 avahi     Ss   ?     2221 00:00:07 avahi-daemon: running [example.net]
```

Here are a few other **extraneous examples of the ps command**:

```
$ ps -C httpd                    Display running httpd processes
  PID TTY        TIME CMD
 1493 ?       00:00:00 httpd
 1495 ?       00:00:00 httpd
```

Note that you need to install an HTTP server, such as Apache, to run an httpd process.

```
$ ps -p 5413 -o pid,ppid,bsdtime,args       Display info for PID 5413
  PID  PPID   TIME COMMAND
 5413     1   0:08 gpm -m /dev/input/mice -t exps2
$ ps -U chris,francois -o pid,ruser,tty,stat,args See info for 2 users
  PID RUSER   TT      STAT COMMAND
 1010 chris   pts/0   Ss   -bash
 5951 francois pts/1  Ss+  /bin/bash
```

Watching Active Processes with top

If you want to **see the processes running on your system on an ongoing basis**, you can use the top command. The top command runs a screen-oriented view of your running processes that is updated continuously. If you start the `top` command with no options, it displays your system's uptime, tasks, CPU usage, and memory usage, followed by a list of your running processes, sorted by CPU usage. Here's an example:

```
$ top
top - 01:39:43 up 4 days,  1:53,  6 users,  load average: 1.25, 1.08, 1.11
Tasks: 119 total,   1 running, 117 sleeping,   0 stopped,   1 zombie
Cpu(s): 46.8% us,  3.3% sy,  0.0% ni, 49.5% id,  0.0% wa,  0.3% hi,  0.0% si
Mem:    482992k total,   472688k used,    10304k free,    24312k buffers
Swap: 5863716k total,   534512k used,  5329204k free,    68072k cached

  PID USER      PR  NI  VIRT  RES  SHR S %CPU %MEM    TIME+  COMMAND
 2690 root      15   0  344m  76m 7116 S 32.2 16.2  2349:08 X
 2778 chris     15   0 16212 7992 4836 S  1.7  1.7  4:30.61 metacity
22279 chris     15   0  227m 109m  23m S  1.0 23.3 34:34.00 firefox-bin
```

Here are examples of other options you can use to **start top to continuously display running processes**:

```
$ top -d 5          Change update delay to 5 seconds (from default 3)
$ top -u francois   Only see processes of effective user name francois
$ top -p 190,2690   Only display processes 190 and 2690
$ top -n 10         Refresh the screen 10 times before quitting
$ top -b            Run in non-interative non-screen-oriented mode
```

The last example (`top -b`) formats the output of `top` in a way that is suitable for output to a file, as opposed to redrawing the same screen for interactive viewing. This can be used to create a log of processes, for example when hunting down that runaway processes that eats up all your resources in the middle of the night. Here's how to **run top and log the output** for 10 hours:

```
$ top -b -n 12000 > myprocesslog
```

When `top` is running, you can **update and sort the process list in different ways**. To **immediately update the process list**, press Space or Enter. Press Shift+n to **sort by PID**. Press Shift+p to **sort by CPU usage**. Press Shift+m to **sort by memory usage**. Press Shift+t to **sort by CPU time consumed**. You can also change the column to sort by using the < (**sort column to left**) or > (**sort column to right**) characters. Or, press f and **select the letter of the column you want to sort by** when the list of columns appears.

There are several ways to **change the behavior of top as it's running**. Press d and type a number representing seconds to **change the delay between refreshes**. Press u and enter a user name to **only display processes for the selected user**. To **view only a select number of processes**, type n and type the number you want to see. Press = at any point to **return to the original top display**.

You can **act on any of the running processes** in different ways. To **signal (kill) a running process**, type **k** followed by the PID of the process you want to send the signal to. Then type **9** to end it or a different signal number to send that signal to the process. To **give a process higher or lower run priority**, type **n** and then add a negative number (to increase priority) or a positive number (to reduce priority).

If you want to **find more information about how to use top**, type **?** during a `top` session. The man page also has a lot of information about how to use `top`:

```
$ man top          View the top man page
```

When you are done using top, type **q** to exit.

Finding and Controlling Processes

Changing a running process first means finding the process you want to change, then modifying the processing priority or sending the process a signal to change its behavior. If you are looking for a particular process, you might find it tough to locate it in a large list of processes output by ps or top. The pgrep command offers ways of searching through your active processes for the ones you are looking for. The renice command lets you change the processing priority of running processes. The kill, pkill, and killall commands let you send signals to running processes (including signals to end those processes).

Using pgrep to Find Processes

In its most basic form, you can use pgrep to search for a command name (or part of one) and produce the process ID of any process that includes that name. For example:

```
$ pgrep init          Show PID for any process including 'init' string
1
2689
```

Because we know there is only one init command running, we next use the -l option to see each process's command name (to learn why two processes showed up):

```
$ pgrep -l init       Show PID and name for any process including 'init' string
1 init
2689 xinit
```

You can also **search for processes that are associated with a particular user:**

```
$ pgrep -lu chris     List all processes owned by user chris
2551 sshd
2552 bash
2803 vim
```

Probably the most useful way to use pgrep is to have it **find the process IDs of the running processes and pipe those PIDs to another command** to produce the output. Here are some examples (look for other commands if metacity or firefox aren't running):

```
$ ps -p `pgrep metacity`       Search for metacity and run ps (short)
  PID TTY          TIME CMD
```

```
  2778 ?          00:05:00 metacity
$ ps -fp $(pgrep nautilus)          Search for nautilus and run ps (full)
UID        PID PPID  C STIME TTY     TIME CMD
chris     5907 5840  0 Sep05 ?    00:00:26 nautilus --no-default-window --s
# sudo# renice -5 $(pgrep firefox)  Search for firefox, improve its priority
20522: old priority 0, new priority -5
20557: old priority 0, new priority -5
```

Any command that can take a process ID as input can be combined with pgrep in these ways. As the previous example of pgrep illustrates, you can use commands such as renice to change how a process behaves while it is running.

Using fuser to Find Processes

Another way to locate a particular process is by what the process is accessing. The fuser command can be used to find which processes have a file or a socket open at the moment. After the processes are found, fuser can be used to send signals to those processes.

The fuser command is most useful for finding out if files are being held open by processes on mounted file systems (such as local hard disks or Samba shares). Finding those processes allows you to close them properly (or just kill them if you must) so the file system can be unmounted cleanly.

Here are some examples of the fuser command for listing processes that have files open on a selected file system:

```
$ fuser -mauv /boot          Verbose output of processes with /boot open
                USER        PID ACCESS COMMAND
/boot/grub/:    root       3853 ..c.. (root)bash
                root      19760 ..c.. (root)bash
                root      28171 F.c.. (root)vi
                root      29252 ..c.. (root)man
                root      29255 ..c.. (root)sh
                root      29396 F.c.. (root)vi
```

The example just shown displays the process ID for running processes associated with /boot. They may have a file open, a shell open, or be a child process of a shell with the current directory in /boot. Specifically in this example, there are two bash shells open in the /boot file system, two vi commands with files open in /boot, and a man command running in /boot. The -a shows all processes, -u indicates which user owns each process, and -v produces verbose output.

Here are other examples using fuser to show processes with files open:

```
$ fuser /boot               Show parent PIDs for processes opening /boot
/boot:       19760c 29396c
$ fuser -m /boot            Show all PIDs for processes opening /boot
/boot:       3853c 19760c 28171c 29396c 29252c 29255c
```

```
$ fuser -u /boot          Show PIDs/user for this shell open in /boot
/boot:       19760c(root) 29396c(root) 29252c(root) 29255c(root)
```

After you know which processes have files open, you can close those processes manually or kill them. Close processes manually if at all possible, because simply killing processes can leave files in an unclean state! Here are examples of using fuser to kill or send other signals to all processes with files open to a file system:

```
$ sudo fuser -k /boot      Kill all processes with /boot files open (SIGKILL)
$ fuser -l                 List supported signals
HUP INT QUIT ILL TRAP ABRT IOT BUS FPE KILL USR1 SEGV USR2 PIPE ALRM TERM
STKFLT CHLD CONT STOP TSTP TTIN TTOU URG XCPU XFSZ VTALRM PROF WINCH IO
PWR SYS UNUSED
$ sudo fuser -k -HUP /boot Send HUP signal to all processes with /boot open
```

Changing Running Processes

Even after a process is running, you can change its behavior in different ways. With the renice command, shown earlier, you can adjust a running process's priority in your system's scheduler. With the nice command, you can determine the default priority and also set a higher or lower priority at the time you launch a process.

Another way you can change how a running process behaves is to send a signal to that process. The kill and killall commands can be used to send signals to running processes. Likewise, the pkill command can send a signal to a process.

Adjusting Processor Priority with nice

Every running process has a *nice* value that can be used to tell the Linux process scheduler what priority should be given to that process. Positive values of niceness actually give your process a lower priority. The concept came about during the days of large, multi-user Unix systems where you could be "nice" by running a non-urgent process at a lower priority so other users had a shot at the CPU.

Niceness doesn't enforce scheduling priority, but is merely a suggestion to the scheduler. To see your current nice value, you can type the nice command with no options:

```
$ nice          Run nice to determine current niceness
0
```

The default nice value is 0. You can use the nice command to run a process at a higher or lower priority than the default. The priority number can range from –20 (most favorable scheduling priority) to 19 (least favorable scheduling priority). Although the root user can raise or lower any user's nice value, a regular user can only lower the priorities of a process (setting a higher nice value).

> **WARNING!** *Proceed with caution when assigning negative nice values to processes. This can possibly crash your machine if critical system processes lose their high priority.*

Here are a few examples of starting a command with `nice` to **change a command's nice value:**

```
$ nice -n 12 nroff -man a.roff | less   Format man pages at low priority
$ sudo nice -n -10 gimp                 Launch gimp at higher priority
```

When a process is already running, you can **change the process's nice value using the renice command.** Here are some examples of the `renice` command:

```
$ renice +2 -u francois                 Renice francois' processes +2
$ renice +5 4737                        Renice PID 4737 by +5
$ sudo renice -3 `pgrep -u chris spamd` Renice chris' spamd processes -3
9688: old priority -1, new priority -3
20279: old priority -1, new priority -3
20282: old priority -1, new priority -3
```

The backticks are used in the previous command line to indicate that the output of the `pgrep` command (presumably PIDs of `spamd` daemons run by chris) is fed to the `renice` command.

The niceness settings for your processes are displayed by default when you run `top`. You can also see niceness settings using `-o nice` when you produce custom output from the `ps` command.

Running Processes in the Background and Foreground

When you run a process from a shell, it is run in the foreground by default. That means that you can't type another command until the first one is done. By adding an ampersand (`&`) to the end of a command line, you can run that command line in the background. Using the `fg`, `bg`, and `jobs` commands, along with various control codes, you can move commands between background and foreground.

In the following sequence of commands, we start the GIMP image program from a Terminal window. After that is a series of control keys and commands to **stop and start the process and move it between foreground and background:**

```
$ gimp                      Run gimp in the foreground
<Ctrl+z>                    Stop process and place in background
[1]+  Stopped       gimp
$ bg 1                      Start process running again in background
$ fg 1                      Continue running process in foreground
gimp
<Ctrl+c>                    Kill process
```

Note that processes placed in the background are given a job ID number (in this case, 1). By placing a percentage sign in front of the number (for example, `%1`) you can identify a particular background process to the `bg` and `fg` commands or simply type the number with the command (as in `fg 1`). With one or more background jobs running at the current shell, you can **use the jobs command to manage your background jobs**:

```
$ jobs                  Display background jobs for current shell
[1]     Running              gimp &
[2]     Running              xmms &
[3]-    Running              gedit &
[4]+    Stopped              gtali
$ jobs -l               Display PID with each job's information
[1]   31676 Running            gimp &
[2]   31677 Running            xmms &
[3]- 31683 Running             gedit &
[4]+ 31688 Stopped             gtali
$ jobs -l %2            Display information only for job %2
[2]   31677 Running            xmms &
```

The processes running in the `jobs` examples might have been done while you were logged in (using `ssh`) to a remote system, but want to **run remote GUI applications on your local desktop**. By running those processes in the background, you can have multiple applications running at once, while still having those applications associated with your current shell. Once a process is running, you can **disconnect the process from the current shell using the disown command**:

```
$ disown %3             Disconnect job %3 from current shell
$ disown -a             Disconnect all jobs from current shell
$ disown -h             Protect all jobs from HUP sent to current shell
```

After you have disowned a process, you can close the shell without also killing the process.

> **NOTE** With `fg`, `bg`, or `disown`, *if you don't indicate which process to act on, the current job is used. The current job has a plus sign (+) next to it.*

The `fg` and `bg` commands manipulate running processes by moving those processes to the foreground or background. Another way to manipulate running commands is to send signals directly to those processes. A common way to send signals to running processes is with the `kill` and `killall` commands.

Killing and Signaling Processes

You can stop or change running processes by sending signals to those processes. Commands such as `kill` and `killall` can send signals you select to running processes, which as their names imply, is often a signal to kill the process.

Signals are represented by numbers (9, 15, and so on) and strings (`SIGKILL`, `SIGTERM`, and so on). Table 9-2 shows standard signals you can send to processes in Linux.

Table 9-2: Standard Signals to Send to Processes

Signal Number	Signal Name	Description
1	SIGHUP	Hang up from terminal or controlling process died
2	SIGINT	Keyboard interrupt
3	SIGQUIT	Keyboard quit
4	SIGILL	Illegal instruction
6	SIGABRT	Abort sent from abort function
8	SIGFPE	Floating point exception
9	SIGKILL	Kill signal
11	SIGSEGV	Invalid memory reference
13	SIGPIPE	Pipe broken (no process reading from pipe)
14	SIGALRM	Timer signal from alarm system call
15	SIGTERM	Termination signal
30,10,16	SIGUSR1	User-defined signal 1
31,12,17	SIGUSR2	User-defined signal 2
20,17,18	SIGCHLD	Child terminated or stopped
19,18,25	SIGCONT	Continue if process is stopped
17,19,23	SIGSTOP	Stop the process
18,20.24	SIGTSTP	Stop typed at terminal
21,21,26	SIGTTIN	Terminal input for background process
22,22,27	SIGTTOU	Terminal output for background process

The kill command can send signals to processes by process ID or job number while the killall command can signal processes by command name. Here are some examples:

```
$ kill 28665                      Send SIGTERM to process with PID 28665
$ kill -9 4895                    Send SIGKILL to process with PID 4895
$ kill -SIGCONT 5254              Continue a stopped process (pid 5254)
$ kill %3                         Kill the process represented by job %3
$ killall spamd                   Kill all spamd daemons currently running
$ killall -SIGHUP sendmail        Have sendmail processes reread config files
```

The SIGKILL (9) signal, used generously by trigger-happy novice administrators, should be reserved as a last resort. It does not allow the targeted process to exit cleanly but forces it to end abruptly. This can potentially result in loss or corruption of data handled by that process. The SIGHUP signal was originally used on Unix systems to indicate that a terminal was being disconnected from a mainframe (such as from a hang-up of a dial-in modem). However, daemon processes, such as sendmail and httpd, were implemented to catch SIGHUP signals as an indication that those processes should reread configuration files.

Running Processes Away from the Current Shell

If you want a process to continue to run, even if you disconnect from the current shell session, there are several ways to go about doing that. You can use the nohup command to run a process in a way that it is impervious to a hang-up signal:

```
$ nohup updatedb &            Run updatedb with no ability to interrupt
# nohup nice -9 gcc hello.c &  Run gcc uninterrupted and higher priority
```

Using nohup is different than running the command with an ampersand alone because with nohup the command will keep running, even if you exit the shell that launched the command.

The nohup command was commonly used in the days of slow processors and dial-up connections (so you didn't have to stay logged in to an expensive connection while a long compile completed). Also, today using tools such as screen (described in Chapter 14) you can keep a shell session active, even after you disconnect your network connection to that shell.

Scheduling Processes to Run

Commands associated with the cron facility can be used to set a command to run at a specific time (including now) so that it is not connected to the current shell. The at command runs a command at the time you set:

```
$ at now +1 min       Start command running in one minute
at> updatedb
at> <Ctrl+d> <EOT>
job 5 at Mon Aug 20 20:37:00 2007
$ at teatime          Start command at 4pm today
$ at now +5 days      Start a command in five days
$ at 06/25/08         Start a command at current time on June 25, 2008
```

Another way to run a command that's not connected with the current shell is with the batch command. With batch, you can set a command to start as soon as the processor is ready (load average below .8):

```
$ batch               Start command running immediately
at> find /mnt/isos | grep jpg$ > /tmp/mypics
at> <Ctrl+d> <EOT>
```

Note that after the `at` or `batch` commands you see a secondary `at>` prompt. Type the command you want to run at that prompt and press Enter. After that, you can continue to enter commands. When you are done, press Ctrl+d on a line by itself to queue the commands you entered to run.

After the commands are entered, you can **check the queue of at jobs that are set** to run by typing the `atq` command:

```
$ atq
11              Wed Sep  5 21:10:00 2007 a francois
10              Fri Aug 24 21:10:00 2007 a francois
8               Thu Aug 23 20:53:00 2007 a francois
```

Regular users can only see their own at jobs that are queued. The root user can see everyone's queued `at` jobs. If you want to **delete an at job from the queue**, use the `atrm` command:

```
$ atrm 11                       Delete at job number 11
```

The `at` and `batch` commands are for queuing up a command to run as a one-shot deal. You can use the cron facility to **set up commands to run repeatedly**. These commands are scripted into cron jobs which are scheduled in crontab files. There is one system crontab file (`/etc/crontab`). Also, each user can create a personal crontab file that can launch commands at times that the user chooses. To **create a personal crontab file**, type the following.

```
$ crontab -e                    Create a personal crontab file
```

The `crontab -e` command opens your crontab file (or creates a new one) using the `vi` text editor. Here are examples of several entries you could add to a crontab file:

```
15 8 * * Mon,Tue,Wed,Thu,Fri mail chris < /var/project/stats.txt
* * 1 1,4,7,10 * find / | grep .doc$ > /var/sales/documents.txt
```

The first crontab example shown sends a mail message to the user named `chris` by directing the contents of `/var/project/stats.txt` into that message. That mail command is run Monday through Friday at 8:15 a.m. In the second example, on the first day of January, April, July, and October, the `find` command runs to look for every `.doc` file on the system and sends the resulting list of files to `/var/sales/documents.txt`.

The last part of each crontab entry is the command that is run. The first five fields represent the time and date the command is run. The fields from left to right are: minute (0 to 59), hour (0 to 23), day of the month (0 to 31), month (0 to 12 or Jan, Feb, Mar, Apr, May, Jun, Jul, Aug, Sep, Oct, Nov, or Dec), and day of the week (0 to 7 or Sun, Mon, Tue, Wed, Thu, Fri, or Sat). An asterisk (*) in a field means to match any value for that field.

Here are some **other options with the crontab command**:

```
# crontab -eu chris          Edit another user's crontab (root only)
$ crontab -l                 List contents of your crontab file
15 8 * * Mon,Tue,Wed,Thu,Fri mail chris < /var/project/stats.txt
* * 1 1,4,7,10 * find / | grep .doc$ > /var/sales/documents.txt
$ crontab -r                 Delete your crontab file
```

The traditional way to configure system cron jobs was to add them to the system crontab. Although this is still an option, Ubuntu provides an easier way to create hourly, daily, weekly, and monthly cron jobs, by **associating the command you want to run with a cron directory**. Simply create a script that you want to run. Then copy the script to the /etc/cron.hourly, /etc/cron.daily, /etc/cron.weekly, or /etc/cron.monthly directory. The command will then run in the time frame indicated by the directory (hourly, daily, weekly, or monthly).

An alternative to the cron facility is the anacron facility. With anacron, as with cron, you can configure commands to run periodically. However, anacron is most appropriate for machines that are not on all the time. If a command is not run because the computer was off during the scheduled time, the next time the computer is on, the anacron facility makes sure that the commands that were missed during the downtime are run after the system resumes.

Summary

Watching and working with the processes that run on your Linux system are important activities to make sure that your system is operating efficiently. Using commands such as ps and top, you can view the processes running on your system. You can also use pgrep to search for and list particular processes.

With commands such as nice and renice, you can adjust the recommended priorities at which selected processes run. When a process is running, you can change how it is running or kill the process by sending it a signal from the kill or killall command.

After launching a command from the current shell, you can set that command's process to run in the background (bg) or foreground (fg). You can also stop and restart the process using different control codes.

To schedule a command to run at a later time, you can use the at or batch command. To set up a command to run repeatedly at set intervals, you can use the cron or anacron facilities.

10

Managing the System

Without careful management, the demands on your Linux system can sometimes exceed the resources you have available. Being able to monitor your system's activities (memory, CPU, and device usage) over time can help you make sure that your machine has enough resources to do what you need it to. Likewise, managing other aspects of your system, such as the device drivers it uses and how the boot process works, can help avoid performance problems and system failures.

This chapter is divided into several sections that relate to ways of managing your Ubuntu or other Linux system. The first section can help you monitor the resources (processing power, devices, and memory) on your Linux system. The next section describes how to check and set your system clock. Descriptions of the boot process and subsequent run levels follow. The last sections describe how to work with the kernel and related device drivers, as well as how to view information about your computer's hardware components.

Monitoring Resources

Ubuntu, Debian, and other Linux systems do a wonderful job of keeping track of what they do. If you care to look, you can find lots of information about how your CPU, hard disks, virtual memory, and other computer resources are being used.

You can go to where the Linux kernel stores real-time information about your system by directly viewing the contents of files in the /proc file system (see Appendix C). An alternative, however, is to use commands to view information about how your computer's virtual memory, processor, storage devices, and network interfaces are being used on your system.

There are commands that can monitor several different aspects of your system's resources. Because this book is not just a man page, however, we have divided the following sections by topic (monitoring memory, CPU, and storage devices) rather than by the commands that do them (top, vmstat, and iostat).

> **NOTE**   *Some of the applications described in this section are installed by default in Ubuntu, in packages such as the procps package. To use* iostat *or* sar, *however, you need to install the sysstat package. Install the sysstat package with the following command:*
>
> $ **sudo apt-get install sysstat**

Monitoring Memory Use

Few things will kill system performance faster than running out of memory. Commands such as free and top let you see basic information about how your RAM and swap are being used. The vmstat command gives detailed information about memory use and can run continuously. The slabtop command can show how much memory the kernel (slab cache) is consuming.

The free command provides the quickest way to **see how much memory is being used** on your system. It shows the total amount of RAM (Mem:) and swap space (Swap:), along with the amount currently being used. Here are examples of the free command:

```
$ free          List memory usage in kilobytes (-k default)
            total       used       free     shared    buffers     cached
Mem:       742476     725108      17368          0     153388     342544
-/+ buffers/cache:    229176     513300
Swap:     1020116         72    1020044
$ free -m       List memory usage in megabytes
            total       used       free     shared    buffers     cached
Mem:          725        706         18          0        148        333
-/+ buffers/cache:       223        501
Swap:         996          0        996
$ free -b       List memory usage in blocks
            total       used       free     shared    buffers     cached
Mem:      760295424  742510592   17784832          0  157114368  350765056
-/+ buffers/cache: 234631168  525664256
Swap: 1044598784      73728 1044525056
$ free -mt      List memory usage with totals displayed (Swap + Mem)
            total       used       free     shared    buffers     cached
Mem:          725        708         16          0        149        334
-/+ buffers/cache:       223        501
Swap:         996          0        996
Total:       1721        708       1013
$ free -g        List memory usage in gigabytes
$ free -s 5      Continuously display memory usage every 5 seconds
```

To avoid wasting RAM and speed up applications, Linux uses as much otherwise unused RAM as possible for the disc cache. For that reason, the first line of output from free that often shows little free RAM can be misleading. We recommend you pay closer attention to the second line of output, which shows the amount of RAM actually available for applications. That amount is 501MB in this example:

```
-/+ buffers/cache:        223        501
```

One way to guess how much memory you need on a system is to go to another computer running Ubuntu, then open every application you think you may be running at once. Run free with the total option (free -t) to see how much memory is being used. Then make sure that your new system has at least that much total memory (with most or all of it preferably being available in RAM).

The top command provides a means of watching the currently running processes, with those processes sorted by CPU usage or memory (see Chapter 9 for a description of top for watching running processes). However, you can also use top to **watch your memory usage in a screen-oriented way.** Here is an example:

```
$ top
top - 14:14:59 up 3 days, 18:26,  1 user,  load average: 0.11, 0.04, 0.01
Tasks: 114 total,   3 running, 111 sleeping,   0 stopped,   0 zombie
Cpu(s):  0.0%us,  0.0%sy,  0.0%ni,100.0%id,  0.0%wa,  0.0%hi,  0.0%si,  0.0%st
Mem:     742476k total,    727232k used,     15244k free,    153708k buffers
Swap:  1020116k total,        72k used,  1020044k free,    343924k cached
  PID USER      PR  NI  VIRT  RES  SHR S %CPU %MEM    TIME+  COMMAND
 2347 root      34  19 89552  77m 5636 S  0.0 10.7  6:05.75 yum-updatesd
 2797 chris     18   0 80612  27m  18m S  0.0  3.8  0:01.29 nautilus
 2814 chris     15   0 44420  22m  20m S  0.0  3.1  0:00.17 nm-applet
```

To exit top, press q. Like the output for free, top shows total of memory usage for RAM (Mem:) and swap space (Swap:). However, because top is screen oriented and provides ongoing monitoring, you can watch memory usage change every three seconds (by default). With top running, press Shift+m and the running processes will be displayed in memory-use order (so you can watch which processes are consuming the most memory). The most useful column to analyze a process' memory usage is RES, which shows the process' actual physical RAM usage, also known as resident size. The %MEM column is based on this resident size.

For a more detailed view of your virtual memory statistics, use the vmstat command. With vmstat you can **view memory use over a given time period,** such as since the previous reboot or using a sample period. The following example shows vmstat redisplaying statistics every three seconds:

```
$ vmstat 3
procs -----------memory---------- --swap-- ----io---- --system-- -----cpu-----
 r  b   swpd   free   buff  cache   si   so    bi    bo   in   cs us sy id wa st
 1  0  97740  32488  3196 148360    0    0     0     1   26 3876 85 15  0  0  0
 1  1  98388   7428  3204 151472    0  216     0   333   30 3200 82 18  0  0  0
 1  0 113316   8148  2980 146968    0 4980     4  5121   79 3846 77 23  0  0  0
```

2	0	132648	7472	2904	148488	0	6455	3	6455	90	3644	83	17	0	0	0
2	0	147892	8088	2732	144208	0	5085	9	5220	79	3468	84	16	0	0	0
1	0	157948	7680	2308	134812	0	3272	12	3296	69	3174	77	23	0	0	0
3	0	158348	7944	1100	123888	21	144	25	275	26	3178	86	14	0	1	0
2	0	166116	7320	568	120280	11	2401	20	2403	51	3175	84	16	0	0	0
3	0	181048	7708	648	119452	53	4852	796	4984	123	1783	86	13	0	1	0

To exit vmstat, press Ctrl+c. The vmstat example shows a 30-second time period where more than 100 applications are started. Notice that when the free space goes from 32488 kilobytes to 7428 kilobytes (RAM is filling up), data begins being moved to the swap area (see the 216 under the so column). Because the swap area resides on the hard disk, you can see that the block written to disk device (bo) increases as the swap out increases. You can see the amount of swap space being used increasing under the swpd column.

The CPU is also straining in the example, with no idle time showing (id 0). Notice also that when some of the applications need to be swapped back in (see the last three lines of output), the processor has to wait on two occasions for input/output to complete (wa 1).

Here are some other options for using vmstat:

```
$ vmstat -S m           Display output in 1000k megabytes
$ vmstat -S M           Display output in 1024k megabytes
$ vmstat -S k           Display output in 1000-byte kilobytes
$ vmstat -S K           Display output in 1024-byte kilobytes
$ vmstat -n 2 10        Output every two seconds, repeat 10 times
$ vmstat -s | less      Display event counters and memory statistics
$ vmstat -S M -s | less Display statistics in megabytes
         725 M total memory
         717 M used memory
         486 M active memory
         175 M inactive memory
           7 M free memory
           1 M buffer memory
         120 M swap cache
         996 M total swap
         802 M used swap
         193 M free swap
             . . .
```

The previous example shows various memory statistics (-s) output in megabytes (-S M), which we find more convenient to get a general view of memory usage. The other examples show how to display vmstat output in megabytes and kilobytes (in both marketing and technical terms). After that, the -n 2 10 option tells vmstat to repeat every set number of seconds (2) for a limited number of times (10).

With commands such as ps and top, you can see how much memory each application is consuming on your system. The kernel itself, however, has its own memory cache to keep track of its resources, called the *kernel slab*. You can use the vmstat command to display kernel slab memory cache statistics (from /proc/slabinfo) as follows:

```
$ vmstat -m | less     Page through kernel slab memory cache
Cache              Num    Total   Size   Pages
nf_nat:help          2      13     308     13
nf_nat:base          0       0     276     14
bridge_fdb_cache     0       0      64     59
   . . .
ext3_inode_cache  1236    2928     488      8
ext3_xattr          29     156      48     78
   . . .
```

The slab memory cache information shows each cache name, the number of objects active for that cache type, the total number of objects available for that cache type, the size of the cache (in bytes), and the number of pages for each cache. You can **display kernel slab memory cache information in a screen-oriented view** (similar to the top command) using slabtop:

```
$ slabtop
Active / Total Objects (% used)    : 49127 / 70942 (69.2%)
Active / Total Slabs (% used)      : 3094 / 3094 (100.0%)
Active / Total Caches (% used)     : 101 / 145 (69.7%)
Active / Total Size (% used)       : 8830.29K / 12013.73K (73.5%)
Minimum / Average / Maximum Object : 0.01K / 0.17K / 128.00K

 OBJS ACTIVE  USE OBJ SIZE  SLABS OBJ/SLAB CACHE SIZE NAME
11600   4303  37%   0.13K    400       29     1600K dentry_cache
 2928   1246  42%   0.48K    366        8     1464K ext3_inode_cache
 4355   2535  58%   0.28K    335       13     1340K radix_tree_node
  219    219 100%   4.00K    219        1      876K size-4096
 4128   3485  84%   0.16K    172       24      688K filp
```

The slabtop output updates every three seconds. By default, slab caches are sorted by the number of objects (first column) in each cache. By pressing c you can sort by cache size instead (as shown in the previous example).

Monitoring CPU Usage

An overburdened CPU is another obvious place to look for performance problems on your system. The vmstat command, shown earlier, can produce basic statistics relating to CPU usage (user activity, system activity, idle time, I/O wait time, and time stolen from a virtual machine). The iostat command (from the sysstat package), however, can generate more detailed reports of CPU utilization.

Here are two examples of using iostat to **display a CPU utilization report:**

```
$ iostat -c 3       CPU stats every 3 seconds (starting apps)
Linux 2.6.21-1.3194.fc7 (davinci)      08/10/2007
```

```
avg-cpu:   %user    %nice %system %iowait   %steal    %idle
            0.50     0.00    0.00    0.00     0.00    99.50
avg-cpu:   %user    %nice %system %iowait   %steal    %idle
           28.71     0.00    5.45   18.32     0.00    47.52
avg-cpu:   %user    %nice %system %iowait   %steal    %idle
           98.99     0.00    1.01    0.00     0.00     0.00
avg-cpu:   %user    %nice %system %iowait   %steal    %idle
           99.50     0.00    0.50    0.00     0.00     0.00


$ iostat -c 3        CPU stats every 3 seconds (copying files)
Linux 2.6.21-1.3194.fc7 (davinci)         08/10/2007
avg-cpu:   %user    %nice %system %iowait   %steal    %idle
            0.50     0.00    0.00    0.00     0.00     0.00
avg-cpu:   %user    %nice %system %iowait   %steal    %idle
            0.50     0.00   24.88   74.63     0.00     0.00
avg-cpu:   %user    %nice %system %iowait   %steal    %idle
            0.50     0.00   10.00   89.50     0.00     0.00
avg-cpu:   %user    %nice %system %iowait   %steal    %idle
            0.50     0.00   17.41   82.09     0.00     0.00
avg-cpu:   %user    %nice %system %iowait   %steal    %idle
            0.00     0.00   14.65   85.35     0.00     0.00
```

The first `iostat` example above starts with a quiet system, then several applications started up. You can see that most of the processing to start the applications is being done in user space. The second `iostat` example shows a case where several large files are copied from one hard disk to another. The result is a high percentage of time being spent at the system level, also known as *kernel space* (in this case, reading from and writing to disk partitions). Note that the file copies also result in a higher amount of time waiting for I/O requests to complete (%iowait).

Here are examples using `iostat` to **print CPU utilization reports with timestamps**:

```
$ iostat -c -t          Print time stamp with CPU report
Linux 2.6.21-1.3194.fc7 (davinci)        08/10/2007

Time: 9:28:03 AM
avg-cpu:   %user    %nice %system %iowait   %steal    %idle
            0.50     0.00    0.00    0.00     0.00    99.50
$ iostat -c -t 2 10       Repeat every 2 seconds for 10 times
```

The `dstat` command (dstat package) is available as an alternative to `iostat` for **viewing information about your CPU usage** (as well as other performance-related items). One advantage of `dstat` over other tools is that it more precisely shows the units of measurement it is displaying (such as kilobytes or megabytes) and also uses colors to differentiate the data. Here is an example of `dstat` for displaying CPU information:

```
$ dstat -t -c 3         View CPU usage continuously with time stamps
---time--- ----total-cpu-usage----
__epoch___|usr sys idl wai hiq siq
1189727284|  0   0 100   0   0   0
1189727287|  1   0  99   0   0   0
```

```
1189727290|   3   0   97   0   0   0
1189727293|   0   0  100   0   0   0
1189727296|   5   0   95   0   0   0
1189727299|   1   0   99   0   0   0
1189727302|   3   0   97   0   0   0
1189727305|   0   0  100   0   0   0
1189727308|   3   0   96   0   1   0
1189727311|   1   0   99   0   0   0
1189727314|   0   0  100   0   0   0
1189727317|   0   0  100   0   0   0
1189727320|   1   0   99   0   0   0
1189727323|   5   0   95   0   0   0
1189727326|   3   0   97   0   0   0
1189727329|   3   0   97   0   0   0
1189727332|   2   0   98   0   0   0
1189727335|   5   0   95   0   0   0
```

In this example, the output includes a date/time values based on the start of the epoch (-t) for the CPU report (-c) that is produced every three seconds (3). This report runs continuously until you stop it (Ctrl+c).

If you want to find out specifically which processes are consuming the most processing time, you can use the top command. Type top, then press Shift+p to sort by CPU usage (this is the default sorting order):

```
$ top                    Display running processes and sort by CPU usage
Tasks: 120 total,   3 running, 116 sleeping,   0 stopped,   1 zombie
Cpu(s): 86.8% us,  6.0% sy,  0.0% ni,  3.3% id,  4.0% wa,   0.0% hi,   0.0% si
Mem:    482992k total,   476884k used,      6108k free,     1220k buffers
Swap:  5863716k total,  1166252k used,  4697464k free,    52984k cached

  PID USER      PR  NI  VIRT  RES  SHR S %CPU %MEM    TIME+  COMMAND
 9648 chris     16   0  309m 123m  16m R 72.6 26.1 287:55.22 firefox-bin
  552 root      15   0  762m  65m 5732 S 15.6 14.0   4388:27 X
```

The full output would show many more processes, all sorted by current CPU usage (%CPU column). In this example, Firefox web browser (72.6%) and the X display server (15.6%) are consuming most of the CPU. If you decided you wanted to kill the Firefox process, you could type k followed by the process ID of Firefox (9648) and the number 9 signal (if for some reason you couldn't just close the Firefox window normally).

If you want **information about the processor itself**, you can view information directly from the /proc/cpuinfo file. Here is an example:

```
$ cat /proc/cpuinfo       View CPU information from /proc
processor       : 0
vendor_id       : AuthenticAMD
cpu family      : 6
model           : 4
model name      : AMD Athlon(tm) processor
stepping        : 4
```

193

```
cpu MHz         : 1340.080
cache size      : 256 KB
   ...
flags           : fpu vme de pse tsc msr pae mce cx8 apic mtrr pge mca cmov pat
pse36 mmx fxsr syscall mmxext 3dnowext 3dnow up
bogomips        : 2680.91
clflush size    : 32
```

An interesting thing to note about your CPU are the flags that represent features that it supports. Some features in Ubuntu require that particular CPU extensions associated with those flags be on for the Ubuntu feature to work. For example, to use the Xen virtualization para-virtualized guests, the pae flag must be set. To run fully virtualized guests, the CPU must have either the vmx flag (for Intel processors) or svm flag (for AMD processors) extension support.

Similar information about your processor(s) is collected by the system at the very beginning of the boot process, and can be obtained by looking at the beginning of the output of the dmesg command.

Monitoring Storage Devices

Basic information about storage space available to your Linux file systems can be seen using commands such as du and df (as described in Chapter 7). If you want details about how your storage devices are performing, however, commands such as vmstat and iostat can be useful.

Some of the same kind of output from the iostat command shown earlier can be used to tell if bottlenecks occur while doing disk reads and writes. Here's an example:

```
$ iostat 3       Check disk reads and writes per disk
Linux 2.6.21-1.3194.fc7 (davinci)      08/11/2007

avg-cpu:  %user   %nice %system %iowait  %steal   %idle
          13.15    0.60    0.59    0.16    0.00   85.49
Device:            tps   Blk_read/s   Blk_wrtn/s   Blk_read   Blk_wrtn
sda               1.09        32.08        58.94   16086324   29554312
sdb               0.29         5.27        11.23    2644482    5631348

avg-cpu:  %user   %nice %system %iowait  %steal   %idle
           1.00    0.00   42.14   45.15    0.00   11.71
Device:            tps   Blk_read/s   Blk_wrtn/s   Blk_read   Blk_wrtn
sda             411.37     66515.05         2.68     198880          8
sdb              68.23         2.68     14696.99          8      43944

avg-cpu:  %user   %nice %system %iowait  %steal   %idle
           0.67    0.00   41.00   58.33    0.00    0.00
Device:            tps   Blk_read/s   Blk_wrtn/s   Blk_read   Blk_wrtn
sda             239.67     52530.67       106.67     157592        320
sdb             236.00         0.00     55077.33          0     165232
```

The first part of the output of iostat shows averages of CPU usage since the last reboot. The next part reflects processing that occurs when a large amount of data is copied from the first disk (sda) to the second disk (sdb). High iowait values indicate that disk input/output is the bottleneck on the system. In other words, faster disk writing would improve performance more than a faster CPU.

The vmstat command can also list statistics about your disks. Here's an example of using vmstat to list information about disk reads and writes:

```
$ vmstat -d          Display disk read, write, and input/output statistics
disk- -----------reads----------- ------------writes-------- ----IO---
       total merged  sectors    ms  total merged sectors ms   cur  sec
  ...
sda 332773  74844 19022380 2524211 245477 3473801 29758560 37140075   0 1372
sdb  79963 253716  2646922 2158000  76044  977122  8428140 12489809   0  506
```

The Linux system in this example has two hard disks (sda and sdb). You can see the total number of sectors successfully read and written from those hard disks. You can also see how many seconds were spent on input/output (IO) for those disks. Furthermore, you can see if there any I/O operations in progress, and you can also list read/write information for selected disk partitions. Here is an example:

```
$ vmstat -p sda1       Display read/write stats for a disk partition
sda1           reads       read sectors   writes   requested writes
               174060         12993689     2778        22224
```

Unfortunately the preceding command does not work with softraid md partitions, lvm partitions, and some hardware RAID driver-specific devices.

If you want to find out what files and directories are currently open on your storage devices, you can use the lsof command. This command can be particularly useful if you are trying to unmount a file system that keeps telling you it is busy. You can check what open file is preventing the unmount and decide if you want to kill the process holding that file open and force an unmount of the file system. Here is an example of lsof:

```
$ lsof | less     List processes holding files and directories open
COMMAND    PID  USER   FD     TYPE DEVICE   SIZE    NODE NAME
init         1  root  cwd      DIR   8,5    4096       2 /
init         1  root  rtd      DIR   8,5    4096       2 /
init         1  root  txt      REG   8,5   38620 2049530 /sbin/init
  ...
bash     23857 chris  cwd      DIR   8,1    4096 2719746 /mnt/sda1/dx
```

The first files shown as being open are those held open by the init process (the first running process on the system). Files held open by system processes (such as udevd) and daemons (such as sshd and syslogd) follow init. Eventually, you will see files held open by individual users (which are probably the ones you are interested in if you are unable to unmount a disk partition).

> **NOTE** *You may see permission restrictions unless you run the* `sudo`
> *command first:*
>
> ```
> $ sudo lsof | less
> ```

When you are looking at the `lsof` output, you want to see the name of the file
or directory that is open (`NAME`), the command that has it open (`COMMAND`), and
the process ID of that running command (`PID`). As is often the case when a file
system you want to unmount is being held open, the `/mnt/sda1` file system is
being held open by a `bash` shell in the preceding example (`/mnt/sda1/dx` is the
bash shell's current working directory). In fact, instead of piping `lsof` output to
`less` or `grep`, here are a few other ways you can find what you are looking for
from `lsof` output:

```
$ lsof -c bash            List files open by bash shells
$ lsof -d cwd             List directories open as current working directory
$ lsof -u chris           List files and directories open by user chris
$ lsof /mnt/sda1          List anything open on /mnt/sda1 file system
$ lsof +d /mnt/sda1/dx    List anything open under /mnt/sda1/dx directory
```

As noted previously, you may need to use the `sudo` command to acquire the root permissions to view all the output of the `lsof` command.

Mastering Time

Keeping correct time on your Linux system is critical to the system's proper function-
ing. Your computer running Linux keeps time in two different ways: a system clock
(which Linux uses to keep track of time) and a hardware clock (that sets the system
time when Linux boots up).

The system time is what is used to set timestamps for file creation, process runtimes,
and anything else where date and time are used. System time can be viewed and set
manually (with the `date` command) or automatically (with the `ntpd` service).

The hardware clock is part of the motherboard's CMOS and runs on a battery attached
to the motherboard when the system is powered off. You set the hardware clock with
the `hwclock` command.

There are many other tools that can be used to work with time in Linux systems. For
example, there are tools for checking time in different ways, such as using `clockdiff`
(to measure clock difference between computers) and `uptime` (to see how long your
system has been up).

Changing Time/Date with Graphical Tools

Graphical tools in Ubuntu and and other Linux systems for changing the date, time and time zone used on your system include the Date and Time Settings window (`sudo time-admin` command). That window can also be used to enable the Network Time Protocol (NTP), to automatically synchronize your Linux system's date and time with a selected time server over the network. You may need to install NTP support, available as a handy button-click on the Date and Time Settings window.

The Date/Time Properties window saves the settings and choices you make. During Ubuntu startup, the system reads these settings to set your time zone and whether your system is using UTC time.

Your Linux system's time zone is set based on the contents of the `/etc/localtime` file. You can set a new time zone immediately by copying the file representing your time zone from a subdirectory of `/usr/share/zoneinfo`. For example, to change the current time zone to that of America/Chicago, you could do the following:

```
$ sudo cp /usr/share/zoneinfo/America/Chicago /etc/localtime
```

This can also be accomplished by creating a symlink:

```
$ sudo ln -s /usr/share/zoneinfo/America/Chicago /etc/localtime
```

To change the time zone permanently, set it in the Date and Time Settings window to the time zone you want. For example, `America/Chicago`.

Displaying and Setting Your System Clock

The `date` command is the primary command-based interface for viewing and changing date and time settings, if you are not having that done automatically with NTP. Here are examples of `date` commands for **displaying dates and times** in different ways:

```
$ date                              Display current date, time and time zone
Sun Aug 12 01:26:50 CDT 2007
$ date '+%A %B %d %G'               Display day, month, day of month, year
Sunday August 12 2007
$ date '+The date today is %F.'     Add words to the date output
The date today is 2007-08-12
$ date --date='4 weeks'             Display date four weeks from today
Sun Sep  9 10:51:18 CDT 2007
$ date --date='8 months 3 days'     Display date 8 months 3 days from today
Tue Apr 15 10:59:44 CDT 2008
$ date --date='4 Jul' +%A           Display day on which July 4 falls
Wednesday
```

Although our primary interest in this section is time, since we are on the subject of dates as well, the cal command is a quick way to **display dates by month**. Here are examples:

```
$ cal                    Show current month calendar (today is highlighted)
    August 2007
Su Mo Tu We Th Fr Sa
          1  2  3  4
 5  6  7  8  9 10 11
12 13 14 15 16 17 18
19 20 21 22 23 24 25
26 27 28 29 30 31
$ cal 2007               Show whole year's calendar
                          2007
       January              February              March
Su Mo Tu We Th Fr Sa   Su Mo Tu We Th Fr Sa   Su Mo Tu We Th Fr Sa
    1  2  3  4  5  6                1  2  3                 1  2  3
 7  8  9 10 11 12 13    4  5  6  7  8  9 10    4  5  6  7  8  9 10
14 15 16 17 18 19 20   11 12 13 14 15 16 17   11 12 13 14 15 16 17
21 22 23 24 25 26 27   18 19 20 21 22 23 24   18 19 20 21 22 23 24
28 29 30 31            25 26 27 28            25 26 27 28 29 30 31
   ...
$ cal -j                 Show Julian calendar (numbered from January 1)
August 2007
Sun Mon Tue Wed Thu Fri Sat
            213 214 215 216
217 218 219 220 221 222 223
224 225 226 227 228 229 230
231 232 233 234 235 236 237
238 239 240 241 242 243
```

The date command can also be used to **change the system date and time**. For example:

```
$ sudo date 081215212008        Set date/time to Aug. 12, 2:21PM, 2008
Tue Aug 12 11:42:00 CDT 2008
$ sudo date --set='+7 minutes'   Set time to 7 minutes later
Sun Aug 12 11:49:33 CDT 2008
$ sudo date --set='-1 month'     Set date/time to one month earlier
Sun Jul 12 11:50:20 CDT 2008
```

The next time you boot Ubuntu, the system time will be reset based on the value of your hardware clock (or your NTP server, if NTP service is enabled). And the next time you shut down, the hardware clock will be reset to the system time, in order to preserve that time while the machine is powered off. To change the hardware clock, you can use the hwclock command.

Displaying and Setting Your Hardware Clock

Anyone can use the hwclock command to view hardware clock settings; however, you must have root privileges to change those settings. To use hwclock to **view the current time from your computer's hardware clock**, type the following:

```
$ hwclock -r            Display current hardware clock settings
Sun 12 Aug 2007 03:45:40 PM CDT   -0.447403 seconds
```

Even if your hardware clock is set to UTC time, hwclock displays local time by default. If your system time strays from your hardware clock (for example, if you tried some of the date commands shown previously), you can **reset your system clock from your hardware clock** as follows:

```
$ sudo hwclock --hctosys    Reset system clock from hardware clock
```

Likewise if your hardware clock is set incorrectly (for example, if you replaced the CMOS battery on your motherboard), you can **set the hardware clock from your system clock** as follows:

```
# hwclock --systohc    Reset hardware clock from system clock
```

Over time your hardware clock can drift. Because the clock tends to drift the same amount each day, hwclock can keep track of this drift time (which it does in the /etc/adjtime file). You can **adjust the hardware clock time** based on the adjtime file as follows:

```
$ sudo hwclock --adjust    Adjust hardware clock time for drift
```

To **set the hardware clock to a specific time**, you can use the --set option. Here is an example:

```
$ sudo hwclock --set --date="3/18/08 18:22:00"    Set clock to new date/time
```

In this example, the hardware clock is set to March 18, 2008 at 6:22 p.m. This update does not immediately affect the system clock.

Using Network Time Protocol to Set Date/Time

When you install Ubuntu, you are given the opportunity to set your system date and time. An option at that time is to use preconfigured Network Time Protocol (NTP) servers to automatically get the current date and time when your system reboots. If you choose that option, the installer will setup the ntpd daemon and use it to keep your time synchronized.

If you didn't configure NTP to set time for your system when you first installed your Linux system, you can do so later by **turning on the ntpd service**. You can either install the service from the Date and Time Settings window with a click of the button, or enter commands.

Here is how to enable the service from the command line:

```
$ sudo apt-get install ntp    Install ntp package if necessary, start the service
```

The ntpd service uses information in the /etc/ntpd.conf file. You can specify the name or IP address of the time server to query for the time, for example.

Whether you install ntpd manually or let the installer do it automagically, the resulting setup turns your machine into a time server, listening on UDP port 123. Unless you have very specific needs (and your own GPS or atomic clock), running ntpd on your machine can be both a waste of resources and a security risk. For that reason, some system administrators prefer using ntpdate (often in a daily cronjob) to set their system time via NTP:

```
$ sudo ntpdate pool.ntp.org
15 Aug 00:37:12 ntpdate[9706]:
adjust time server 66.92.68.11 offset 0.009204 sec
```

If you try running ntpdate while ntpd is running, you will get the following error:

```
$ sudo ntpdate pool.ntp.org
15 Aug 00:37:00 ntpdate[9695]: the NTP socket is in use, exiting
```

Note that the ntpdate command has been marked as deprecated and will disappear in the future. It has been replaced by the following options of ntpd:

```
$ sudo ntpd -qg
```

The -q option tells ntpd to exit after setting the clock (as opposed to keep running as a daemon). The -g option prevents ntpd from panicking if the system clock is off by more than 1000 seconds.

Managing the Boot Process

When a computer first starts up, the basic input/output system (BIOS) looks to its boot order settings to determine where to find the operating system to boot. Typically, if a bootable medium has not been inserted into a removable drive (CD, DVD, floppy disk, and so on), the BIOS looks to the master boot record (MBR) on the first bootable hard disk. At this point, for most Linux systems, control of the boot process is handed to the *boot loader*.

For Ubuntu, and, in fact, most Linux systems these days, the Grand Unified Boot Loader (GRUB) is the boot loader that is used by default. GRUB is a replacement for LILO, which was the most popular Linux boot loader during the 1990s. GRUB can be set up to boot not only your Linux system, but also to boot any other operating systems installed on your hard disks (Windows, BSD, or others). GRUB can also include boot options with each bootable operating system to refine the boot process, such as to turn on or off support for a particular type of hardware.

Once a Linux system is selected to boot from the boot loader, the boot loader loads the kernel. The following dilemma then occurs: the kernel needs to mount the root file system on the hard drive. This requires the appropriate storage drivers (block device kernel modules). And those drivers are located on the hard drive itself! To break that vicious cycle, a small initial ramdisk (initrd) containing the block device modules is mounted by the boot loader. This allows the Linux kernel to read the root file system. After that, the init process takes over and begins starting the system services, based on the *run level* that is set for the system.

The following sections describe commands for modifying the boot loader, startup scripts, and run levels associated with your Linux system.

Using the GRUB Boot Loader

Assuming GRUB was set up when you first installed Ubuntu, the settings for your boot loader are stored in the /boot/grub/menu.1st file. Any changes you make to that file are picked up automatically when you reboot Ubuntu. Here's an example of the contents of the /boot/grub/menu.1st file:

```
default=0
timeout=5


hiddenmenu

title Ubuntu, kernel 2.6.20-16-generic
root (hd0,0)
kernel          /vmlinuz-2.6.20-16-generic
root=UUID=db2dac48-a62e-4dbe-9529-e88a57b15bac ro quiet splash

initrd          /initrd.img-2.6.20-16-generic
```

This example shows only one bootable operating system (Ubuntu), although the default file normally lists a number of variants, such as a recovery mode version of Ubuntu. The default=0 line says that the first title entry is booted by default. The timeout=5 line says that GRUB pauses five seconds at the splash screen before booting. The hiddenmenu line indicates that you won't see the list of bootable titles when the boot splash screen appears (press a key during the timeout period to see the menu).

The actual boot entry (`title Ubuntu`) points to the first partition on the first hard disk (`hd0,0`), which contains the kernel and initial RAM disk (initrd) to be booted. To change how that kernel boots, you can add options to the end of the kernel line. Or you can add entirely new title entries to boot different kernels or operating systems.

Some available boot options are described in Table 2-1 in Chapter 2. Options you might want to add to the end of the kernel line include 3 (to boot into runlevel 3, text mode) or `ide=nodma` (to turn off DMA if your system is having hard disk errors).

In normal circumstances, you don't need to run any commands to have changes to `menu.1st` picked up by your boot loader. When you reboot, the `menu.1st` file is read directly from the hard disk. However, if your MBR becomes corrupted for some reason and your system won't boot, you may need to reload the GRUB boot loader.

To reinstall GRUB on your hard disk's MBR, boot a Ubuntu live CD or install CD in rescue mode and follow the instructions to change root (chroot) to the hard disk partition containing your Ubuntu system. Then, assuming that you're booting from your computer's first SATA hard disk, type the following to **reload the boot loader to the MBR**:

```
$ sudo grub-install /dev/sda
```

The boot loader should now be installed on your hard disk's MBR. If your `menu.1st` file is correct, your system should be able to reboot from hard disk now.

In addition, you can use the `update-grub` command to create the `menu.1st` file from questions you answer.

```
$ sudo update-grub
```

Repairing the initial ramdisk (initrd)

The initrd is a file located in `/boot` with a name like `initrd.img-2.6.20-16-generic`. If your initrd becomes corrupted, or if you need to add new block device drivers to it, run the `mkinitrd` command. First, make sure you make a copy of your existing initrd file. Then run the following commands:

```
$ sudo apt-get install initrd-tools
$ sudo mkinitrd -o /boot/ initrd.img-2.6.20-16-generic
```

Replace the kernel version in the example above (2.6.20-1.2320.fc5) with your own kernel version. Alternatively, to use the currently running kernel version, you can use:

```
$ sudo mkinitrd -o /boot/initrd.img-`uname -r` `uname -r`
```

Unfortunately, you will often realize that you need to rebuild your initrd after it is too late, as you witness a kernel panic during the root file system mount stage of boot. When that occurs, boot into rescue mode as described in the previous section and run `mkinitrd` after `chroot`ing to the proper hard disk partition.

Controlling Startup and Run Levels

After the kernel has started up, it hands control of the system to the `init` process. The `init` process becomes the first running process on the system (PID 1), directing the start-up of other processes based on the contents of the `/etc/inittab` file, the default run level, and the `init` scripts set to run at that run level.

The default run level is typically set to 5 for desktop systems and 3 for server systems (based on the value passed to the `telinit` command in the `/etc/event.d/rc-default` file). As noted earlier, that value can be overridden by adding a different run level number (S, 1, 2, 3, 4, or 5) to the end of the kernel boot line from the boot screen.

Most Linux administrators leave the basic startup features alone and focus on which services are turned on or off at the selected run level. The mechanism for starting run level scripts in Ubuntu, and similar systems is based on the System V Init facility (sysvinit and initscripts packages), used originally in AT&T UNIX System V systems.

> **NOTE** *Even though Ubuntu uses the upstart system rather than the init system, you can still change run levels with the* `init` *or* `telinit` *command.*

This section contains commands for working with system initialization scripts and changing run levels. As root, you can use the `runlevel` command to see the current run level:

```
$ runlevel          Display current and previous run levels
N 2
```

Because the system in this example booted directly to run level 3, there is no previous run level (N). To change the current run level, you can use the `init` command:

```
$ sudo init 5       Change the current run level to 5 (X Desktop)
```

In this example, the current run level changes from the previous level (in this case, 3) to run level 5 (which starts the X Window graphical user interface). You can also use the q option to the `init` command to reexamine the /etc/inittab file and start or stop processes based on changes made to that file:

```
$ sudo init q       Start or stop changed processes in inittab file
```

Note that running `init q` does not start or stop System V services. It is used mostly when tinkering with the `getty`s defined in the files in the `/etc/event.d` directory.

To manage services, you can use the `chkconfig` and `service` commands. For example, to start the NTP service immediately, you could type this:

```
$ sudo /etc/init.d/ntp start          Start Samba service immediately
Starting NTP server ntpd                    [  OK  ]
```

Each service comes with a shell script in the `/etc/init.d` directory. You can pass `start` or `stop` options to each service. The format is:

```
sudo /etc/init.d/service_to_control start
sudo /etc/init.d/service_to_control stop
```

Most of the scripts in the `/etc/init.d` directory support start and stop options, while some support other features as well. Here's how to use `service` to start and stop services:

```
$ /etc/init.d/ntp                      Show usage statement (with no options)
Usage: /etc/init.d/ntp {start|stop|restart|try-restart|force-reload|status}

$ sudo /etc/init.d/ntp restart         Restart NTP service (first off, then on)
 * Stopping NTP server ntpd                [ OK ]
 * Starting NTP server ntpd                [ OK ]
$ sudo /etc/init.d/ntp try-restart     Restart NTP service (if already running)
 * Stopping NTP server ntpd                [  OK  ]
 * Starting NTP server ntpd                [  OK  ]
$ sudo /etc/init.d/ntp force-reload      Reload settings in config file
 * Stopping NTP server ntpd                [  OK  ]
 * Starting NTP server ntpd                [  OK  ]
$ sudo /etc/init.d/ntp  status         Check if the NTP service is running (smbd)
 * NTP server is running.
$ sudo /etc/init.d/ntp stop            Stop NTP service
 * Stopping NTP server ntpd                [  OK  ]
```

Any of the `init` scripts contained in `/etc/init.d` can be started in this way, but not all scripts support all the features just shown. Most `init` scripts, however, will show their usage statement with no option (as shown in the first example above).

Although the previous commands start the run level script service immediately, to have a service start automatically at boot time or during a run level change, you can use the `update-rc.d` command. In addition, most installation scripts for services will automatically turn a service on for the next time you boot. With `update-rc.d`, you can turn services on, or turn them off on a per-run level basis. Here are examples:

```
$ sudo update-rc.d ntp defaults        Turn on the NTP service
```

> **NOTE** *The documentation for the* `update-rc.d` *command recommends you not use this command to manage the run levels of your system. See the online man page for the* `update-rc.d` *command for details.*

Although you can use the `init` command to change to any run level, including `init 0` (shut down) and `init 6` (reboot), there are also specific commands for stopping Linux.

The advantages of commands such as halt, reboot, poweroff, and shutdown are that they include options to let you **stop some features before shutdown occurs**. For example:

> **WARNING!** *Don't try the following commands if you don't intend to actually turn off your system, especially on a remote system.*

```
$ sudo reboot              Reboot the computer
$ sudo halt -n             Don't run sync to sync hard drives before shutdown
$ sudo halt -h             Put hard drives in standby mode before halting
$ sudo shutdown 10         Shutdown in ten minutes after warning the users
$ sudo shutdown -r 10      Reboot in ten minutes after warning the users
$ sudo shutdown 10 'Bye!'  Send custom message to users before shutdown
```

Besides the reboot and init 6 commands, you can also use the old PC keystrokes Ctrl+Alt+Del to reboot your computer.

Straight to the Kernel

In general, when the kernel starts up on your Linux system, you shouldn't have to do too much with it. However, there are tools for checking the kernel that is in use and for seeing information about how the kernel started up. Also, if something goes wrong or if there is some extra support you need to add to the kernel, there are tools to do those things.

To find out **what kernel is currently running on your system**, type the following:

```
$ uname -r        Display name of kernel release
2.6.20-16-generic
$ uname -a        Display all available kernel info
Linux server.domain.com #2 SMP Fri Aug 31 00:55:27 UTC 2007 i686 GNU/Linux
```

When the kernel starts, messages about what occurs are placed in the kernel ring buffer. You can **display the contents of the kernel ring buffer** using the dmesg command:

```
$ dmesg |less
[    0.000000] Linux version 2.6.20-16-generic (root@terranova) (gcc version 4.1
.2 (Ubuntu 4.1.2-0ubuntu4)) #2 SMP Fri Aug 31 00:55:27 UTC 2007 (Ubuntu 2.6.20-1
6.31-generic)
[    0.000000] BIOS-provided physical RAM map:
[    0.000000] sanitize start
[    0.000000] sanitize end
   ...
[   15.935761] CPU: L1 I cache: 32K, L1 D cache: 32K
[   15.935763] CPU: L2 cache: 2048K
[   15.935765] CPU: Physical Processor ID: 0
[   15.935767] CPU: Processor Core ID: 0
[   15.935768] CPU: After all inits, caps: bfebfbff 20100000 00000000 00003940 0
000e3bd 00000000 00000001
```

If that buffer fills up, it may no longer contain the beginning of the recorded information. In that case, you can use less /var/log/dmesg.

Other information of interest about kernel processing can be found in the /var/log files — in particular, the messages file. You can page through those files as follows:

```
$ sudo cat /var/log/messages* | less        Page through /var/log/messages
Aug  5 21:55:46 davinci syslogd 1.4.2: restart.
Aug  6 22:12:03 davinci kernel: eth0: link up, 100Mbps, lpa 0x45E1
Aug  6 22:13:06 davinci kernel: eth0: link down
Aug  6 22:13:07 davinci kernel: eth0: link up, 100Mbps, lpa 0x45E1
Aug 10 10:53:46 davinci init: Switching to runlevel: 3
```

In the best circumstances, all the hardware connected to your computer should be detected and configured with the proper Linux drivers. In some cases, however, either the wrong driver is detected or the necessary driver may not be available on your system. For those cases, Linux offers ways of listing loadable kernel modules and adding new ones to your system.

The lsmod command lets you **view the names of the loaded modules**, their size, and what other modules are using them. Here is an example:

```
$ lsmod
Module              Size  Used by
   ...
parport_pc         29797  1
parport            38025  2 lp,parport_pc
snd_ens1371        28769  1
gameport           19017  1 snd_ens1371
snd_rawmidi        26561  1 snd_ens1371
snd_ac97_codec     96357  1 snd_ens1371
ac97_bus            6465  1 snd_ac97_codec
snd_timer          24773  2 snd_seq,snd_pcm
soundcore          11553  2 snd
e100               37193  0
```

If you want to **find out more information about a particular module**, you can use the modinfo command. Here's an example:

```
$ modinfo snd_ens1371
filename:       /lib/modules/2.6.21-1.3194.fc7/kernel/sound/pci/
                snd-ens1371.ko
description:    Ensoniq/Creative AudioPCI ES1371+
license:        GPL
author:         Jaroslav Kysela <perex@suse.cz>, Thomas Sailer
                <sailer@ife.ee.ethz.ch>
srcversion:     411FDA312BD30C6B2A8F6E7
alias:          pci:v00001102d00008938sv*sd*bc*sc*i*
alias:          pci:v00001274d00005880sv*sd*bc*sc*i*
alias:          pci:v00001274d00001371sv*sd*bc*sc*i*
depends:        snd-pcm,snd,snd-rawmidi,gameport,snd-ac97-codec
vermagic:       2.6.21-1.3194.fc7 SMP mod_unload 686 4KSTACKS
```

```
parm:    index:Index value for Ensoniq AudioPCI soundcard. (array of int)
parm:    id:ID string for Ensoniq AudioPCI soundcard. (array of charp)
parm:    enable:Enable Ensoniq AudioPCI soundcard. (array of bool)
parm:    joystick_port:Joystick port address. (array of int)
```

If you decide you need to **add or remove a loadable module** to get some hardware item on your system working properly, you can use the `modprobe` command. You can also use `modprobe` to **list all available modules and remove modules**. Here are examples:

```
$ modprobe -l | grep c-qcam          List all modules, then look for c-qcam
/lib/modules/2.6.21-1.3228.fc7/kernel/drivers/media/video/c-qcam.ko
$ sudo modprobe c-qcam               Load module for Color QuickCam
$ sudo modprobe -r c-qcam            Remove module for Color QuickCam
```

> **NOTE** *You may hear about the command* insmod. insmod *is to* modprobe *what* rpm *is to* apt-get: modprobe *can intelligently load module dependencies. For that reason, we recommend you use only* modprobe.

You can **control kernel parameters with the system running** using the `sysctl` command. You can also add parameters permanently to the `/etc/sysctl.conf` file, so they can load as a group or at each reboot. Here are some examples:

```
$ sudo sysctl -a | less              List all kernel parameters
kernel.panic = 0
kernel.exec-shield = 1
  ...
$ sudo sysctl kernel.hostname        List value of particular parameter
$ sudo sysctl -p                     Load parms from /etc/sysctl.conf
$ sudo sysctl -w kernel.hostname=joe Set value of kernel.hostname
```

As noted earlier, if you want to change any of your kernel parameters permanently, you should add them to the `/etc/sysctl.conf` file. Parameter settings in that file are in the form *parameter = value*.

Poking at the Hardware

If you just generally want to find out more about your computer's hardware, you can use the following commands. The `lspci` command **lists information about PCI devices** on your computer:

```
$ lspci                      List PCI hardware items
00:00.0 Host bridge: VIA Technologies, Inc. VT8375 [KM266/KL266] Host Bridge
00:01.0 PCI bridge: VIA Technologies, Inc. VT8633 [Apollo Pro266 AGP]
00:10.0 USB Controller: VIA Technologies, Inc. VT82xxxxx UHCI USB 1.1
00:11.0 ISA bridge: VIA Technologies, Inc. VT8235 ISA Bridge
00:12.0 Ethernet controller: VIA Technologies, Inc. VT6102 [Rhine-II]
01:00.0 VGA compatible controller: S3 Inc. VT8375 [ProSavage8 KM266/KL266]
  ...
$ lspci -v                   List PCI hardware items with more details
$ lspci -vv                  List PCI hardware items with even more details
```

Using the `dmidecode` command, you can **display information about your computer's hardware components,** including information about what features are supported in the BIOS. Here is an example:

```
$ sudo dmidecode | less          List hardware components
$ sudo dmidecode 2.7
SMBIOS 2.3 present.
32 structures occupying 919 bytes.
Table at 0x000F0100.

Handle 0x0000, DMI type 0, 20 bytes.
BIOS Information
 Vendor: Award Software International, Inc.
 Version: F2
 Release Date: 10/06/2003
  . . .
Processor Information
 Socket Designation: Socket A
 Type: Central Processor
 Family: Athlon
 Manufacturer: AMD
 ID: 44 06 00 00 FF FB 83 01
 Signature: Family 6, Model 4, Stepping 4
 Flags:
        FPU (Floating-point unit on-chip)
        VME (Virtual mode extension)
        DE (Debugging extension)
```

You can use the `hdparm` command to **view and change information relating to your hard disk.**

> **WARNING!** *Although it's safe to view information about features of your hard disks, it can potentially damage your hard disk to change some of those settings.*

Here are some examples of printing information about your hard disks:

```
$ sudo hdparm /dev/sda         Display hard disk settings (SATA or SCSI drive)
/dev/sda:
 IO_support    =  0 (default 16-bit)
 readonly      =  0 (off)
 readahead     = 256 (on)
 geometry      = 30401/255/63, sectors = 488395055, start = 0
$ sudo hdparm /dev/hda         Display hard disk settings (IDE drive)
$ sudo hdparm -I /dev/sda      Display detailed drive information
/dev/sda:
ATA device, with non-removable media
        Model Number:      FUJITSU MPG3409AT   E
        Serial Number:     VH06T190RV9W
        Firmware Revision: 82C5
 . . .
```

Summary

Ubuntu and other Linux systems make it easy for you to watch and modify many aspects of your running system to make sure it is operating at peak performance. Commands such as `free`, `top`, `vmstat`, `slabtop`, `iostat`, and `dstat` let you see how your system is using its memory, CPU, and storage devices. Using commands such as `date`, `hwclock`, and `cal`, as well as services such as NTP, you can watch and manage your system's date and time settings.

To manage the features that are set and services that come up when you boot your system, you can modify features associated with your GRUB boot loader and system run levels. You can start, stop, list, add, and remove individual system services using commands such as `service` and `chkconfig`. Commands such as `reboot`, `halt`, and `shutdown` let you safely stop or reboot your computer.

When it comes to managing your computer's hardware, commands such as `lsmod`, `modinfo`, and `modprobe` let you work with loadable modules. You can view information about your hardware with such commands as `lspci`, `dmidecode`, and `hdparm`.

11

Managing Network Connections

Connecting to a network from Linux is often as easy as attaching your computer's network interface card to your ISP's hardware (such as a DSL or cable modem) and rebooting. However, if your network interface doesn't come up or requires some manual setup, there are many commands available for configuring network interfaces, checking network connections, and setting up special routing.

This chapter covers many useful commands for configuring and working with your network interface cards (NICs), such as `ethtool`, `mii-tool`, and `ifconfig`. More specifically, it covers ways of configuring wired Ethernet, wireless Ethernet, and modem network hardware. With your hardware connected and network interfaces in place, the chapter describes commands such as `netstat`, `dig`, `ip`, and `ping` for getting information about your network.

Configuring Networks from the GUI

When you first install Ubuntu, the installer lets you configure any wired Ethernet cards attached to your computer, with the use of a DHCP server detected on your network. Alternatively, you can set a static IP address, along with your hostname and IP addresses for your gateway machine and name servers. After installation, there are also graphical tools for configuring your network interfaces.

The Network Configuration window (select System ⇨ Administration ⇨ Network from the GNOME desktop) offers a GUI for configuring your network interface, network hardware, DNS servers, host list, and even IPsec virtual private networks. You can configure both dynamic (DHCP, bootp) and static IP addresses. You can even set up static network routes.

In some cases, however, your network interfaces may not be working. Likewise, there may be ways you want to work with your network interfaces that are not supported from the GUI. For those cases, the following sections describe how to work with your network interfaces from the command line.

Managing Network Interface Cards

If the network hardware on your computer didn't immediately come up and let you connect to the Internet, there are some steps you should go through to troubleshoot the problem:

❑ Verify that your network interface card (NIC) is properly installed and that the cable is connected to your network (ISP's CPE, switch, and so on).

❑ After the cable is connected, make sure you have a link with no speed or duplex mismatches.

❑ If all else fails, consider replacing your NIC with known-good spare to isolate a hardware failure.

To check your link from Linux, and to set speed and duplex, there are two commands you can use: the older mii-tool (net-tools package) and the newer ethtool (ethtool package). Use ethtool unless you have a very old NIC and NIC driver that is not compatible with the ethtool command.

To **view the syntax of the ethtool command**, type the following:

```
$ ethtool -h | less          View options to the ethtool command
```

The ethtool command outputs its built-in help to stderr. To be able to page through that help with less, we redirect stderr to stdout.

To **display settings for a specific Ethernet card**, add the interface name to the command. For example, to view card information for eth0, type:

```
$ sudo ethtool eth0                   See settings for NIC at eth0
Settings for eth0:
        Supported ports: [ TP MII ]
        Supported link modes:   10baseT/Half 10baseT/Full
                                100baseT/Half 100baseT/Full
        Supports auto-negotiation: Yes
        Advertised link modes:  10baseT/Half 10baseT/Full
                                100baseT/Half 100baseT/Full
```

```
Advertised auto-negotiation: Yes
Speed: 100Mb/s
Duplex: Full
Port: MII
PHYAD: 1
Transceiver: internal
Auto-negotiation: on
Supports Wake-on: g
Wake-on: g
Current message level: 0x00000007 (7)
Link detected: yes
```

You will need root permissions to acquire information about the Ethernet interface, hence the use of the `sudo` command in the previous example.

To find out about the driver being used for a particular network card, use the `-i` option:

```
$ sudo ethtool -i eth0        Display driver information for NIC
driver: e1000
version: 7.3.15-k2-NAPI
firmware-version: 0.5-7
bus-info: 0000:04:00.0
```

Use the `-S` option to **display detailed statistics for a NIC**:

```
$ sudo ethtool -S eth0        Show statistics for NIC at eth0
NIC statistics:
    rx_packets: 1326384
    tx_packets: 773046
    rx_bytes: 1109944723
    tx_bytes: 432773480
    rx_errors: 5
    tx_errors: 2
    rx_dropped: 0
    tx_dropped: 0
    multicast: 0
    collisions: 0
    rx_length_errors: 0
    rx_over_errors: 0
    rx_crc_errors: 5
    rx_frame_errors: 0
    rx_fifo_errors: 0
    rx_missed_errors: 0
    tx_aborted_errors: 0
    tx_carrier_errors: 2
  ...
```

The `ethtool` command can be used to **change NIC settings** as well as display them. To turn off auto-negotiation and hard-set the NIC to 100 Mpbs, full duplex, type this:

```
$ sudo ethtool -s eth0 speed 100 duplex full autoneg off   Change NIC settings
```

To turn off auto-negotiation and hard-set the speed to 10 Mpbs, half-duplex, type this:

```
$ sudo ethtool -s eth0 speed 10 duplex half autoneg off     Change NIC settings
```

The changes just made to your NIC settings are good for the current session. When you reboot, however, those setting will be lost. To make these settings stick at the next reboot or network restart, you need to create a new script to get executed at boot time. The following steps describe how to do this.

1. Choose a name for your new script, such as eth_options, and then create the script in the /etc/init.d directory:

```
$ sudo vi /etc/init.d/eth_options
```

2. Insert the following text into this new script:

```
#!/bin/sh
ETHTOOL="/usr/sbin/ethtool"
ETHTOOL_OPTS="speed 10 duplex half autoneg off"
DEV="eth0"
case "$1" in
start)
    echo -n "Setting $DEV options to $ETHTOOL_OPTS...";
    $ETHTOOL -s $DEV $ETHTOOL_OPTS;
    echo " done.";;
stop)
    ;;
esac
exit 0
```

3. The specific settings you desire should be placed into the variable ETHTOOL_OPTS. For example:

```
ETHTOOL_OPTS="speed 10 duplex half autoneg off"
```

You can also change the DEV variable, which points to the first Ethernet interface, eth0.

4. Next, you need to set up the script as an executable file:

```
$ sudo chmod +x /etc/init.d/eth_options
```

5. Then, set up the symbolic links to run your new script under the different run levels:

```
$ sudo update-rc.d eth_options defaults
 Adding system startup for /etc/init.d/eth_options ...
    /etc/rc0.d/K20eth_options -> ../init.d/eth_options
    /etc/rc1.d/K20eth_options -> ../init.d/eth_options
    /etc/rc6.d/K20eth_options -> ../init.d/eth_options
    /etc/rc2.d/S20eth_options -> ../init.d/eth_options
    /etc/rc3.d/S20eth_options -> ../init.d/eth_options
    /etc/rc4.d/S20eth_options -> ../init.d/eth_options
    /etc/rc5.d/S20eth_options -> ../init.d/eth_options
```

You can run your script with the following command:

```
$ sudo /etc/init.d/eth_options start
```

> **NOTE** *You can find tips similar to this at the nixCraft site,* www.cyberciti
> .biz/tips/.

As mentioned earlier, ethtool may not work on some older NICs. So **if you have an older NIC, try using mii-tool** as follows:

```
$ sudo mii-tool          Show negotiated speed and link status of old NIC
eth0: negotiated 100baseTx-FD flow-control, link ok
```

This example was taken from the same machine as the examples above, with the NIC auto-negotiating at 1000 Mbps, full-duplex. The mii-tool command is mis-reading the speed setting. This is why we recommend using mii-tool only as a last resort if ethtool doesn't work with your old NIC.

To **display mii-tool output with more verbosity,** use the -v option:

```
$ sudo mii-tool -v       Show verbose output of settings for old NIC
eth0: negotiated 100baseTx-FD flow-control, link ok
  product info: vendor 00:50:43, model 12 rev 2
  basic mode:   autonegotiation enabled
  basic status: autonegotiation complete, link ok
  capabilities: 100baseTx-FD 100baseTx-HD 10baseT-FD 10baseT-HD
  advertising:  100baseTx-FD 100baseTx-HD 10baseT-FD 10baseT-HD flow-control
  link partner: 100baseTx-FD 100baseTx-HD 10baseT-FD 10baseT-HD flow-control
```

In the example just shown, you can see that each mode (100baseTx and 10baseT) supports both half-duplex (HD) and full duplex (FD). To **disable auto-negotiation and force a particular setting,** use the -F option as follows:

```
$ sudo mii-tool -F 10baseT-FD eth0    Force speed/duplex to 10baseT-FD
```

If you change your mind and later want to **re-enable auto-negotiation,** use the -r option:

```
$ sudo mii-tool -r eth0          Re-enable auto-negotiation for an old NIC
restarting autonegotiation...
```

mii-tool does not provide a capability to save settings like ethtool does, so you have to run it after every reboot. This can be done by adding it at the end of /etc/rc.local.

The netstat command provides another way to **get network interface statistics:**

```
$ netstat -i             Get network interface statistics for eth0
Kernel Interface table
Iface MTU Met RX-OK RX-ERR RX-DRP RX-OVR TX-OK TX-ERR TX-DRP TX-OVR Flg
eth0 1500 0 1757208      6      0      0 996834      4      0      0 BMRU
```

Use the -c option to get netstat to **refresh network interface statistics every second:**

```
$ netstat -ic          Refresh network statistics every second
```

You can **get cleaner (screen-oriented) refreshed output** from netstat by combining it with the watch command as follows:

```
$ watch netstat -i     Refresh network statistics (screen oriented)
Every 2.0s: netstat -i                Wed Aug 22 01:55:48 2007

Kernel Interface table
Iface MTU Met RX-OK RX-ERR RX-DRP RX-OVR TX-OK TX-ERR TX-DRP TX-OVR Flg
eth0 1500 0 1757208     6      0      0 996834     4      0      0 BMRU
```

As the output indicates, the netstat statistics are updated every 2.0 seconds.

Managing Network Connections

Starting and stopping the network interfaces for your wired Ethernet connections to your LAN or the Internet is usually handled automatically at the time you boot and shut down your Ubuntu system. However, you can use the commands in /etc/init.d to start and stop your network interfaces any time you want or update-rc.d to configure whether your network starts automatically.

The ifconfig and ip commands can also be used to configure, activate, and deactivate interfaces. However, on Ubuntu and other Debian derivatives, the commands in the /etc/init.d directory provide simpler tools to start and stop network interfaces. Therefore, in most cases, you should only use ifconfig and ip commands to gather information about your Ethernet interfaces and NICs (as shown later in this section).

Starting and Stopping Ethernet Connections

The reason that your wired Ethernet interfaces just come up in many cases when you boot Ubuntu is that the network service is set to be on when the system enters the common boot run levels (run levels 3 and 5). There is a set of underlying configuration files and scripts that make that happen and a few simple commands that let you control it.

For Ubuntu, control scripts and configuration files are located in the /etc/network/ directory. NICs are configured by editing /etc/network//interfaces. The file looks like the following:

```
auto lo
iface lo inet loopback

auto eth0
iface eth0 inet dhcp
```

```
auto eth1
iface eth1 inet dhcp

auto eth2
iface eth2 inet dhcp

auto ath0
iface ath0 inet dhcp

auto wlan0
iface wlan0 inet dhcp
```

To **get more information on this file**, type the following:

```
$ less /usr/share/doc/network-manager/README.Debian
```

If you change the interfaces file, you need to run the following command:

```
$ sudo /etc/dbus-1/event.d/25NetworkManager restart
```

The script that starts the configured `network-scripts` files is `/etc/init.d/network`. As with other Linux services, you can start and stop the `network` service using the `/etc/init.d/networking` command.

To **take all NICs offline then bring them back online**, allowing any change to the network scripts to take effect, type the following:

```
$ sudo /etc/init.d/networking restart    Shutdown and bring up network interfaces
 * Reconfiguring network interfaces...
There is already a pid file /var/run/dhclient.eth0.pid with pid 9242
killed old client process, removed PID file
Internet Systems Consortium DHCP Client V3.0.4
Copyright 2004-2006 Internet Systems Consortium.
All rights reserved.
For info, please visit http://www.isc.org/sw/dhcp/


Listening on LPF/eth0/00:19:d1:5a:a9:e2
Sending on   LPF/eth0/00:19:d1:5a:a9:e2
Sending on   Socket/fallback
DHCPRELEASE on eth0 to 192.168.1.1 port 67
There is already a pid file /var/run/dhclient.eth0.pid with pid 134993416
Internet Systems Consortium DHCP Client V3.0.4
Copyright 2004-2006 Internet Systems Consortium.
...
                                                         [ OK ]
```

You may see errors for extra interfaces defined but not available on your system, such as wireless interfaces. You can ignore any error that refers to a networking device you have not installed.

Use the start and stop options to **start and stop your network interfaces,** respectively:

```
$ sudo /etc/init.d/networking stop      Shutdown network interfaces
$ sudo /etc/init.d/networking start     Bring up network interfaces
```

To **check the status of your network interfaces,** type the following:

```
$ ifconfig          Check network interface status
eth0      Link encap:Ethernet  HWaddr 00:19:D1:5A:A9:E2
          inet addr:192.168.1.106  Bcast:192.168.1.255  Mask:255.255.255.0
          inet6 addr: fe80::219:d1ff:fe5a:a9e2/64 Scope:Link
          UP BROADCAST RUNNING MULTICAST  MTU:1492  Metric:1
          RX packets:14442 errors:0 dropped:0 overruns:0 frame:0
          TX packets:13080 errors:0 dropped:0 overruns:0 carrier:0
          collisions:434 txqueuelen:1000
          RX bytes:3732823 (3.5 MiB)  TX bytes:1142020 (1.0 MiB)

lo        Link encap:Local Loopback
          inet addr:127.0.0.1  Mask:255.0.0.0
          inet6 addr: ::1/128 Scope:Host
          UP LOOPBACK RUNNING  MTU:16436  Metric:1
          RX packets:35 errors:0 dropped:0 overruns:0 frame:0
          TX packets:35 errors:0 dropped:0 overruns:0 carrier:0
          collisions:0 txqueuelen:0
          RX bytes:2121 (2.0 KiB)  TX bytes:2121 (2.0 KiB)
```

If you have multiple network interfaces, you may want to just **bring one interface up or down.** To do that, use the ifup and ifdown commands:

```
$ sudo ifdown eth0      Take the eth0 network interface offline
$ sudo ifup eth0        Bring the eth0 network interface online
```

When your network interfaces are up, there are tools you can use to view information about those interfaces and associated NICs.

Viewing Ethernet Connection Information

To view the media access control (MAC) address for your NIC and IP address for your TCP/IP connections, you can use the ifconfig command. The following command line **shows the address information and status of your eth0 Ethernet interface:**

```
$ ifconfig eth0
eth0      Link encap:Ethernet  HWaddr 00:D0:B7:79:A5:35
          inet addr:10.0.0.155  Bcast:10.0.0.255  Mask:255.255.255.0
          inet6 addr: fe80::2d0:b7ff:fe79:a535/64 Scope:Link
          UP BROADCAST RUNNING MULTICAST  MTU:1500  Metric:1
          RX packets:1413382 errors:6 dropped:0 overruns:0 frame:6
          TX packets:834839 errors:4 dropped:0 overruns:0 carrier:4
          collisions:0 txqueuelen:1000
          RX bytes:1141608691 (1.0 GiB)  TX bytes:470961026 (449.1 MiB)
```

In this example, the eth0 interface is the first Ethernet interface on the computer. The MAC address (HWaddr) of the NIC is 00:D0:B7:79:A5:35. You can see eth0's IP address (10.0.0.155), broadcast address (10.0.0.255), and subnet mask (255.255.255.0). Other information includes the number of packets received and transmitted, as well as problems (errors, dropped packets, and overruns) that occurred on the interface.

To **get information on both active and inactive NICs,** use the -a option:

```
$ ifconfig -a
```

Instead of using ifconfig (and several other commands described in this chapter), you can use the newer ip command. The ip command was made to show information about your network interfaces, as well as changing settings for network devices, routing, and IP tunnels. Here the ip command is used to **show information about the eth0 interface:**

```
$ ip addr show eth0
2: eth0: <BROADCAST,MULTICAST,UP,LOWER_UP> mtu 1500 qdisc pfifo_fast qlen 1000
    link/ether 00:d0:b7:79:a5:35 brd ff:ff:ff:ff:ff:ff
    inet 10.0.0.155/24 brd 10.0.0.255 scope global eth0
    inet6 fe80::2d0:b7ff:fe79:a535/64 scope link
       valid_lft forever preferred_lft forever
```

The ip command allows for shorthand syntax. If you're familiar with the Cisco IOS command line interface, the ip command works the same way. For example, instead of typing ip addr show, you could type the following to **see information on all interfaces:**

```
$ ip a
```

The ip command can operate on multiple network components, known as *objects*. One of these objects is addr, which allows ip to configure network addresses. We will cover other objects of the ip command below.

To **see how the ip command is used,** use the help option. Along with the help option, you can identify an ip object to get information on using that object:

```
$ ip help          View ip usage statement
Usage: ip [ OPTIONS ] OBJECT { COMMAND | help }
       ip [ -force ] [-batch filename
where  OBJECT := { link | addr | route | rule | neigh | ntable | tunnel|
                   maddr | mroute | monitor | xfrm }
       OPTIONS := { -V[ersion] | -s[tatistics] | -r[esolve] |
                    -f[amily] { inet | inet6 | ipx | dnet | link } |
                    -o[neline] | -t[imestamp] }
$ ip addr help     View help for the addr object
$ ip route help    View help for the route object
$ ip tunnel help   View help for the tunnel object
```

Understanding subnetwork masks can be confusing if you're not used to them. You may find `ipcalc` (from the ipcalc package) useful to **calculate a host computer's netmask from its CIDR IP address:**

```
$ ipcalc -bmn 192.168.1.100/27
Address:   192.168.1.100
Netmask:   255.255.255.224 = 27
Wildcard:  0.0.0.31
=>
Network:   192.168.1.96/27
HostMin:   192.168.1.97
HostMax:   192.168.1.126
Broadcast: 192.168.1.127
Hosts/Net: 30                    Class C, Private Internet
```

In the example just shown, the netmask (which indicates which part of an IP address represents the network and which represents the host) is 255.255.255.224. That was derived from the /27 value at the end of the IP address 192.168.1.100.

Using Wireless Connections

Setting up wireless connections in Linux has been tricky in the past, primarily due to the fact that open source drivers have not been available for the vast majority of wireless LAN cards on the market. More recent releases of Ubuntu have shown a marked improvement.

Wireless configuration is an area where we would suggest you use the GUI tools (in particular, the Network Configuration window described earlier in this chapter, or Network Manager) to do basic configuration. You may need to add wireless tools packages to get this to work, such as wireless-tools and bcm43xx-fwcutter packages, which are available from the Ubuntu repositories. Likewise, you may need firmware that is available in the following packages: ipw2100-source, ipw2200-firmware, and zd1211-firmware packages.

If you are not able to configure your wireless LAN card using the Network Configuration window, you might be able to get your wireless card working using drivers and tools available from Atheros (`www.atheros.com`), the MadWifi (`www.madwifi.org`) project, or the Ndiswrapper project (`ndiswrapper.sourceforge.net`). Many packages of software from those projects are available from the standard Ubuntu repositories, described in Chapter 2.

If you need help **determining exactly what wireless card you have,** type the following:

```
$ lspci | grep -i wireless        Search for wireless PCI cards
01:09.0 Network controller: Broadcom Corporation BCM4306 802.11b/g
    Wireless LAN Controller (rev 03)
```

Assuming that your wireless card is up and running, there are some useful commands in the wireless-tools package you can use to view and change settings for your wireless cards. In particular, the iwconfig command can help you work a with your wireless LAN interfaces. The following **scans your network interfaces for supported wireless cards** and lists their current settings:

```
$ iwconfig
eth0      no wireless extensions.
eth1      IEEE 802.11-DS  ESSID:""  Nickname:"HERMES I"
          Mode:Managed  Frequency:2.457 GHz  Access Point: Not-Associated
          Bit Rate:11 Mb/s   Tx-Power=15 dBm   Sensitivity:1/3
          Retry limit:4   RTS thr:off   Fragment thr:off
          Encryption key:off
          Power Management:off
```

Wireless interfaces may be named wlanX or ethX, depending on the hardware and driver used. You may be able to obtain more information after setting the link up on the wireless interface:

```
$ ip link set eth1 up
$ iwconfig eth1

eth1      IEEE 802.11-DS  ESSID:""  Nickname:"HERMES I"
          Mode:Managed  Frequency:2.457 GHz  Access Point: None
          Bit Rate:11 Mb/s   Tx-Power=15 dBm   Sensitivity:1/3
          Retry limit:4   RTS thr:off   Fragment thr:off
          Encryption key:off
          Power Management:off
          Link Quality=0/92  Signal level=134/153  Noise level=134/153
          Rx invalid nwid:0  Rx invalid crypt:0  Rx invalid frag:0
          Tx excessive retries:0  Invalid misc:0   Missed beacon:0
```

The settings just shown can be modified in a lot of ways. Here are some ways to **use iwconfig to modify your wireless interface settings**. In the following examples, we operate on a wireless interface named wlan0. These operations may or may not be supported, depending on which wireless card and driver you are using.

```
$ sudo iwconfig wlan0 essid "MyWireless"    Set essid to MyWireless
$ sudo iwconfig wlan0 channel 3             Set the channel to 3
$ sudo iwconfig wlan0 mode Ad-Hoc           Change from Managed to Ad-Hoc mode
$ sudo iwconfig wlan0 ap any                Use any access point available
$ sudo iwconfig wlan0 sens -50              Set sensitivity to -50
$ sudo iwconfig wlan0 retry 20              Set MAC retransmissions to 20
$ sudo iwconfig wlan0 key 1234-5555-66      Set encryption key to 1234-5555-66
```

The essid is sometimes called the Network Name or Domain ID. Use it as the common name to identify your wireless network. Setting the channel lets your wireless LAN operate on that specific channel.

With `Ad-Hoc` mode, the network is composed of only interconnected clients with no central access point. In `Managed/Infrastructure` mode, by setting `ap` to a specific MAC address, you can force the card to connect to the access point at that address, or you can set `ap` to `any` and allow connections to any access point.

If you have performance problems, try adjusting the sensitivity (`sens`) to either a negative value (which represents dBm) or positive value (which is either a percentage or a sensitivity value set by the vendor). If you get retransmission failures, you can increase the `retry` value so your card can send more packets before failing.

Use the `key` option to set an encryption key. You can enter hexadecimal digits (XXXX-XXXX-XXXX-XXXX or XXXXXXXX). By adding an `s:` in front of the key, you can enter an ASCII string as the key (as in `s:My927pwd`).

Using Dial-up Modems

Although high-speed DSL, cable modem, and wireless LAN hardware have become widely available, there may still be times when a phone line and a modem are your only way to get on the Internet. Linux offers both graphical and command line tools for configuring and communicating with modems.

As with other network connections in Ubuntu, dial-up modem connections can be configured using the Network Configuration window. Most external serial modems will work with Linux without any special configuration. Most hardware PCI modems will also work. However, many software modems (also sometimes called Winmodems) often will not work in Linux (although some can be configured with special drivers, and are therefore referred to as Linmodems).

Instead of describing the contortions you must go through to get some Winmodems working in Linux, we recommend that you purchase either a modem that connects to an external serial port or a hardware modem. If you want to try configuring your Winmodem yourself, refer to the Linmodems site (`www.linmodems.org`).

If you are not able to get your modem working from the Network Configuration window, there are some commands you can try. First try the `wvdialconf` command to try to scan any modems connected to your serial ports and create a configuration file:

```
$ sudo wvdialconf /etc/wvdial.conf    Scan serial ports, create config file
Scanning your serial ports for a modem.

ttyS0: ATQ0 V1 E1 -- OK
ttyS0: ATQ0 V1 E1 Z -- OK
  ...
```

In this example, a modem was found on the COM1 port (serial port `/dev/ttyS0`). Further output should show which speeds are available and various features that are supported. The configuration information that results is, in this case, written to the file /etc/wvdial.conf. Here's an example of what that file might look like:

```
[Dialer Defaults]
Modem = /dev/ttyS0
Baud = 115200
Init1 = ATZ
Init2 = ATQ0 V1 E1 S0=0 &C1 &D2 S11=55 +FCLASS=0
;Phone =
;Username =
;Password =
```

Open wvdial.conf in a text editor and remove the comment characters (;) from in front of the Phone, Username, and Password entries. Then add the phone number you need to dial to reach your ISP's bank of dial-in modems. Next add the user name and password you need to log in to that modem connection.

To **use the dial-up entry** you just configured, you can use the wvdial command:

```
$ sudo wvdial                     Dial out and connect to your ISP
--> WvDial: Internet dialer version 1.54.0
--> Initializing modem.
--> Sending: ATZ
ATZ
OK
--> Modem initialized.
  . . .
```

After the connection is established between the two modems, a Point-to-Point Protocol (PPP) connection is created between the two points. After that, you should be able to start communicating over the Internet.

If you find that you are not able to communicate with your modem, there are some ways of querying your computer's serial ports to find out what is going wrong. The first thing to check at the low level is that your /dev/ttyS? device talks to the hardware serial port.

By default, the Linux system knows of four serial ports: COM1 (/dev/ttyS0), COM2 (/dev/ttyS1), COM3 (/dev/ttyS2), and COM4 (/dev/ttyS3). To **see a listing of those serial ports**, use the setserial command (from the setserial package) with the -g option, as follows:

```
$ setserial -g /dev/ttyS0 /dev/ttyS1 /dev/ttyS2 /dev/ttyS3 See port info
/dev/ttyS0, UART: 16550A, Port: 0x03f8, IRQ: 4
/dev/ttyS1, UART: unknown, Port: 0x02f8, IRQ: 3
/dev/ttyS2, UART: unknown, Port: 0x03e8, IRQ: 4
/dev/ttyS3, UART: unknown, Port: 0x02e8, IRQ: 3
```

To see more detailed information on your serial ports, use the -a option:

```
$ setserial -a /dev/ttyS0          View serial port details
/dev/ttyS0, Line 0, UART: 16550A, Port: 0x03f8, IRQ: 4
        Baud_base: 115200, close_delay: 50, divisor: 0
        closing_wait: 3000
        Flags: spd_normal skip_test
$ setserial -ga /dev/ttyS0 /dev/ttyS1   Check multiple port details
```

The setserial command can also be used to re-map physical serial ports to logical /dev/ttyS? devices. Unless you're running kernel 2.2 with a jumper-configured ISA serial card, you won't need this. Modern Linux systems running on modern hardware make COM1 and COM2 serial ports work right out of the box, so we won't cover these options.

The stty command is another command you can use to work with serial ports. To view the current settings for the COM1 port (ttyS0), type the following:

```
$ stty -F /dev/ttyS0 -a          View tty settings for serial port
speed 9600 baud; rows 0; columns 0; line = 0;
intr = ^C; quit = ^\; erase = ^?; kill = ^U; eof = ^D; eol = <undef>; eol2 =
<undef>; swtch = <undef>; start = ^Q; stop = ^S;
susp = ^Z; rprnt = ^R; werase = ^W; lnext = ^V; flush = ^O; min = 1; time = 0;
-parenb -parodd cs8 hupcl -cstopb cread clocal -crtscts
-ignbrk -brkint -ignpar -parmrk -inpck -istrip -inlcr -igncr icrnl ixon -ixoff -
iuclc -ixany -imaxbel -iutf8
opost -olcuc -ocrnl onlcr -onocr -onlret -ofill -ofdel nl0 cr0 tab0 bs0 vt0 ff0
isig icanon iexten echo echoe echok -echonl -noflsh -xcase -tostop -echoprt
echoctl echoke
```

The dialer will typically change these settings as needed, although you can use the stty command to change these settings as well. Refer to the stty man page (man stty) for descriptions of any of the tty settings.

You can talk directly to the modem or other serial devices using the minicom command (from the minicom package). In fact, it can be useful to troubleshoot dialing by issuing AT commands to the modem using minicom. The first time you run minicom, use -s to enter setup mode:

```
$ minicom -s          Create your modem settings
+-----[configuration]-----+
| Filenames and paths     |
| File transfer protocols |
| Serial port setup       |
| Modem and dialing       |
| Screen and keyboard     |
| Save setup as dfl       |
| Save setup as..         |
| Exit                    |
| Exit from Minicom       |
+-------------------------+
```

Let's forget about modems for a moment and assume you want to use COM1 to connect to a Cisco device at 9600 baud. Use the arrow keys to navigate to Serial port setup and press Enter to select it. Press a to edit the serial device and change that device to /dev/ttyS0. Next, press e for port settings and when the Comm Parameters screen appears, press e for 9600 baud. To toggle off hardware flow control, press f. Press Enter to return to the configuration screen.

To change modem parameters, select modem and dialing. Then clear the init, reset, connect, and hangup strings (which are not appropriate for the Cisco device we're configuring). When that's done, select save setup as dfl (default) from the configuration screen and choose Exit (not Exit from Minicom).

You're now in the minicom terminal. To learn more about how to use minicom, press Ctrl+a, then z for help. When you are done, press Ctrl+a, then x to exit from minicom.

> **WARNING!** *Do not run minicom inside* screen *with the default key bindings! Otherwise, Ctrl+a gets intercepted by* screen*! If you do so by mistake, go to another* screen *window and type:* killall minicom.

Checking Name Resolution

Because IP addresses are numbers, and people prefer to address things by name, TCP/IP networks (such as the Internet) rely on DNS to resolve host names into IP addresses. Ubuntu provides several tools for looking up information related to DNS name resolution.

When you first installed Ubuntu, you either identified Domain Name System (DNS) servers to do name resolution or had them assigned automatically from a DHCP server. That information is then stored in the /etc/resolv.conf file, looking something like the following:

```
nameserver 11.22.33.44
nameserver 22.33.44.55
```

The numbers shown above are replaced by real IP addresses of computers that serve as DNS name servers. When you can connect to working DNS servers, there are commands you can use to query those servers and look up host computers.

The dig command (which should be used instead of the deprecated nslookup command) can be used to look up information from a DNS server. The host command can be used to look up address information for a host name or domain name.

To **search your DNS servers for a particular host name** (www.turbosphere.com in the following examples), use the dig command as follows:

```
$ dig www.turbosphere.com    Search DNS servers set in /etc/resolv.conf
```

Instead of using your assigned name server, you can **query a specific name server**. The following example queries the DNS server at 4.2.2.1:

```
$ dig www.turbosphere.com @4.2.2.1
```

Using dig, you can also **query for a specific record type**:

```
$ dig turbosphere.com mx    Queries for the mail exchanger
$ dig turbosphere.com ns    Queries for the authoritative name servers
```

Use the +trace option to **trace a recursive query** from the top-level DNS servers down to the authoritative servers:

```
$ dig +trace www.turbosphere.com    Recursively trace DNS servers
```

If you just want to **see the IP address of a host computer**, use the +short option:

```
$ dig +short www.turbosphere.com    Display only name/IP address pair
turbosphere.com.
66.113.99.70
```

You can use dig **to do a reverse lookup to find DNS information based on an IP address**:

```
$ dig -x 66.113.99.70            Get DNS information based on IP address
```

You can use host **to do a reverse DNS lookup** as well:

```
$ host 66.113.99.70
70.99.133.66.in-addr.arpa domain name pointer boost.turbosphere.com.
```

To get hostname information for the local machine, use the hostname and dnsdomainname commands:

```
$ hostname              View the local computer's full DNS host name
boost.turbosphere.com
```

You can also use hostname to **set the local hostname temporarily** (until the next reboot). Here's an example:

```
$ sudo hostname server1.example.com    Set local hostname
```

Changing the hostname of a running machine may adversely affect some running daemons. Instead, we recommend you **set the local hostname so it is set each time the system starts up.** Edit the first line in the /etc/hostname file. Here is an example:

```
server1.example.com
```

Troubleshooting Network Problems

Troubleshooting networks is generally done from the bottom layer up. As discussed at beginning of the chapter the first step is to make sure that the physical network layer components (cables, NICs, and so on) are connected and working. Next, check that the links between physical nodes are working. After that, there are lots of tools for checking the connectivity to a particular host.

Checking Connectivity to a Host

When you know you have a link and no duplex mismatch, the next step is to `ping` your default gateway. You should have either configured the default gateway (`gw`) in the `/etc/network/interfaces` file or let the system set up the default gateway from a service such as DHCP. To **check your default gateway in the actual routing table**, use the `ip` command as follows:

```
$ ip route
10.0.0.0/24 dev eth0  proto kernel  scope link  src 10.0.0.155
169.254.0.0/16 dev eth0  scope link
default via 10.0.0.1 dev eth0
```

The gateway for the default route in this example is 10.0.0.1. To **make sure there is IP connectivity to that gateway**, use the `ping` command as follows, passing the address for your default gateway:

```
$ ping 10.0.0.1
PING 10.0.0.1 (10.0.0.1) 56(84) bytes of data.
64 bytes from 10.0.0.1: icmp_seq=1 ttl=64 time=0.382 ms
64 bytes from 10.0.0.1: icmp_seq=2 ttl=64 time=0.313 ms
64 bytes from 10.0.0.1: icmp_seq=3 ttl=64 time=0.360 ms
64 bytes from 10.0.0.1: icmp_seq=4 ttl=64 time=1.43 ms

--- 10.0.0.1 ping statistics ---
4 packets transmitted, 4 received, 0% packet loss, time 2999ms
rtt min/avg/max/mdev = 0.313/0.621/1.432/0.469 ms
```

By default, `ping` continues until you press Ctrl+c. Other `ping` options include the following:

```
$ ping -a 10.0.0.1         Add an audible ping as ping progresses
$ ping -c 4 10.0.0.1       Ping 4 times and exit (default in Windows)
$ ping -q -c 5 10.0.0.1    Show summary of pings (works best with -c)
$ sudo ping -f 10.0.0.1       Send a flood of pings (must be root)
$ ping -i 3 10.0.0.1       Send packets in 3-second intervals
$ sudo ping -I eth0 10.0.0.1   Set source to eth0 (use if multiple NICs)
PING 10.0.0.1 (10.0.0.1) from 10.0.0.155 eth0: 56(84) bytes of data.
$ sudo ping -I 10.0.0.155 10.0.0.1    Set source to 10.0.0.155
```

```
PING 10.0.0.1 (10.0.0.1) from 10.0.0.155 : 56(84) bytes of data.
$ ping -s 1500 10.0.0.1   Set packet size to 1500 bytes
PING 10.0.0.1 (10.0.0.1) 1500(1528) bytes of data.
```

Use the ping flood option with caution. By default, ping sends small packets (56 bytes). Large packets (such as the 1500-byte setting just shown) are good to make faulty NICs or connections stand out.

Checking Address Resolution Protocol (ARP)

If you're not able to ping your gateway, you may have an issue at the Ethernet MAC layer. The Address Resolution Protocol (ARP) can be used to find information at the MAC layer. To view and configure ARP entries, use the arp or ip neighbor command. This example shows arp listing computers in the ARP cache by hostname:

```
$ arp -v          List ARP cache entries by name
Address        HWtype  HWaddress          Flags Mask      Iface
ritchie        ether   00:10:5A:AB:F6:A7  C                eth0
einstein       ether   00:0B:6A:02:EC:98  C                eth0
Entries: 1  Skipped: 0  Found: 1
```

In this example, you can see the names of other computers that the local computer's ARP cache knows about and the associated hardware type and hardware address (MAC address) of each computer's NIC. You can disable name resolution to see those computers' IP addresses instead:

```
$ arp -vn         List ARP cache entries by IP address
Address        HWtype  HWaddress          Flags Mask      Iface
10.0.0.1       ether   00:10:5A:AB:F6:A7  C                eth0
10.0.0.50      ether   00:0B:6A:02:EC:98  C                eth0
Entries: 1  Skipped: 0  Found: 1
```

To delete an entry from the ARP cache, use the -d option:

```
$ sudo arp -d 10.0.0.50        Delete address 10.0.0.50 from ARP cache
```

Instead of just letting ARP dynamically learn about other systems, you can add static ARP entries to the cache using the -s option:

```
$ sudo arp -s 10.0.0.51 00:0B:6A:02:EC:95    Add IP and MAC addresses to ARP
```

To do the same actions with the ip command that you just did with the arp command, use the neighbor object (note that neighbor, nei, and n objects can be used interchangeably):

```
$ ip neighbor
10.0.0.1 dev eth0 lladdr 00:10:5a:ab:f6:a7 DELAY
10.0.0.50 dev eth0 lladdr 00:0b:6a:02:ec:98 REACHABLE
# ip nei del 10.0.0.50 dev eth0
# ip n add 10.0.0.51 lladdr 00:0B:6A:02:EC:95 dev eth0
```

228

To query a subnet to see if an IP is already in use, and to find the MAC address of the device using it, use the `arping` command. The `arping` command is used by `ifup` to avoid IP conflicts when bringing an Ethernet NIC up. Here are examples:

```
$ arping 10.0.0.50              Query subnet to see if 10.0.0.50 is in use
ARPING 10.0.0.50 from 10.0.0.195 eth0
Unicast reply from 10.0.0.50 [00:0B:6A:02:EC:98]  0.694ms
Unicast reply from 10.0.0.50 [00:0B:6A:02:EC:98]  0.683ms
$ sudo arping -I eth0 10.0.0.50  Specify interface to query from
```

Like the `ping` command, the `arping` command continuously queries for the address until the command is ended by typing Ctrl+c. Typically, you just want to know if the target is alive, so you can run one of the following commands:

```
$ arping -f 10.0.0.50    Query 10.0.0.50 and stop at the first reply
$ arping -c 2 10.0.0.51  Query 10.0.0.50 and stop after 2 counts
```

Tracing Routes to Hosts

After verifying that you can ping your gateway and even reach machines that are out-side of your network, you may still have issues reaching a specific host or network. If that's true, you can use traceroute (from the traceroute package) to find the bottleneck or point of failure:

```
$ traceroute boost.turbosphere.com  Follow the route taken to a host
traceroute to boost.turbosphere.com (66.113.99.70),30 hops max,40 byte packets
 1  10.0.0.1 (10.0.0.1)  0.281 ms  0.289 ms  0.237 ms
 2  tl-03.hbci.com (64.211.114.1)  6.213 ms  6.189 ms  6.083 ms
 3  172.17.2.153 (172.17.2.153)  14.070 ms  14.025 ms  13.974 ms
 4  so-0-3-2.ar2.MIN1.gblx.net (208.48.1.117)  19.076 ms  19.053 ms 19.004 ms
 5  so1-0-0-2488M.ar4.SEA1.gblx.net(67.17.71.210)94.697 ms 94.668 ms 94.612ms
 6  64.215.31.114 (64.215.31.114)  99.643 ms  101.647 ms  101.577 ms
 7  dr02-v109.tac.opticfusion.net(209.147.112.50)262.301ms 233.316ms 233.153 ms
 8  dr01-v100.tac.opticfusion.net (66.113.96.1) 99.313 ms 99.401 ms 99.353 ms
 9  boost.turbosphere.com (66.113.99.70)  99.251 ms  96.215 ms  100.220 ms
```

As you can see, the longest hop is between 4 (Global Crossing probably in Minneapolis) and 5 (GC in Seattle). That gap is not really a bottleneck; it just reflects the distance between those hops. Sometimes, the last hops look like this:

```
28  *  *  *
29  *  *  *
30  *  *  *
```

The lines of asterisks (*) at the end of the trace can be caused by firewalls that block traffic to the target. However, if you see several asterisks before the destination, those can indicate heavy congestion or equipment failures and point to a bottleneck.

By default, `traceroute` uses UDP packets, which provides a more realistic per-formance picture than ICMP. That's because some Internet hops will give lower priority to ICMP traffic. If you'd still like to **trace using ICMP packets,** try the following command:

```
$ traceroute -I boost.turbosphere.com   Use ICMP packets to trace a route
```

By default, `traceroute` connects to port 80. You can **set a different port** using the -p option:

```
$ traceroute -p 25 boost.turbosphere.com   Connect to port 25 in trace
```

You can **view IP addresses instead of host names** by disabling name resolution of hops:

```
$ traceroute -n boost.turbosphere.com   Disable name resolution in trace
```

An **alternative to traceroute is the tracepath command,** which also uses UDP to perform the trace:

```
$ tracepath boost.turbosphere.com        Use UDP to trace the route
```

To view and manipulate the kernel's routing table, the `route` command used to be the tool of choice. This is slowly being replaced by the `ip route` command. For the most part, the Ubuntu network scripts rely on `ip route`. But it doesn't hurt to be familiar with both commands, because `route` is still quite commonly used.

You can use the old `route` command to **display your local routing table.** Here are two examples of the `route` command, with and without DNS name resolution:

```
$ route              Display local routing table information
Kernel IP routing table
Destination   Gateway   Genmask        Flags Metric Ref   Use Iface
10.0.0.0      *         255.255.255.0  U     0      0       0 eth0
default       ritchie   0.0.0.0        UG    0      0       0 eth0
$ route -n           Display routing table without DNS lookup
Kernel IP routing table
Destination   Gateway   Genmask        Flags Metric Ref   Use Iface
10.0.0.0      *         255.255.255.0  U     0      0       0 eth0
0.0.0.0       10.0.0.1  0.0.0.0        UG    0      0       0 eth0
```

You can **add a default gateway** using the gw option:

```
$ sudo route add default gw 10.0.0.2     Add 10.0.0.2 as default gateway
```

You can **add a new route to your network** by specifying either the interface (eth0) or IP address of the gateway (such as gw 10.0.0.100):

```
$ sudo route add -net 192.168.0.0 netmask 255.255.255.0 eth0
$ sudo route add -net 192.168.0.0 netmask 255.255.255.0 gw 10.0.0.100
```

You can **delete a route** using the del option:

```
$ sudo route del -net 192.168.0.0 netmask 255.255.255.0   Delete a route
```

Using the newer ip command, you can do the same activities just shown with the `route` command. Here are three different ways to show the same basic routing information:

```
$ ip route show          Display basic routing information
10.0.0.0/24 dev eth0  proto kernel  scope link  src 10.0.0.195
169.254.0.0/16 dev eth0  scope link
default via 10.0.0.1 dev eth0
$ ip route               Display basic routing (example #2)
$ ip r                   Display basic routing (example #3)
```

Here are some examples for **adding and deleting routes with ip**:

```
$ sudo ip r add 192.168.0.0/24 via 10.0.0.100 dev eth0  Add route to interface
$ sudo ip r add 192.168.0.0/24 via 10.0.0.100           Add route no interface
$ sudo ip r del 192.168.0.0/24                          Delete route
```

To **make a new route permanent,** edit the `/etc/network/interfaces` file and place the information about the new route in that file. For example, to add the route added with the `ip` command above, add the following lines to `/etc/network/interfaces`:

```
iface eth0 inet static
address 192.168.0.0
netmask 255.255.255.0
gateway 10.0.0.100
```

Displaying netstat Connections and Statistics

The tools above cover network troubleshooting mostly at the network layer (layer 3). To **display information about packets sent between transport-layer protocols (TCP and UDP), and ICMP,** you can use the `netstat` command:

```
$ netstat -s | less      Show summary of TCP, ICMP, UDP activities
```

You can see a **list of all TCP connections,** including which process is handling the connection:

```
$ sudo netstat -tanp            View active TCP connections
Active Internet connections (servers and established)
Proto Recv-Q Send-Q Local Address  Foreign Address  State  PID/Program name
tcp        0      0 127.0.0.1:631   0.0.0.0:*        LISTEN 2039/cupsd
tcp        0      0 127.0.0.1:25    0.0.0.0:*        LISTEN 2088/sendmail
  ...
```

You can also **view active UDP connections** as follows:

```
$ sudo netstat -uanp            View active UDP connections
Active Internet connections (servers and established)
Proto Recv-Q Send-Q Local Address    Foreign Address State PID/Program name
udp        0      0 0.0.0.0:631       0.0.0.0:*            2039/cupsd
udp        0      0 192.168.122.1:123 0.0.0.0:*            2067/ntpd
  ...
```

231

To narrow your output from netstat to daemons bound to a TCP port, look for the word listen. For example:

```
$ sudo netstat -tanp | grep -i listen    View daemons listening to a port
```

The command just shown is a great way to resolve port usage conflicts between daemons.

Other Useful Network Tools

If you'd like to see header information about packets as they are sent and received by your system, use tcpdump. The tcpdump command has a lot of advanced features, most of which revolve around filtering and finding a needle in a haystack of packets. If you run tcpdump on a remote machine, your screen will be flooded with all the ssh traffic between your client and the remote machine. To get started without having to learn too much about how tcpdump filtering works, run the following command:

```
$ sudo tcpdump | grep -v ssh    Find packets except those associated with ssh
```

If you'd like to dig deeper into packet-level traffic, use wireshark (formerly known as ethereal). Install the wireshark package. You can run wireshark with X over ssh on a remote machine. Wireshark is a very powerful packet sniffer that rivals the best commercial tools.

To explore networks and remote machines and see what services they offer, use nmap. The nmap command (from the nmap package) is the most common port scanner. It was even featured in the movie *The Matrix Reloaded*! Make sure that you are explicitly authorized to scan the systems or networks you are scanning. The nmap command is part of the nmap package and can be run as a user, but several scan types require root privileges.

Here's how to do a basic host scan with nmap:

```
$ sudo nmap 10.0.0.1    Scan ports on computer at 10.0.0.1
```

To get maximum verbosity from nmap, use the -vv option:

```
$ sudo nmap -vv 10.0.0.1    Show maximum verbosity from nmap output
```

To use nmap to scan an entire network, use the network address as an argument. In the following example, we add the -sP option to tell nmap to perform a simple ping sweep:

```
$ sudo nmap -vv -sP 10.0.0.0/24    Scan hosts on an entire network
```

You can be very specific about the information that nmap gathers for you. In the following example, the -P0 option tells nmap not to use ping (this is good for scanning machines that don't respond to ping). The -O option displays OS fingerprinting for the machine you are scanning. The -p 100-200 option tells nmap to scan only ports 100 through 200:

```
$ sudo nmap -vv -P0 -O -p 100-200 10.0.0.1   No ping, OS fingerprint, ports 100-200
```

The nmap command has a lot more options for advanced usage. Refer to the nmap man page (man nmap) for further information.

Summary

Nearly every aspect of the network connections from your Ubuntu system can be configured, checked, and monitored using command-line tools. You can view and change settings of your NICs using ethtool and mii-tool commands. You can view network statistics with netstat.

To start and stop your network, commands such as service, chkconfig, ifup, and ifdown are easy manage. When a connection is established, you can see statistics about that connection using ifconfig and ip commands.

Besides using wired Ethernet cards, other network hardware such as wireless LAN cards and dial-up modems are supported in Linux. Use commands such as iwconfig to work with wireless interfaces, and wvdialconf and minicom to configure modems.

To check DNS name resolution, use the dig, host, and hostname commands. Commands for checking connectivity and routes to a host include ping, arp, traceroute, and ip.

12

Accessing Network Resources

In the time it takes to fire up a graphical FTP client, you could already have downloaded a few dozen files from a remote server using command line tools. Even when a GUI is available, commands for transferring files, web browsing, sharing directories, and reading mail can be quick and efficient to use. When no GUI is available, they can be lifesavers.

This chapter covers commands for accessing resources (files, e-mail, shared directories, and online chats) over the network.

Running Commands to Browse the Web

Text-mode web browsers provide a quick way to check that a web server is working or to get information from a web server when a useable GUI isn't available. The once-popular lynx text-based browser was supplanted in most Linux systems by the links browser, which was later replaced by elinks. (Typing links now runs elinks.) To use a command line browser, you need to install one of these programs, with package names that match the command names: lynx, links, and elinks respectively. In most cases, if you want a command line web browser, install the elinks package.

The elinks browser runs in a terminal window. Aside from not displaying images in the terminal, elinks can handle most basic HTML content and features: tables, frames, tabbed browsing, cookies, history, mime types, and simple cascading style sheets. You can even use your mouse to follow links and select menu items.

IN THIS CHAPTER

Web browsing with elinks

Wget, curl, lftp, and scp for file transfers

Sharing directories with NFS, Samba, and SSHFS

IRC chats with irssi

Mail and mutt e-mail clients

Because `elinks` supports multiple colors, as long as the terminal you are using supports multiple colors, it's easy to spot links and headings in the text. (Colors may not work within a `screen` session.) Here are some examples of `elinks` command lines:

```
$ elinks                          Prompts for file name or URL
$ elinks www.handsonhistory.com   Opens file name or URL you request
```

If you have a mouse available, click near the top of the terminal window to see the menu. Select the menu name or item you want. Select a link to go to that link. Table 12-1 shows `elinks` keyboard navigation keys.

Table 12-1: Control Keys for Using elinks

Keys	Description	Keys	Description
Esc (or F9/F8)	Toggle menu on and off (then use arrow keys or mouse to navigate menus).	=	View page information.
Down arrow	Go to next link or editable field on page.	Ctrl+r	Reload page.
Up arrow	Go to previous link or editable field on the page.	a	Bookmark current page.
Right arrow or Enter	Go forward to highlighted link. Enter text in highlighted form field.	t	Open new browser tab.
Left arrow	Go back to previous page.	>	Go to next tab.
/	Search forward.	<	Go to previous tab.
?	Search backwards.	c	Close current tab.
n	Find next.	d	Download current link.
N	Find previous.	D	View downloads.
PageUp	Scroll one page up.	A	Add current link to bookmarks.
PageDown	Scroll one page down.	s	View bookmarks.
g	Go to a URL.	v	View current image.
q or Ctrl+c	Exit elinks.	h	View global history manager.

You can add global settings for `elinks` to `/etc/elinks.conf`. Per-user settings are stored in each user's `$HOME/.elinks` directory. Type `man elinkskeys` to see available settings.

Transferring Files

Commands in Linux for downloading files from remote servers (HTTP, HTTPS, FTP, or SSH) are plentiful and powerful. You might choose one command over another because of the specific options you need. For example, you may want to perform a download over an encrypted connection, resume an aborted download, or do recursive downloads. This section describes how to use wget, ftp, lftp, scp, and scftp.

Downloading Files with wget

Sometimes you need to **download a file from a remote server** using the command line. For example, you find a link to an RPM software package, but the link goes through several HTTP redirects that prevent rpm from installing straight from HTTP. Or you may want to script the automated download of a file, such as a log file, every night.

The wget command can download files from web servers (HTTP and HTTPS) and FTP servers. With a server that doesn't require authentication, a wget command can be as simple as the wget command and the location of the download file:

```
$ wget https://help.ubuntu.com/7.04/common/img/headerlogo.png
```

If, for example, an **FTP server requires a login and password**, you can enter that information on the wget command line in the following forms:

```
$ wget ftp://user:password@ftp.example.com/path/to/file
$ wget --user=user --password=password ftp://ftp.example.com/path/to/file
```

For example:

```
$ wget ftp://chris:mykuulpwd@ftp.linuxtoys.net/home/chris/image.jpg
$ wget --user=chris --password=mykuulpwd \
ftp://ftp.linuxtoys.net/home/chris/image.jpg
```

You can use wget to **download a single web page** as follows:

```
$ wget http://www.wiley.com       Download only the Web page
```

If you open the resulting index.html, you'll have all sorts of broken links. To download all the images and other elements required to render the page properly, use the –p option:

```
$ wget -p http://www.wiley.com       Download Web page and other elements
```

But if you open the resulting index.html in your browser, chances are you will still have all the broken links even though all the images were downloaded. That's because the links need to be translated to point to your local files. So instead, do this:

```
$ wget -pk http://www.wiley.com       Download pages and use local file names
```

And if you'd like wget to keep the original file and also do the translation, type this:

```
$ wget -pkK http://www.wiley.com      Rename to local names, keep original
```

Sometimes an HTML file you download does not have an .html extension, but ends in .asp or .cgi instead. That may result in your browser not knowing how to open your local copy of the file. You can have wget append .html to those files using the -E option:

```
$ wget -E http://www.aspexamples.com      Append .html to downloaded files
```

With the wget command, you can recursively mirror an entire web site. While copying files and directories for the entire depth of the server's file structure, the -m option adds timestamping and keeps FTP directory listings. (Use this with caution, because it can take a lot of time and space.)

```
$ wget -m http://www.linuxtoys.net
```

Using some of the options just described, the following command line results in the most usable local copy of a web site:

```
$ wget -mEkK http://www.linuxtoys.net
```

If you have ever had a large file download (such as a CD or DVD image file) disconnect before it completed, you may find the -c option to wget to be a lifesaver. Using -c, wget resumes where it left off, continuing an interrupted file download. For example:

```
$ wget http://example.com/DVD.iso      Begin downloading large file
  ...
95%[=========  ] 685,251,583 55K/s   Download killed before completion
$ wget -c http://example.com/DVD.iso   Resume download where stopped
  ...
HTTP request sent, awaiting response... 206 Partial Content
Length: 699,389,952 (667), 691,513 (66M) remaining [text/plain]
```

Because of the continue feature (-c), wget can be particularly useful for those with slow Internet connections who need to download large files. If you have ever had a several-hour download get killed just before it finished, you'll know what we mean. (Note that if you don't use the -c when you mean to resume a file download, the file will be saved to a different file: the original name with a .1 appended to it.)

Transferring Files with cURL

The client for URLs application (curl command) provides similar features to wget for transferring files using web and FTP protocols. However, the curl command can also transfer files using other popular protocols, including SSH protocols (SCP and SFTP), LDAP, DICT, Telnet, and File.

Instead of supporting large, recursive downloads (as wget does), curl is designed for *single-shot file transfers*. It does, however, support more protocols (as noted) and some neat advanced features. To use this command, you need to install the curl package. Here are a few interesting examples of **file transfers with curl**:

```
$ curl -O ftp://kernelorg.mirrors.tds.net/pub/linux/kernel/v1.0/patch[6-8].sign
$ curl -OO ftp://kernelorg.mirrors.tds.net/pub/linux/kernel/v2.6/ \
    ChangeLog-2.6.{1,4}
$ curl -O ftp://chris:MyPasswd@ftp.example.com/home/chris/fileA \
    -Q '-DELE fileA'
$ curl -T install.log ftp://chris:MyPasswd@ftp.example.com/tmp/ \
    -Q "-RNFR install.log" -Q "-RNTO Xinstall.log
$ curl ftp://ftp.kernel.org/pub//                    List /pub/ contents
```

The first two commands show how to use square brackets to indicate a range [6-8] and curly brackets for a list {1,4} of characters or numbers to match files.

The third command line illustrates how to add a user name and password (chris:MyPasswd), download a file (fileA) from the server, and then delete the file on the server once the download is done (-Q '-DELE fileA').

The fourth example uploads (-T) the file install.log to an FTP server. Then it renames the remote file to Xinstall.log. The last example tells curl to list the contents of the /pub/ directory at ftp.kernel.org.

Transfering files with FTP Commands

Ubuntu comes with the standard FTP client (ftp command), that works the same way it does on most UNIX and Windows systems. We recommend you use the full-featured, user-friendly lftp instead.

With these FTP clients, you open a session to the FTP server (as opposed to just grabbing a file, as you do with wget and curl). Then you navigate the server much as you would a local file system, getting and putting documents across the network connection. Here are examples of how to **connect to an FTP server with lftp**:

```
$ lftp mirrors.kernel.org                Anonymous connection
lftp mirrors.kernel.org:~>
$ lftp francois@example.com              Authenticated connection
lftp example.com:~>
$ lftp -u francois example.com           Authenticated connection
Password: ******
lftp example.com:~>
$ lftp -u francois,Mypwd example.com     Authentication with password
lftp example.com:~>
$ lftp                                   Start lftp with no connection
lftp :~> open mirrors.kernel.org         Start connection in lftp session
lftp mirrors.kernel.org:~>
```

> **WARNING!** *The fourth example should be avoided in real life. Passwords that are entered in a command line end up stored in clear text in your ~/.bash_history. They may also be visible to other users in the output of* ps auwx.

When a connection is established to an FTP server, you can use a set of commands during the FTP session. FTP commands are similar to shell commands. Just like in a bash shell, you can press Tab to autocomplete file names. In a session, lftp also supports sending multiple jobs to the background (Ctrl+z) and returning them to foreground (wait or fg). These are useful if you want to continue traversing the FTP site while files are downloading or uploading. Background jobs run in parallel. Type jobs to see a list of running background jobs. Type help to see a list of lftp commands.

The following sample lftp session illustrates **useful commands when downloading**:

```
$ lftp mirrors.kernel.org
lftp mirrors.kernel.org:~> pwd                      Check current directory
ftp://mirrors.kernel.org
lftp mirrors.kernel.org:~> ls                       List current directory
drwxr-sr-x   8 400   400   4096 Jul 02 20:19 debian/
drwxr-xr-x   7 537   537     77 May 21 21:37 fedora/
  ...
lftp mirrors.kernel.org:~> cd fedora/releases/7/Live/i386   Change directory
lftp mirrors.kernel.org:...> get Fedora-7-Live-i686.iso     Download a file
Fedora-7-Live-i686.iso at 776398 (1%) 467.2K/s eta:26m {Receiving data}
lftp mirrors.kernel.org:...> <Ctrl+z>               Send download to background
lftp mirrors.kernel.org:...> mget /gnu/ed/*         Get all in /gnu/ed
lftp mirrors.kernel.org:...> !ls                    Run local ls
lftp mirrors.kernel.org:...> bookmark add Live      Bookmark location
lftp mirrors.kernel.org:...> quit                   Close lftp
```

This session logs in as the anonymous user at mirrors.kernel.org. After changing to the directory containing the ISO image I was looking for, I downloaded it using the get command. By typing Ctrl+z, the download could continue while I did other activities. Next, the mget command (which allows wildcards such as *) downloaded all files from the /gnu/ed directory.

Any command preceded by an exclamation mark (such as !ls) is executed by the local shell. The bookmark command saves the current location (in this case, ftp://mirrors.kernel.org/fedora/releases/7/Live) under the name Live, so next time I can run lftp Live to return to the same location. The quit command ends the session.

Here are some **useful commands during an authenticated lftp upload session**. This assumes you have the necessary file permissions on the server:

```
$ lftp chris@example.com
Password: *******
lftp example.com:~> lcd /home/chris/songs    Change to a local directory
lftp example.com:~> cd pub/uploads           Change to server directory
lftp example.com:~> mkdir songs              Create directory on server
```

```
lftp example.com:~> chmod 700 songs          Change remote directory perms
lftp example.com:~> cd songs                 Change to the new directory
lftp example.com:~> put song.ogg tune.ogg    Upload files to server
3039267 bytes transferred
lftp example.com:~> mput /var/songs/*        Upload matched files
lftp example.com:~> quit                     Close lftp
```

The lftp session illustrates how you can use shell command names to operate on remote directories (provided you have permission). The mkdir and chmod commands create a directory and leave permissions open only to your user account. The put command uploads one or more files to the remote server. The mput command can use wildcards to match multiple files for download. Other commands include mirror (to download a directory tree) and mirror -R (to upload a directory tree).

lftp also provides a shell script for **non-interactive download sessions**: lftpget. The syntax of lftpget is similar to that of the wget command:

```
$ lftpget ftp://mirrors.kernel.org/ubuntu/dists/feisty/Release
```

Keep in mind that standard FTP clients are insecure because they do all their work in clear text. So your alternative, especially when security is a major issue, is to use SSH tools to transfer files.

Using SSH Tools to Transfer Files

Because SSH utilities are among the most important tools in a system administrator's arsenal of communications commands, some of the more complex uses of configuring and using SSH utilities are covered in Chapter 13. However, in their most basic form, SSH utilities are the tools you should use most often for basic file transfer.

In particular, the scp command will do most of what you need to get a file from one computer to another, while making that communication safe by encrypting both the password stage and data transfer stage of the process. The ssh command replaces the rcp command as the most popular tool for host-to-host file copies.

> **WARNING!**   *You do not get a warning before overwriting existing files with* scp, *so be sure that the target host doesn't contain any files or directories you want that are in the path of your* scp *file copies.*

Copying Remote Files with scp

To use scp to transfer files, the SSH service (usually the sshd server daemon) must be running on the remote system. Here are some examples of **useful scp commands**:

```
$ scp myfile francois@server1:/tmp/     Copy myfile to server1
Password: ******
$ scp server1:/tmp/myfile .             Copy remote myfile to local working dir
Password: ******
```

Use the -p option to **preserve permissions and timestamps** on the copied files:

```
$ scp -p myfile server1:/tmp/
```

If the SSH service is configured to listen on a port other than the default port 22, use -P to **indicate that port** on the scp command line:

```
$ scp -P 12345 myfile server1:/tmp/     Connect to a particular port
```

To do **recursive copies**, from a particular point in the remote file system, use the -r option:

```
$ scp -r mydir francois@server1:/tmp/     Copies all mydir to remote /tmp
```

Although scp is most useful when you know the exact locations of the file(s) you need to copy, sometimes it's more helpful to browse and transfer files interactively.

Copying Remote Files in sftp and lftp Sessions

The sftp command lets you use an FTP-like interface to **find and copy files over SSH protocols**. Here's an example of how to start an sftp session:

```
$ sftp chris@server1
chris@server1's password: *****
sftp>
```

Use sftp in the same manner as you use regular FTP clients. Type ? for a list of commands. You can change remote directories (cd), change local directories (lcd), check current remote and local directories (pwd and lpwd), and list remote and local contents (ls and lls). Depending on the permission of the user you logged in as, you may be able to create and remove directories (mkdir and rmdir), and change permissions (chmod) and ownership/group (chown and chgrp) of files and directories.

You can also use lftp (discussed earlier in this chapter) as an sftp client. Using lftp adds some user-friendly features such as **path completion** using the Tab key:

```
$ lftp sftp://chris@server1
Password: ********
lftp chris@server1:~>
```

Using Windows File Transfer Tools

In many cases, people need to get files from Linux servers using Windows clients. If your client operating system is Windows, you can use one of the following open source tools to get files from Linux servers:

❑ **WinSCP** (http://winscp.net) — Graphical scp, sftp, and FTP client for Windows over SSH1 and SSH2 protocols.

❑ **FileZilla** (`http://filezilla.sourceforge.net`) — Provides graphical client FTP and SFTP services in Windows, as well as offering FTP server features.

❑ **PSCP** (`www.chiark.greenend.org.uk/~sgtatham/putty/`) — Command line `scp` client that is part of the PuTTY suite.

❑ **PSFTP** (`www.chiark.greenend.org.uk/~sgtatham/putty/`) — Command line `sftp` client that is part of the PuTTY suite.

Sharing Remote Directories

Tools described to this point in the chapter provide atomic file access, where a connection is set up and files are transferred in one shot. In times where more persistent, ongoing access to a remote directory of files is needed, services for sharing and mounting remote file systems can be most useful. Such services include Network File System (NFS), Samba, and SSHFS.

Sharing Remote Directories with NFS

Assuming a server is already running the NFS service (part of the nfs-kernel-server package), you can use `exportfs` and `showmount` commands to see available and mounted shared directories. Mounting a shared directory is done with special options to the standard `mount` command. If you install the nfs-kernel-server package, Ubuntu will start the NFS service.

Viewing and Exporting NFS Shares

Run from the NFS server, the `exportfs` command **shows all shared directories** available from that server:

```
$ sudo /usr/sbin/exportfs -v
/export/myshare    client.example.com(ro,wdelay,root_squash,no_subtree_check)
/mnt/public        <world>(rw,wdelay,root_squash,no_subtree_check)
```

The two directories being shared are `/export/myshare` and `/mnt/public`. The first is only available to host computer `client.example.com`, whereas the second is available to everyone. Options for each share are shown in parenthesis. The first share is available read-only (`ro`), writes to the share are delayed to improve performance when more writes are expected (`wdelay`), and r equests from the root user on the client are mapped into the anonymous UID (`root_squash`). Also, a less thorough check of file system permission is done (`no_subtree_check`). The second share allows read-write mounting (`rw`).

Add and modify shared NFS directories by making changes to the `/etc/exports` file. To get changes to take effect, type any of the following as root:

```
$ sudo /etc/init.d/nfs-kernel-server reload    Reload exported shared directories
```

```
$ sudo exportfs -r                          Reload exported shared directories
$ sudo exportfs -rv                         Verbose reload of exported shares
exporting client.example.com:/export/myshare
exporting *:/mnt/public
```

From the Linux server system, you can use the `showmount` command to see what shared directories are available from the local system. For example:

```
$ sudo /usr/sbin/showmount -e
Export list for server.example.com
/export/myshare  client.example.com
/mnt/public      *
```

From a client Linux system, you can use the `showmount` command to see what shared directories are available from a selected computer. For example:

```
$ sudo /usr/sbin/showmount -e server.example.com
/export/myshare client.example.com
/mnt/public      *
```

Mounting NFS Shares

Use the `mount` command to mount a remote NFS share on the local computer. Here is an example:

```
$ sudo mkdir /mnt/server-share
$ sudo mount server.example.com:/export/myshare /mnt/server-share
```

This example notes the NFS server (`server.example.com`) and the shared directory from that server (`/export/myshare`). The local mount point, which must exist before mounting the share, appears at the end of the command (`/mnt/server-share`).

Pass NFS-specific options to the `mount` command by adding them after the `-o` option:

```
$ sudo mount -o rw,hard,intr server.example.com:/export/myshare /mnt/server-share
```

The `rw` option mounts the remote directory with read-write permissions, assuming that permission is available. With `hard` set, someone using the share will see a `server not responding` message when a read or write operation times out. If that happens, having set the `intr` option lets you interrupt a hung request to a remote server (type Ctrl+c).

By default, NFS version 3 (nfs3) protocol is used to connect to the share. To use NFS version 4, which is designed to work over the Internet and through firewalls, indicate that protocol as the file system type on the command line as follows:

```
$ sudo mount -t nfs4 server.example.com:/ /mnt/server-share
```

244

NOTE *Depending on which version of Ubuntu you are using, the implementation of NFS v4 may not be robust enough for production. It may be safer and/or more reliable to tunnel earlier versions of NFS over SSH. You can find more information on this topic with an Internet search for "nfs ssh", and especially look at* www.howtoforge.com/nfs_ssh_tunneling. *In addition, look at* http://tldp.org/HOWTO/NFS-HOWTO/security.html *for more on NFS security.*

Sharing Remote Directories with Samba

Samba is the open source implementation of the Windows file and print sharing protocol originally known as *Server Message Block* (SMB) and now called *Common Internet File System* (CIFS). There is an implementation of Samba in Linux, as well as in many other operating systems. To use samba, install the packages samba and samba-doc.

Graphical tools for sharing, querying, and mounting shared SMB directories from Windows include the Samba SWAT web-based administration tool. To use the SWAT tool in Linux, install the swat package. Next, read the instructions at https://help .ubuntu.com/community/Swat for details on how you can start SWAT.

Commands for working with Samba shares can be used to query SMB servers, mount directories, and share directories.

Viewing and Accessing Samba Shares

To scan your network for SMB hosts, type the following:

```
$ findsmb
                        *=DMB
                        +=LMB
IP ADDR          NETBIOS NAME  WORKGROUP/OS/VERSION
---------------------------------------------------------------------
192.168.1.1     SERVER1       +[MYWORKGROUP] [Unix] [Samba 3.0.25a-3.fc7]
```

To view a text representation of your network neighborhood (shared directories and printers), use smbtree:

```
$ sudo smbtree
Password: ******
MYGROUP
   \\THOMPSON              Samba Server Version 3.0.25a-3.fc7
      \\THOMPSON\hp2100    HP LaserJet 2100M Printer
      \\THOMPSON\IPC$      IPC Service (Samba Server Version 3.0.25a-3.fc7)
   \\EINSTEIN              Samba Server
      \\EINSTEIN\hp5550    HP DeskJet 5550 Printer
      \\EINSTEIN\IPC$      IPC Service (Samba Server)
```

To **add an existing Linux user as a Samba user,** use the `smbpasswd` command:

```
$ sudo smbpasswd -a francois
New SMB password: ******
Retype new SMB password: ******
Added user francois
```

> **NOTE** *You need to set up a Samba password for yourself to perform any of the commands that ask for a password.*

To **list services offered by a server to an anonymous user,** type the following:

```
$ smbclient -L server
Password: ******
Anynymous login successful
Domain=[MYGROUP] OS=[Unix] Server=Samba 3.0.25a-3.fc7
tree connect failed: NT_STSTUS_LOGON_FAILURE
```

Here's the output from `smbclient` for a specific user named francois:

```
$ smbclient -L server -U francois
Password: ******
Domain=[MYGROUP] OS=[Unix] Server=[Samba 3.0.25a-3.fc7]

        Sharename    Type    Comment
        ---------    ----    -------
        IPC$         IPC     IPC Service (Samba Server Version 3.0.25a-3.fc7)
        hp5550       Printer HP DeskJet 5550 Printer

            Server                Comment
            ---------             -------
            THOMPSON              Samba Server Version 3.0.25a-3.fc7

            Workgroup             Master
            ---------             -------
            MYGROUP               THOMPSON
```

To **connect to a Samba share FTP-style,** type the following:

```
$ smbclient //192.168.1.1/myshare -U francois
Password:
Domain=[MYWORKGROUP] OS=[Unix] Server=[Samba 3.0.25a-3.fc7]
smb: \>
```

As with most FTP clients, type `help` or `?` to see a list of available commands. Likewise, you can use common shell-type commands, such as `cd`, `ls`, `get`, `put`, and `quit`, to **get around on the SMB host.**

Mounting Samba Shares

You can **mount remote Samba shares on your local file system** much as you would a local file system or remote NFS file system. To mount the share:

```
$ sudo mount -t smbfs -o username=francois,password=MySecret \
    //192.168.1.1/myshare /mnt/mymount/
```

> **NOTE** *The Samba file system (*smbfs*) is deprecated and should no longer be used in some Linux distributions; however, this is the type supported on Ubuntu. In other distributions, the preferred method is to indicate CIFS (*-t cifs*) as the file system type when you mount a remote Samba share.*

You can **see the current connections and file locks** on a server using the smbstatus command. This will tell you if someone has mounted your shared directories or is currently using an smbclient connection to your server:

```
$ sudo smbstatus
Samba version 3.0.25a-3.fc7
PID     Username    Group    Machine
-------------------------------------------
 5466   francois         francois 10.0.0.55   (10.0.0.55)


Service    pid   machine    Connected at
-------------------------------------------
myshare    5644  10.0.0.55  Tue Jul  3 15:08:29 2007

No locked files
```

Looking Up Samba Hosts

NetBIOS names are used to identify hosts in Samba. You can **determine the IP address of a computer** using the nmblookup command to broadcast for a particular NetBIOS name on the local subnet as follows:

```
$ nmblookup thompson
querying thompson on 192.168.1.255
192.168.1.1 server1<00>
```

To **find the IP address for a server on a specific subnet,** use the -U option:

```
$ nmblookup -U 192.168.1.255 server1
querying server1 on 192.168.1.255
192.168.1.1 server1<00>
```

Checking Samba Configuration

If you are unable to use a Samba share or if you have other problems communicating with your Samba server, you can test the Samba configuration on the server. The testparm command can be used to **check your main Samba configuration file** (smb.conf):

```
$ testparm
Load smb config files from /etc/samba/smb.conf
Processing section "[homes]"
Processing section "[printers]"
Processing section "[myshare]"
Loaded services file OK.
Server role: ROLE_STANDALONE
Press Enter to see a dump of your service definitions
```

After pressing Enter as instructed, you can see the settings from your smb.conf file. Here's how an entry for the myshare shared directory, used earlier in an example, might appear in the smb.conf file:

```
[myshare]
        path = /home/francois
        username = francois
        valid users = francois
        hosts allow = einstein
        available = yes
```

This entry allows the Samba user francois to access the /home/francois directory (represented by the myshare share name) from the host computer named einstein. The share is shown as being currently available.

The previous example of testparm showed the entries you set in the smb.conf file. However, it doesn't **show all the default entries you didn't set**. You can view those using the -v option. Pipe it to the less command to page through the settings:

```
$ testparm -v | less
```

If you want to **test a configuration file before it goes live**, you can tell testparm to use a file other than /etc/samba/smb.conf:

```
$ testparm /etc/samba/test-smb.conf
```

Sharing Remote Directories with SSHFS

Another magical trick you can do over the SSH protocol is mount remote file systems. Using the SSH file system (sshfs), you can mount any directory from an SSH server that your user account can access from your local Linux system. sshfs provides encryption of the mount operation as well as of all the data being transferred. Another cool aspect of sshfs is that it requires no setup on the server side (other than having SSH service running).

Here is a quick procedure for **mounting a directory of documents from a remote server to a local directory**. Doing this only requires that the remote server is running SSH, is accessible, and that the directory you want is accessible to your user account on the server. Here we are mounting a directory named /var/docs from the host at 10.0.0.50 to a mount point called /mnt/docs on the local system:

```
$ sudo apt-get install sshfs          Install sshfs software
$ sudo mkdir /mnt/docs                 Create mount point
$ sudo sshfs chris@10.0.0.50:/var/docs /mnt/docs  Mount remote directory
```

When you are done using the remote directory, you can **unmount** it with the fusermount command (part of the fuse-utils package):

```
$ sudo fusermount -u /var/docs         Unmount remote directory
```

Chatting with Friends in IRC

Despite the emergence of instant messaging, Internet Relay Chat (IRC) is still used by a lot of people today. Freenode.net has tons of chat rooms dedicated to supporting major open source software projects. In fact, many people stay logged into them all day and just watch the discussions of their favorite Linux projects scroll by. This is known as *lurking*.

The xchat utility is a good graphical, multi-operating system IRC client. You can install just the xchat package or the GNOME bindings in the xchat-gnome package. If you install the latter, from Ubuntu, select Applications ⇨ Internet ⇨ XChat-GNOME IRC Chat. But the elite way to do IRC is to run a text-mode client in screen on an always-on machine, such as an old server. Another similar option is to use an IRC proxy client, also known as a *bouncer*, such as dircproxy (part of the dircproxy package).

The original IRC client was ircII. It allowed the addition of scripts — in some ways similar to macros found in productivity suites — that automated some of the commands and increased usability. The most popular was PhoEniX by Vassago. Then came BitchX, which started as an ircII script and then became a full-blown client. Today, most people use irssi. To **install and launch irssi** from Ubuntu, type:

```
$ sudo  apt-get install irssi
$ irssi -n JayJoe199x
```

In this example, the user name (nick) is set to JayJoe199x (you should choose your own). You should see a blue status bar at the bottom of the screen indicating that you are in Window 1, the status window. If this is the first time you've run irssi, the program will display help messages pointing you to the documentation. IRC commands are preceded with a / character. For example, to **connect to the freenode server**, type:

```
/connect chat.freenode.net
```

If you didn't add your user name on the command line, you are connected to chat
.freenode.net with the user name you are logged in under. On IRC, a chat room
is called a *channel* and has a pound sign (#) in front of the name. Next, try joining the
#centos IRC channel:

```
/join #centos
```

Your screen should look similar to Figure 12-1.

Figure 12-1: irssi connected to #centos on Freenode

NOTE   *As an Ubuntu user, you may want to join the #ubuntu channel.*

You are now in the channel in Window 2, as indicated in the status bar. Switch among
the irssi windows by typing Alt+1, Alt+2, and so on (or Ctrl+n and Ctrl+p). Note
that the Alt+1, Alt+2, and so on keys won't work inside a gnome-terminal window,
because the gnome-terminal eats those keystrokes. To get help at any time, type /help
command, where *command* is the name of the command you want more information
on. Help text will output in the status window, not necessarily the current window.

To add to the IRC chat, simply type a message and press Enter to send the message to
those in the channel. Type /part to leave a channel. Type /quit to exit the program.

There is a lot more to irssi. You can customize it and improve your experience significantly. Refer to the irssi documentation (www.irssi.org/documentation) for
more information about how to use irssi.

Using Text-Based E-mail Clients

Most Mail User Agents (MUAs) are GUI-based these days. So if you began using e-mail
in the past decade or so, you probably think of Evolution, Kmail, Thunderbird, or (on
Windows systems) Outlook when it comes to e-mail clients. On the first Unix and Linux
systems, however, e-mail was handled by text-based applications.

If you find yourself needing to check e-mail on a remote server or other text-based
environment, venerable text-based mail clients are available and still quite useful. In
fact, some hard core geeks still use text-based mail clients exclusively, touting their
efficiency and scoffing at HTML-based messages.

The mail clients described in this chapter expect your messages to be stored in standard MBOX format on the local system. That means that you are either logged into the mail server or you have already downloaded the messages locally (for example, by using POP3 or similar).

NOTE *Text-based mail clients can be used to read mail already downloaded by other mail clients. For example, you could open your Evolution mail Inbox file by typing* mail -f $HOME/.evolution/mail/loc/Inbox.

Managing E-mail with mail

The oldest command, and easiest to use when you just want a quick check for messages in the root user's mailbox on a remote server, is the mail command (/bin/mail), part of the mailx package. Although mail can be used interactively, it is often used for sending script-based emails. Here are some examples:

```
$ mail -s 'My Linux version' chris@example.com < /etc/lsb-release
$ ps auwx | mail -s 'My Process List' chris@example.com
```

The two mail examples just shown provide quick ways to mail off some text without having to open a GUI mail application. The first example sends the contents of the /etc/lsb-release file to the user chris@example.com. The subject (-s) is set to 'My Linux Version'. In the second example, a list of currently running processes (ps auwx) is sent to the same user with a subject of 'My Process List'.

NOTE *Before you can use the command line mail program, you must configure the package. There are many possible issues with mail servers that depend on your Internet Service Provider, or ISP. The configuration process is started as part of the installation when you run the following command:*

```
$ sudo apt-get install mailx
```

Used interactively, by default the mail command opens the mailbox set by your current shell's $MAIL value. For example:

```
$ echo $MAIL
/var/spool/mail/chris
```

NOTE *You may need to set this environment variable. The value should be /var/spool/mail/username, such as* chris *in this example. On Ubuntu,* MAIL *is not set by default, as the* mail *command is not installed by default.*

To read the mail for the root user, run the following command:

```
$ sudo mail
Mail version 8.1 6/6/93.  Type ? for help.
"/var/spool/mail/root": 25 messages 25 new
>U  1 logwatch@ab.1  Fri Jun 15 20:03  44/1667  "Logwatch for ab (Linux)"
```

```
U  2 logwatch@ab.1  Sat Jun 16 04:32  87/2526  "Logwatch for ab (Linux)"
   3 logwatch@ab.1  Sun Jun 17 04:32  92/2693  "Logwatch for ab (Linux)"
N  4 logwatch@ab.1  Fri Jun 22 09:28  44/1667  "Logwatch for ab (Linux)"
N  5 MAILER-DAEMON@ab  Fri Jun 22 09:28  93/3348  "Warning: could not send "
&
```

The current message has a greater-than sign (>) next to it. New messages have an N at the beginning, unread (but not new) messages have a U, and if there is no letter, the message has been read. The prompt at the bottom (&) is ready to accept commands.

At this point, you are in command mode. You can use simple commands to **move around** and **perform basic mail functions** in mail. Type ? to see a list of commands, or type the number of the message you want to see. Type v3 to open the third message in the vi editor. Type h18 to see a list of message headers that begins with message 18. To reply to message 7, type r7 (type your message, then put a dot on a line by itself to send the message). Type d4 to delete the fourth message (or d4-9 to delete messages four through nine). Type !bash to escape to the shell (then exit to return to mail).

Before you exit mail, know that any messages you view will be copied from your mailbox file to your $HOME/mbox file when you exit, unless you preserve them (pre*). To have all messages stay in your mailbox, exit by typing x. To save your changes to the mailbox, type q to exit.

You can open any file that is in MBOX format when you use mail. For example, if you are logged in as one user, but want to open the mailbox for the user chris, type this:

```
$ sudo mail -f /var/spool/mail/chris
```

Managing E-mail with mutt

If you want to use a command line mail client on an ongoing basis, we recommend you use mutt instead of mail. The mail command has many limitations, such as not being able to send attachments without encoding them in advance (such as with the uuencode command), while mutt has many features for handling modern e-mail needs. The mutt command is part of the mutt package, which you need to install to use this command. Configure mutt by editing /etc/Muttrc. You also need to configure sendmail to allow for sending e-mail.

Like mail, mutt can also be used to pop off a message from a script. mutt also adds the capability to **send attachments**. For example:

```
$ mutt -s "My Linux Version" -a /etc/lsb-release \
     chris@example.com < email-body.txt
$ mutt -s "My Linux Version" -a /etc/lsb-release \
     chris@example.com < /dev/null
```

The first example just shown includes the file `email-body.txt` as the body of the message and attaches the file `/etc/lsb-release` as an attachment. The second example sends the attachment, but has a blank message body (< `/dev/null`).

You can **begin your mutt mail session** (assuming your default mailbox is `$MAIL`) by simply typing `mutt`:

```
$ mutt
/home/chris/Mail does not exist. Create it? ([yes]/no): y


q:Quit  d:Del  u:Undel  s:Save  m:Mail  r:Reply  g:Group  ?:Help

   1 O   Jun 16 logwatch@ab      (  69) Logwatch for ab (Linux)
   2 O   Jun 18 logwatch@ab      ( 171) Logwatch for ab (Linux)
   3 O   Jun 18 Mail Delivery S ( 219) Warning: could not send message
   4 O   Jun 19 logwatch@ab      (  33) Logwatch for ab (Linux)

--Mutt: /var/spool/mail/root [Msgs:22 New:2 Old:20 63K]--(date/date)--(all)--
```

Because `mutt` is screen-oriented, it is easier to use than `mail`. As with `mail`, you **use key commands to move around in mutt.** As usual, type `?` to get help. Hints appear across the top bar to help you with your mail. Use the up and down arrow keys to highlight the messages you want to read. Press Enter to view the highlighted message. Use PageUp and PageDown to page through each message. Press `i` to return to the message headers.

Search forward for text using slash (/) or backwards using Escape slash (Esc-/). Type n to search again. Press Tab to jump to the next new or unread message. Or go to the previous one using Esc-Tab. Type s to save the current message to a file. Type d to delete a message and u to undelete it.

To send a new mail message, type m. After adding the recipient and subject, a blank message opens in `joe` (or whatever you have your `$EDITOR` set to). After exiting the message body, type a to add an attachment, if you like. Type ? to see other ways of manipulating your message, headers or attachments. Type y to send the message or q to abort the send.

When you are done, type x to exit without changing your mailbox; type q to exit and incorporate the changes you made (messages read, deleted, and so on).

Summary

Network access commands provide quick and efficient ways to get content you need over a network. The `elinks` web browser is a popular screen-oriented command for browsing the web or taking a quick look at any HTML file. Dozens of commands are available to download files over FTP, HTTP, SSH, or other protocols, including `wget`, `curl`, `lftp`, and `scp`.

For more ongoing access to remote directories of files, this chapter covers how to use NFS, Samba, and SSHFS command tools. You can do IRC chats, which are popular among open source projects, using the `irssi` command. For text-based e-mail clients, you have choices such as the `mail` and `mutt` commands.

13

Doing Remote System Administration

Most professional Linux administrators do not run a graphical interface on their Internet servers. As a result, when you need to access other computers for remote administration, you will almost surely need to work from the command line at some time. Luckily there are many feature-rich Linux commands to help you do so.

Tools associated with the Secure Shell (SSH) service not only allow remote login and file transfer, but they also offer encrypted communication to keep your remote administration work secure. With tools such as Virtual Network Computing (VNC), you can have a server's remote desktop appear on your local client computer. These and other features for doing remote systems administration are described in this chapter.

IN THIS CHAPTER

Configuring SSH

Using SSH for remote login

Using SSH to do tunneling

Using SSH to provide proxy service

Using SSH with private keys

Using screen remote multiplexing terminal

Accessing remote Windows desktops

Sharing remote Linux desktops with VNC

Doing Remote Login and Tunneling with SSH

Linux's big brother Unix grew up on university networks. At a time when the only users of these networks were students and professors, and with networks mostly isolated from each other, there was little need for security.

Applications and protocols that were designed in those times (the 1970s and 1980s) reflect that lack of concern for encryption and authentication. SMTP is a perfect example of that. This is also true of the first generation of Unix remote tools: telnet, ftp (file transfer protocol), rsh (remote shell), rcp (remote copy), rexec (remote execution), and rlogin (remote login). These tools send user credentials and traffic in clear text. For that reason, they are very dangerous to use on the public, untrusted Internet, and have become mostly deprecated and replaced with the Secure Shell (SSH) commands (ssh, scp, sftp commands and related services).

Although there are still some uses for the legacy remote commands (see the "Using Legacy Communications Tools" sidebar), most of this section describes how to use SSH commands to handle most of your needs for remote communications commands.

Using Legacy Communications Tools

Despite the fact that SSH provides better tools for remote communications, legacy communications commands, sometimes referred to as "r" commands, are still included with most major Linux distributions. Some of these tools will perform faster than equivalent SSH commands because they don't need to do encryption. So some old-school Unix administrators may use them occasionally on private networks or still include them in old scripts. Although for the most part you should ignore these legacy remote commands, one of these commands in particular can be useful in some cases: `telnet`.

The `telnet` command is still used to communicate with some network appliances (routers, switches, UPSes, and so on) that do not have the horsepower to run an `ssh` daemon. Even though it poses a security risk, some appliance manufacturers include `telnet` support anyway.

One good way to use the `telnet` command, however, is for troubleshooting many Internet protocols such as POP3, SMTP, HTTP, and others. Under the hood, these plain-text protocols are simply automated telnet sessions during which a client (such as a browser or mail user agent) exchanges text with a server. The only difference is the TCP port in use. Here is an example of how you could telnet to the HTTP port (80) of a web server:

```
$ telnet www.example.com 80
Trying 208.77.188.166...
Connected to www.example.com.
Escape character is '^]'.
GET / HTTP/1.0
          Enter a second carriage return here
HTTP/1.1 200 OK
```

Similarly, you can telnet to a mail server on port 25 (SMTP) and 110 (POP3) and issue the proper commands to troubleshoot e-mail problems. For more complete descriptions of using the `telnet` command to troubleshoot network protocols, refer to *Linux Troubleshooting Bible* (ISBN 076456997X, Wiley Publishing, 2004), pages 505 and 508.

If you need to forcibly exit your telnet session, type the escape sequence (Ctrl+] by default). This will stop sending your keyboard input to the remote end and bring you to `telnet`'s command prompt where can type `quit` or `?` for more options.

Configuring SSH

Nowadays, the Swiss Army knife of remote system administration is Secure Shell (SSH). SSH commands and services replace all the old remote tools and add strong encryption, public keys, and many other features. The most common implementation of SSH in the Linux world is OpenSSH (www.openssh.com), maintained by the OpenBSD project. OpenSSH provides both client and server components.

To install the OpenSSH server, run the following command:

```
$ sudo apt-get install openssh-server
```

Here are a few facts about SSH:

❑ For Windows, you can use the Linux SSH tools within Cygwin (www.cygwin.com). But unless you're already using Cygwin (a Linux-like environment for Windows), we recommend PuTTY (www.chiark.greenend.org/uk/sgatatham/putty). PuTTY is a powerful open source Telnet/SSH client.

❑ Use SSH version 2 whenever possible, because it is the most secure. Some SSH-enabled network appliances may only support older, less secure versions. OpenSSH supports all versions. Some older versions of Ubuntu accepted SSH v1 and v2 connections. Newer releases accept version 2 by default.

❑ In Ubuntu, run /etc/init.d/ssh start to **start the SSH service** (sshd daemon). To configure the service, edit the /etc/ssh/sshd_config file.

❑ To **configure the ssh client,** edit the /etc/ssh/ssh_config file.

If you prefer to use graphical tools to administer your remote Linux system, you can enable *X11 Tunneling* (also called *X11 Port Forwarding*). With X11 Tunneling enabled (on both the SSH client and server), you can start an X application on the server and have it displayed on the client. All communication across that connection is encrypted.

Ubuntu comes with X11 forwarding turned on (X11Forwarding yes) for the server (sshd daemon). You still need to enable it on the client side. To **enable X11 forwarding on the client for a one-time session,** connect with the following command:

```
$ ssh -X francois@myserver
```

To **enable X11 forwarding permanently for all users,** add ForwardX11 yes to /etc/ssh/ssh _config . To enable it permanently for a specific user only, add the line to that user's ~.ssh/config. Once that setting has been added, the -X option is no longer required to use X11 Tunneling. Run ssh to connect to the remote system as you would normally. To test that the tunneling is working, run xclock after ssh'ing into the remote machine, and it should appear on your client desktop.

SSH Tunneling is an excellent way to securely use remote graphical tools!

Logging in Remotely with ssh

To **securely log in to a remote host,** you can use either of two different syntaxes to specify the user name:

```
$ ssh -l francois myserver
$ ssh francois@myserver
```

However, `scp` and `sftp` commands (discussed in Chapter 12) only support the *user@server* syntax, so we recommend you get used to that one. If you don't specify the user name, `ssh` will attempt to log in using the same user you are logged in as locally. Once connected, if you need to **forcibly exit your ssh session**, type the escape sequence of a tilde followed by a period (~.).

Accessing SSH on a Different Port

For security purposes, a remote host may have its **SSH service listening a different port** than the default port number 22. If that's the case, use -p option to `ssh` to contact that service:

```
$ ssh -p 12345 francois@turbosphere.com    Connect to SSH on port 12345
```

Using SSH to Do Tunneling (X11 Port Forwarding)

With SSH tunneling configured as described earlier, the SSH service forwards X Window System clients to your local display. However, tunneling can be used with other TCP-based protocols as well.

Tunneling for X11 Clients

The following sequence of commands illustrates **starting an SSH session, then starting a few X applications so they appear on the local desktop:**

```
$ ssh francois@myserver                        Start ssh connection to myserver
francois@myserver's password: *******
[francois@myserver ~}$ echo $DISPLAY           Show the current X display entry
localhost:10.0                                 SSH sets display to localhost:10.0
[francois@myserver ~}$ xeyes&                  Show moving desktop eyes
[francois@myserver ~}$ gnome-cups-manager&     Configure remote printers
[francois@myserver ~}$ gksu services-admin&    Change system services
```

Tunneling for CUPS Printing Remote Administration

X11 is not the only protocol that can be tunneled over SSH. You can **forward any TCP port** with SSH. This is a great way to configure secure tunnels quickly and easily. No configuration is required on the server side.

For example, `myserver` is a print server with the CUPS printing service's web-based user interface enabled (running on port 631). That GUI is only accessible from the local machine. On the following client PC, we tunnel to that service using `ssh` with the following options:

```
$ ssh -L 1234:localhost:631 myserver
```

This example forwards port 1234 on the client PC to localhost port 631 on the server. We can now browse to http://localhost:1234 on the client PC. This will be redirected to cupsd listening on port 631 on the server.

Tunneling to an Internet Service

Another example for using SSH tunneling is when your **local machine is blocked from connecting to the Internet,** but you can get to another machine (myserver) that has an Internet connection. The following example lets you visit the Google.com web site (HTTP, TCP port 80) across an SSH connection to a computer named myserver that has a connection to the Internet:

```
$ ssh -L 12345:google.com:80 myserver
```

With this example, any connection to the local port 12345 is directed across an SSH tunnel to myserver, which in turn opens a connection to Google.com port 80. You can now browse to http://localhost:12345 and use myserver as a relay to the Google.com web site. Since you're only using ssh to forward a port and not to obtain a shell on the server, you can add the -N option to **prevent the execution of remote commands:**

```
$ ssh -L 12345:google.com:80 -N myserver
```

Using SSH as a SOCKS Proxy

The previous example demonstrates that you can forward a port from the client to a machine other than the server. In the real world, the best way to **get your browser traffic out of your local network via an encrypted tunnel** is using the SSH built-in SOCKS proxy feature. For example:

```
$ ssh -D 12345 myserver
```

The dynamic (-D) option of ssh lets you log in to myserver (as usual). As long as the connection is open, all requests directed to port 12345 are then forwarded to myserver. Next, set your browser of choice to use localhost port 12345 as a SOCKS v5 proxy and you're good to go. Do not enter anything on the fields for HTTP and other protocols. They all work over SOCKS. See the Firefox Connections Settings window in Figure 13-1.

To test your setup, try disconnecting your ssh session and browsing to any web site. Your browser should give you a proxy error.

From a Windows client, the same port forwarding can be accomplished in Putty by selecting Connection ⇨ SSH ⇨ Tunnels.

Figure 13-1: Use the Firefox Connections Settings window for proxy configuration.

Using ssh with Public Key Authentication

Up to this point, we've only used `ssh` with the default password authentication. The `ssh` command also supports public key authentication. This offers several benefits:

❏ **Automated logins for scripts and cron jobs**: By assigning an empty passphrase, you can use `ssh` in a script to log in automatically. Although this is convenient, it is also dangerous, because anybody who gets to your key file can connect to any machine you can. Configuring for automatic login can also be done with a passphrase and a key agent. This is a compromise between convenience and security, as explained below.

❏ **A two-factor authentication:** When using a passphrase-protected key for interactive logins, authentication is done using two factors (the key and the passphrase) instead of one.

Using Public Key Logins

Here's the process for **setting up key-based communications** between two Linux systems. In the following example, we use empty passphrases for no-password logins. If you prefer to protect your key with a passphrase, simply enter it when prompted during the first step (key pair creation).

On the client system, run the following `ssh-keygen` command **to generate the key pair** while logged in as the user that needs to initiate communications:

```
$ ssh-keygen
Generating public/private rsa key pair.
Enter file in which to save the key (/home/chris/.ssh/id_rsa): <Enter>
Enter passphrase (empty for no passphrase): <Enter>
Enter same passphrase again: <Enter>
Your identification has been saved in /home/chris/.ssh/id_rsa.
Your public key has been saved in /home/chris/.ssh/id_rsa.pub.
The key fingerprint is:
ac:db:a4:8e:3f:2a:90:4f:05:9f:b4:44:74:0e:d3:db chris@host.domain.com
```

Note that at each prompt, you pressed the Enter key to create the default key file name and to enter (and verify) an empty passphrase. You now have a private key that you need to keep very safe, especially since in this procedure you didn't protect it with a passphrase.

You also now have a public key (`id_rsa.pub`), which was created by the previous command. This public key needs to be installed on hosts you want to connect to. The content of `~/.ssh/id_rsa.pub` needs to be copied (securely) to `~/.ssh/authorized_keys2` for the user you want to `ssh` to on the remote server. The `authorized_keys2` file can contain more than one public key, if multiple users use `ssh` to connect to this account.

Log in to the *remote server* system as the user that you will want to `ssh` with the key. If you don't already have a `~/.ssh` directory, the first step is to create it as follows:

```
$ cd
$ mkdir .ssh
$ chmod 700 .ssh
```

The next step is to copy (securely) the public key file from the client and put it in an authorized keys file on the server. This can be accomplished using `scp`. For example, assuming a client system named `myclient` and a client user named `chris`, type the following on the server:

```
$ scp chris@myclient:/home/chris/.ssh/id_rsa.pub .    Get client id_rsa.pub
$ cat id_rsa.pub >> ~/.ssh/authorized_keys2           Add to your keys
$ chmod 600 ~/.ssh/authorized_keys2                   Close permissions
$ rm id_rsa.pub                    Delete public key after copying its content
```

This procedure can also be accomplished by editing the `~/.ssh/authorized_keys2` text file on the server and copy/pasting the public key from the client. Make sure you do so securely over ssh, and make sure not to insert any line breaks in the key. The entire key should fit on a single line, even if it wraps on your screen.

Then from the client (using the client and server user accounts you just configured), you can just ssh to the server and the key will be used. If you set a passphrase, you will be asked for it as you would for a password.

Saving Private Keys to Use from a USB Flash Drive

If you'd like to **store your private key** somewhere safer than your hard drive, you can use a USB flash drive (sometimes called a thumbdrive or pen drive):

```
$ mv ~/.ssh/id_rsa /media/THUMBDRIVE1/myprivatekey
```

And then, when you want **to use the key,** insert the USB drive and type the following:

```
$ ssh -i /media/THUMBDRIVE1/myprivatekey chris@myserver
```

Using keys with passphrases is more secure than simple passwords, but also more cumbersome. To make your life easier, you can use ssh-agent to **store unlocked keys for the duration of your session.** When you add an unlocked key to your running ssh-agent, you can run ssh using the key without being prompted for the passphrase each time.

To see what the ssh-agent command does, run the command with no option. A three-line bash script appears when you run it, as follows:

```
$ ssh-agent
SSH_AUTH_SOCK=/tmp/ssh-SkEQZ18329/agent.18329; export SSH_AUTH_SOCK;
SSH_AGENT_PID=18330; export SSH_AGENT_PID;
echo Agent pid 18330;
```

The first two lines of the output just shown need to be executed by your shell. Copy and paste those lines into your shell now. You can avoid this extra step by starting ssh-agent and having the bash shell evaluate its output by typing the following:

```
$ eval `ssh-agent`
Agent pid 18408
```

You can now unlock keys and add them to your running agent. Assuming you have already run the ssh-keygen command to create a default key, let's **add that default key** using the ssh-add command:

```
$ ssh-add
Enter passphrase for /home/chris/.ssh/id_rsa: *******
Identity added: /home/chris/.ssh/id_rsa (/home/chris/.ssh/id_rsa)
```

Next you could add the key you stored on the USB thumbdrive:

```
$ ssh-add /media/THUMBDRIVE1/myprivatekey
```

Use the -l option to ssh-add to **list the keys stored in the agent:**

```
$ ssh-add -l
2048 f7:b0:7a:5a:65:3c:cd:45:b5:1c:de:f8:26:ee:8d:78 /home/chris/.ssh/id_rsa
```

```
(RSA)
2048 f7:b0:7a:5a:65:3c:cd:45:b5:1c:de:f8:26:ee:8d:78
/media/THUMBDRIVE1/myprivatekey (RSA)
```

To **remove one key from the agent,** for example the one from the USB thumbdrive, run `ssh-add` with the `-d` option as follows:

```
$ ssh-add -d /media/THUMBDRIVE1/myprivatekey
```

To **remove all the keys stored in the agent,** use the `-D` option:

```
$ ssh-add -D
```

Using screen: A Rich Remote Shell

The `ssh` command gives you only one screen. If you lose that screen, you lose all you were doing on the remote computer. That can be very bad if you were in the middle of something important, such as a 12-hour compile. And if you want to do three things at once, for example `vi httpd.conf`, `tail -f error_log`, and `service httpd reload`, you need to open three separate `ssh` sessions.

Essentially, `screen` is a terminal multiplexer. If you are a system administrator working on remote servers, `screen` is a great tool for managing a remote computer with only a command line interface available. Besides allowing multiple shells sessions, `screen` also lets you disconnect from it, and then reconnect to that same `screen` session later.

The `screen` software package is installed by default with Ubuntu.

To **use screen,** run the `ssh` command from a client system to connect to the Linux server where `screen` is installed. Then simply type the following command:

```
$ screen
```

If you ran `screen` from a Terminal window, you should first see a welcome message asking for pizza and beer, and then see a regular bash prompt in the window. To control `screen`, press the Ctrl+a key combo, followed by another keystroke. For example, Ctrl+a followed by ? (noted as Ctrl+a, ?) displays the help screen. With `screen` running, here are some commands and control keys you can use to operate `screen`.

```
$ screen -ls                                 List active screens
There is a screen on:
        7089.pts-2.myserver     (Attached)   Shows screen is attached
1 Socket in /var/run/screen/S-francois.
$ Ctrl+a, a                                  Change window title
Set window's title to: My Server            Type a new title
$ Ctrl+a, c                                  Create a new window
$ Ctrl+a, "                                  Show active window titles
Num Name                    Flags
  0 My Server                                Up/down arrows change windows
  1 bash
```

```
$ Ctrl+a, d                              Detach screen from terminal
$ screen -ls                             List active screens
There is a screen on:
        7089.pts-2.myserver   (Detached)  Shows screen is detached
1 Socket in /var/run/screen/S-francois.
```

The screen session just shown resulted in two windows (each running a bash shell) being created. You can create as many as you like and name them as you choose. Also, instead of detaching from the screen session, you could have just closed it by exiting the shell in each open window (type exit or Ctrl+d).

When the screen session is detached, you are returned to the shell that was opened when you first logged into the server. You can reconnect to that screen session as described in the following section, "Reconnecting to a screen Session."

Table 13-1 shows some other useful control key sequences available with screen.

Table 13-1: Control Keys for Using screen

Keys	Description
Ctrl+a, ?	Show help screen.
Ctrl+a, c	Create new window.
Ctrl+a, d	Detach screen from terminal. The screen session and its windows keep running.
Ctrl+a, "	View list of windows.
Ctrl+a, '	Prompt for number or name of window to switch to.
Ctrl+a, n	View next window.
Ctrl+a, p	View previous window.
Ctrl+a, [	Terminal's vertical scroll is disabled in screen. These keys turn on screen's scrollback mode. Press Enter twice to exit.
Ctrl+a, Shift+a	Rename current window.
Ctrl+a, w	Show the list of window names in the title bar.

Reconnecting to a screen Session

After you detach from a screen session, you can return to that screen again later (even after you log out and disconnect from the server). **To reconnect** when only one screen is running, type the following:

```
$ screen -r
```

If there are several `screen` sessions running, `screen -r` won't work. For example, this shows what happens when two detached `screen` sessions are running:

```
$ screen -r
There are several suitable screens on:
        7089.pts-2.myserver     (Detached)
        7263.pts-2.myserver     (Detached)
Type "screen [-d] -r [pid.]tty.host" to resume one of them.
```

As the output suggests, you could identify the `screen` session you want by its name (which, by default, is a combination of the session's process ID, tty name, and host-name). For example:

```
$ screen -r 7089.pts-2.myserver
```

Naming screen Sessions

Instead of using the default names, you can create more descriptive names for your screen sessions when you start `screen`. For example:

```
$ screen -S mysession
$ screen -ls
There is a screen on:
        26523.mysession (Attached)
```

Sharing screen Sessions

The `screen` command also allows the sharing of screens. This feature is great for tech support, because each person connected to the session can both type into and watch the current session. Creating a named screen, as in the preceding section, makes this easier. Then another person on a different computer can `ssh` to the server (using the same user name) and type the following:

```
$ screen -x mysession
```

Just as with `screen -r`, if there's only one screen running, you don't need to specify which screen you're connecting to:

```
$ screen -x
```

Using a Remote Windows Desktop

Many system administrators who become comfortable using a Linux desktop prefer to do administration of their Windows systems from Linux whenever possible. Linux provides tools such as rdesktop and tsclient, which allow you to connect to a Windows system running Windows Terminal Services.

To be able to connect to your Windows system desktop from Linux, you have to enable Remote Desktop from your Windows system. To do that from Windows XP (and others)

265

right-click My Computer and select Properties. Then choose the Remote tab from the System Properties window and select the Allow users to connect remotely to this computer check box. Select which users you want to let connect to the Windows box and click OK.

Now, from Linux, you can use either `rdesktop` or `tsclient` (a graphical wrapper around `rdesktop`) to connect to the Windows system using Remote Desktop Protocol (RDP). Ubuntu comes with both of these applications installed.

Connecting to a Windows Desktop with tsclient

If you are used to using Windows' Remote Desktop Connection (formerly known as *Terminal Services Client*) to connect from one Windows box to another, you will probably find the tsclient tool a good way to connect to a Windows desktop from Linux. Running `tsclient` opens a Terminal Server Client window that mimics the Windows remote desktop client's user interface.

When the tsclient package is installed, launch tsclient by selecting Applications ➪ Internet ➪ Terminal Server Client from the GNOME desktop or by typing the following from the shell:

```
$ tsclient &
```

Figure 13-2 shows the Terminal Server Client window.

Figure 13-2: Terminal Server Client (tsclient) connects to Windows desktops.

Probably all you need to enter on this screen is the name or IP address of the Windows system. You will probably be prompted for user name and password, depending on how the Windows system is configured. Select different tabs to further refine your connection to the remote Windows desktop.

Note that `tsclient` can also be used as a client for VNC and XDMCP.

Connecting to a Windows Desktop with rdesktop

If you prefer not to use the `tclient` wrapper described above, you can **log in to a remote Windows desktop** using the `rdesktop` command. The `rdesktop` command requests a login to the Windows machine, then opens the Windows desktop for the user after you log in. Here are examples of the `rdesktop` command:

```
$ rdesktop 172.16.18.66           Login to desktop at IP address
$ rdesktop -u chris -p M6pyXX win1  Identify user/password for host win1
$ rdesktop -f win1                 Run rdesktop in full-screen mode
$ rdesktop -0 -r sound:local win1  Direct sound from server to client
$ rdesktop -E win1                 Disable client/server encryption
```

If you disable client/server encryption, the login packet is encrypted, but everything after that is not. Although this can improve performance greatly, anyone sniffing your LAN would be able to see your clear-text communications (including any interactive logins after the initial login packet). Other `rdesktop` options that can improve performance or your Windows desktop include -m (don't send mouse motion events), -D (hide window manager's decorations), and -K (don't override window manager key bindings).

Using Remote Linux Desktop and Applications

The X Window System (X) should not be run on typical production servers for security and performance reasons. But thanks to the client-server nature of X, you can run an X-enabled program on a remote machine with its graphical output directed to your desktop. In that relationship, the application running from the remote machine is referred to as the *X client*, and your desktop is the *X server*. When running remote X applications on untrusted networks or the Internet, use SSH forwarding as described earlier. On trusted LANs, do it without SSH, as described here.

By default, your X desktop will not allow remote X applications to connect (pop up) on your desktop. You can **allow remote apps on your desktop** using the `xhost` command. On your local Linux display, use the `xhost` command to control which remote machines can connect to X and display applications on your desktop. Here are examples of `xhost`:

```
$ xhost                    List allowed hosts
access control enabled, only authorized clients can connect
```

267

```
$ xhost +              Disable access control (dangerous)
access control disabled, clients can connect from any host
$ xhost -              Re-enable access control
access control enabled, only authorized clients can connect
$ xhost remotemachine  Add an allowed host
remotemachine being added to access control list
```

Access control should be completely disabled only for troubleshooting purposes. However, with access enabled for a particular host machine (remotemachine in this case), you can do the following from a shell on the remote computer to have X applications from that machine appear on the local desktop (in this case called localmachine):

```
$ export DISPLAY=localmachine:0    Set the DISPLAY to localmachine:0
$ xterm &                          Open remote Terminal on local
$ xclock &                         Open remote clock on local
$ gtali &                          Open remote dice game on local
```

After setting the DISPLAY variable on remotemachine to point to localmachine, any application run from that shell on remotemachine should appear on Desktop 0 on local-machine. In this case, we started the Terminal window, clock, and game applications.

> **NOTE**   *On recent versions of Ubuntu, the X server doesn't listen for TCP connections by default. To allow remote X connections, edit the* /etc/gdm/ gdm.conf-custom *file on the X server as follows:*
>
> [security]
> DisallowTCP=false
>
> *Then restart X Window.*

Sharing X applications in this way between Linux and UNIX hosts is pretty easy. However, it is not trivial to use across other computer platforms. If your desktop runs Windows, you have to run an X server. A free solution is Cygwin, which includes an X server. There are also feature-rich commercial X servers, but they can be very expensive. To share remote desktops across different operating system platforms, we suggest you use Virtual Network Computing (VNC).

Sharing Desktops Using VNC

Virtual Network Computing (VNC) consists of server and client software that lets you assume remote control of a **full desktop display from one computer on another**. In Ubuntu, the vncviewer command comes pre-installed to access a remote desktop on your display (client), but you need the vncserver package to share a desktop from your computer (server). To install the vncserver package, type the following:

```
$ sudo apt-get install vncserver
```

VNC clients and servers are available for, and interoperable with, many different operating systems. VNC servers are available on Linux, Windows (32-bit), Mac OS X, and UNIX systems. VNC clients are offered on those, and many other types of systems (including OS/2, PalmOS, and even as a Java application running in a web browser).

Setting Up the VNC Server

From your Linux desktop, we'll assume you are using the default display (DISPLAY=:0) as your local desktop. So we'll set out to create independent displays accessible via VNC. To start, open the /etc/vnc.conf file on the Linux system acting as your VNC server (as root user) using any text editor:

```
# vi /etc/vnc.conf
```

In that file, verify the settings. Note that the configuration file is used each time you run the vncserver program.

Then as each user, run the vncpasswd command to create the password each of those users will need to connect to their own desktops on the VNC server. In our example, we run the following as the user francois:

```
$ vncpasswd
Password: *******
Verify: *******
```

Finally, you can start the VNC server (vncserver). Type the following as root user:

```
$ vncserver
```

> **NOTE** By default, vncserver is not set up as a system service. See Chapter 11 for more on defining commands as services.

If you are using the iptables firewall built into your system, make sure you open the port(s) for VNC. Each display runs on its own port. Display number N is accessed on TCP port 5900+N. For example, display 1 is accessible on port 5901. Refer to Chapter 14 for more details on iptables.

Starting Up the VNC Client

With the VNC server running, you can connect to a desktop on that server from any of the client systems mentioned earlier (Windows, Linux, Mac OS X, Unix, and so on). For example, assuming your VNC server is on a system named myserver, you could type the following command to **start that remote desktop** from another Linux system:

```
$ vncviewer myserver:1          Connect as francois on display 1
$ vncviewer myserver:2          Connect as chris on display 2
```

Unless you define some commands to start up, you will only see the background screen for an X Window System display, with cross-hatching. To get beyond this, you need to run X Window programs on the server system, or from your client system, pointing to the VNC X display. For example:

```
$ xterm -display myserver:1 &
$ metacity --display myserver:1 &
```

> **NOTE** *Most X Window programs specify which X server to use (the VNC server in this example) with a* -display *option. The metacity window manager, however, uses two leading dashes for* --display.

You can also use `tsclient` to connect; for this example, you would just specify `myserver:1` as the computer and VNC as the protocol.

Using VNC on Untrusted Networks with SSH

VNC is a considered to be an insecure protocol. The password is sent using fairly weak encryption, and the rest of the session is not encrypted at all. For that reason, when using VNC over an untrusted network or Internet, we recommend you tunnel it over SSH.

For a general description of how the SSH service works, refer to the "Doing Remote Login and Tunneling with SSH" section earlier in this chapter. To forward VNC display 2 (port 5902) on the computer named `myserver`, to the same local port, type the following:

```
$ ssh -L 5902:localhost:5902 myserver
```

> **NOTE** *If you start using VNC routinely, you may want to look at* tightvnc *(in the package of the same name). Although it's not included with Ubuntu,* tightvnc *is another open source implementation of the VNC protocol, under active development and with newer features and optimizations. These features include built-in ssh tunneling.*

Sharing a VNC Desktop with Vino

If you're running GNOME and would like to **share your existing GNOME desktop** (`display :0`), you can do so with Vino (vino package). From the GNOME Desktop panel, select System ➪ Preference ➪ Remote Desktop to display the Remote Desktop Preferences window (`vino-preferences` command) shown in Figure 13-3.

In the Remote Desktop Preferences window, selecting the Allow other users to view your desktop check box lets remote VNC viewers view your desktop. Selecting the Allow other users to control your desktop check box lets others actually manipulate your desktop with their mouse and keyboard.

Figure 13-3: Vino lets remote users view, and possibly control, your desktop.

If the Ask you for confirmation check box is selected, a remote request to view your desktop causes a pop-up window to okay the connection before the requestor can see your desktop. Selecting the Require the user to enter this password check box is a good idea, to prevent those without a password from viewing your desktop. (Be sure the password is at least eight characters.)

As the Remote Desktop Preferences window notes, you can use vncviewer from another Linux system (with the address and display number shown) to display the shared desktop to another system. However, VNC clients from many different operating systems should work as well.

Summary

If you ever find yourself in a position where you need to administer multiple Linux systems, you have a rich set of commands with Linux for doing remote system administration. The Secure Shell (SSH) facility offers encrypted communications between clients and servers for remote login, tunneling, and file transfer.

Virtual Network Computing (VNC) lets one Linux system share its desktop with a client system so that the remote desktop appears right on the client's desktop. With tools such as Vino, you can even share a desktop in such a way that the VNC server and client can both work from the same desktop at the same time.

14

Locking Down Security

Securing your Linux system means first restricting access to the user accounts and services on that system. After that, security means checking that no one has gotten around the defenses you have set up.

Ubuntu, Debian, and other systems based on those Linux distributions are designed to be secure by default. That means that there are no user accounts with blank passwords, and that most network services (Web, FTP, and so on) are off by default (even if their software is installed).

Although many of the commands covered in this book can be used to check and improve the security of your Linux system, some basic Linux features are particularly geared toward security. For example, secure user accounts with good password protection, a solid firewall, and consistent logging (and log monitoring) are critical to having a secure Linux system. Commands related to those features, plus some advanced features, such as SELinux and tripwire, are covered in this chapter.

Working with Users and Groups

During most Linux installation procedures, you are asked to assign a password to the root user (for system administration). Then you might be asked to create a user name of your choice and assign a password to that as well (for everyday computer use). We encourage you to always log in as a regular user and only su or sudo to the root account when necessary. Once Linux is installed, you can use commands or graphical tools to add more users, modify user accounts, and assign and change passwords.

IN THIS CHAPTER

Add user accounts and change user settings with useradd

Change user accounts with usermod

Delete users with userdel

Add, change, and manage passwords with passwd

Manage groups with groupadd, groupmod, and groupdel

See who's logged in with last, lastb, and who

Configure firewalls with iptables

Manage log files with logrotate and logwatch

Check out advanced security with SELinux, tripwire, and APT

Ubuntu enhances security by disabling logins as root, by default. Instead, during installation, you set up a user, with a password, who can perform administrative functions. On Ubuntu, use the sudo command to perform individual root commands. The sudo command prompts for the administrative password, typically your password. This way, you avoid most issues of performing some command as root that you did not intend.

Managing Users the GUI Way

For an Ubuntu desktop system with X, you can manage users and groups with the User Manager window (System ⇨ Administration ⇨ Users and Groups). When managing user accounts for servers, one option is to use web-based GUIs. The most commonly used general-purpose tool is Webmin (www.webmin.com). Make sure you do not run Webmin on its default port (10000) for security reasons. You can also use special-purpose web interfaces. For example, there are many web hosting automation GUIs, such as cPanel (www.cpanel.com), Plesk (www.swsoft.com/plesk), and Ensim (www.ensim.com).

Adding User Accounts

To **add new users,** you can use the useradd command. The only option that is required to add a new user is the user name you are adding. You can see some of the default settings for adding a new user by entering the -D option:

```
$ useradd -D            Show useradd default values
GROUP=100               Set group ID to 100 (users)
HOME=/home              Set base home directory to /home
INACTIVE=-1             Password expiration is disabled (-1)
EXPIRE=                 Don't set date to disable user account
SHELL=/bin/sh           Set the default shell to /bin/bash
SKEL=/etc/skel          Copy default config files from /etc/skel to $HOME
CREATE_MAIL_SPOOL=no    Create a mail spool directory
```

Ubuntu and other Debian systems override the default group (100) and create a new group for every user. By default, the user ID assigned to the first user created is 1000 and the group ID is also 1000. The group name is the same as the user name. The home directory is the user name appended to /home. So, for example, if you created the first regular user account on the system as follows:

```
$ sudo useradd -m willz
```

The result would be a new user account with a willz user name (UID 1001) and willz group name (GID 1001). The -m option tells useradd to create a home directory of /home/willz, and copy a set of configuration files (each beginning with a ".") to the home directory from /etc/skel. The account would remain active indefinitely (no expiration date). **Add a password** as follows, and in most cases that's all you need to do to have a working user account.

```
$ sudo passwd horatio
Changing password for user horatio
New UNIX password: ********
Retype new UNIX password: ********
passwd: all authentication tokens updated successfully.
```

NOTE   *Remember to use strong, non–dictionary-based passwords.*

There are many options you can enter to **override the defaults** when you create a user.
Combine the different options as you choose. Here are some examples:

`$ sudo useradd -u 1101 -g 1300 skolmes`	`Use specific UID and GID for user`
`$ sudo useradd -m -d /home/jj jones`	`Create /var/x/jj home directory`
`$ sudo useradd -G support,sales timd`	`Add user to support and sales groups`
`$ sudo useradd -c "Tom G. Lotto" tlot`	`Add user's full name to comment field`
`$ sudo useradd -s /bin/tcsh joeq`	`Assign a new default shell (tcsh); you`
	`must install this shell`
`$ sudo useradd -e 2008-04-01 jerry`	`Add account to expire April 01, 2008`
`$ sudo useradd -f 0 jdoe`	`Create a disabled account`
`$ sudo useradd -s /sbin/nologin billt`	`Keep user from shelling in`
`$ sudo useradd billyq`	`Prevent creation of home directory, no -m`

Before you can add a user to a group, that group must exist (see the `groupadd` command in the "Adding Groups" section later in this chapter). A user must belong to
one initial group that can be defined with –g and can also belong to supplementary
groups, defined with –G.

To **list the group(s) that a user belongs to**, use the `groups` command:

`$ groups francois`	`List the groups that a user belongs to`
`francois ftpusers`	

The *add account to expire* example (–e) is useful for setting an expiration date for a
user that you know to be temporary. Change the default shell to `nologin` when you
want a user to be able to access the computer (via FTP, POP3, and so on), but you
don't want to allow access to a regular Linux login shell. Likewise, the last example,
with no –m to create a home directory, might allow a user to access a machine, but
not have a home directory. Note that in all the examples, unless you provide the –m
option, the `useradd` command will not create the home directory for the user.

Changing useradd Defaults

The default values you get when you create a new user account with `useradd` (default
shell, GID, expire dates, and so on) are set by values in the `/etc/login.defs` and
`/etc/default/useradd` files. You can edit those files to change defaults or run the
`useradd` command with the –D option to list or selectively change values:

`$ useradd -D`	`List default settings for useradd`
`$ sudo useradd -D -b /home2 -s /bin/csh`	`Set default base dir and shell`
`$ sudo useradd -D -e 2009-01-01`	`Set all new users to expire in 2009`

As noted earlier, files and directories from the /etc/skel directory are copied to the new user's home directory when the account is created when you pass the -m option. Those files include some bash shell files and a link to an example directory. You can add other files and directories to /etc/skel so that each new user gets them. For example, if you are configuring a web server, you might create public_html and public_ftp directories for users to add web pages and files they want to share.

Modifying User Accounts

After a user account is created, you can **change values for that account with the usermod com-mand**. Most options are the same ones you would use with useradd. For example:

```
$ sudo usermod -c "Thomas Lotto" tlot     Change user's name in comment field
$ sudo usermod -s /bin/sh joeq            Change default shell to sh
$ sudo usermod -L swanson                 Lock the user account named swanson
$ sudo usermod -U travis                  Unlock user account named travis
```

Note that the last two examples lock and unlock a user account, respectively. Locking a user account does not remove the user's account from the system or delete any of the user's files and directories. However, it does keep the user from logging in. Locking an account can be useful if an employee is leaving the company, but the work in that employee's files needs to be passed to another person. Under those circumstances, lock-ing the user instead of deleting it prevents the files owned by that user from appearing as belonging to an unassigned UID.

Because a regular user can't use the useradd or usermod command, there are special commands for **changing personal account information**. Here are examples:

```
$ chsh -s /bin/sh                     Change current user's shell to /bin/sh
$ sudo chsh -s /bin/sh francois       Change a user's shell to /bin/sh
$ sudo chfn \
     -o "B-205"              \        Change office number
     -h "212-555-1212"       \        Change home phone number
     -w "212-555-1957"                Change office phone number
$ finger francois
Login: francois                        Name: Francois Caen
Directory: /home/francois              Shell: /bin/bash
Office: B-205, 212-555-1212       Home Phone: 212-555-1957
On since Sat Aug  4 13:39 (CDT) on tty1    4 seconds idle
No mail.
No Plan.
```

The information changed above with the chfn command and displayed with finger are stored in the fifth field of the /etc/password file for the selected user. (The /etc/passwd file can only be edited directly by the root user, and should only be edited using the vipw command and extreme caution.)

On other versions of Linux, you can use the -f option to chfn to change your real, or full name. On Ubuntu, the permission to do this is turned off by default. You can change this by editing /etc/login.defs. Look for the following line:

```
CHFN_RESTRICT           rwh
```

and change this to:

```
CHFN_RESTRICT           frwh
```

Deleting User Accounts

With the userdel command, you can **remove user accounts** from the system, as well as other files (home directories, mail spool files, and so on) if you choose. Here are examples:

```
# userdel jimbo              Delete user, not user's home directory
# userdel -r lily            Delete user, home directory, and mail spool
```

Managing Passwords

Adding or changing a password is usually done quite simply with the passwd command. However, there are additional options available with passwd that let an administrator manage such things as user account locking, password expiration, and warnings to change passwords. Besides passwd, there are commands such as chage, chfn, and vipw, for working with user passwords.

Regular users can **change only their own passwords**, whereas the root user can change the password for any user. For example:

```
$ passwd                            Change a regular user's own password
Changing password for user chris.
Changing password for chris.
(current) UNIX password: ********
New UNIX password: *
BAD PASSWORD: it's WAY too short
New UNIX password: *********
Retype new UNIX password: *********
passwd: password updated successfully
$ sudo passwd joseph                Root can change any user's password
Changing password for user joseph.
New UNIX password: *
Retype new UNIX password: *
passwd: password updated successfully
```

In the first example, a regular user (chris) changes his own password. Even while logged in, the user must type the current password before entering a new one. Also, passwd keeps a regular user from setting a password that is too short, based on a dictionary word, doesn't have enough different characters, or is otherwise easy to guess. The root user, in the second example, can change any user password without the old password.

Passwords should be at least eight characters, be a combination of letters and other characters (numbers, punctuation, and so on), and not include real words. Make passwords easy to remember but hard to guess.

A system administrator can use passwd to **lock and unlock user accounts**. For example:

```
$ sudo passwd -l carl              Lock the user account (carl)
Locking password for user carl.
passwd: Success
$ sudo passwd -u carl              Unlock a locked user account (carl)
Unlocking password for user carl.
passwd: Success
$ sudo passwd -u jordan            Fails to unlock account with blank password
Unlocking password for user jordan.
passwd: Warning: unlocked password would be empty.
passwd: Unsafe operation (use -f to force)
```

Locking a user account with passwd causes an exclamation mark (!) to be placed at the front of the password field in the /etc/shadow file (where user passwords are stored). When a user account is unlocked, the exclamation mark is removed and the user's previous password is restored.

An administrator can use the passwd command to **require users to change passwords regularly**, as well as **warn users when passwords are about to expire**. To use the password expiration feature, the user account needs to have had password expiration enabled. The following examples use passwd to modify password expiration:

```
$ sudo passwd -n 2 vern      Set minimum password life to 2 days
$ sudo passwd -x 300 vern    Set maximum password life to 300 days
$ sudo passwd -w 10 vern     Warn of password expiration 10 days in advance
$ sudo passwd -i 14 vern     Days after expiration account is disabled
```

In the first example, the user must wait at least two days (-n 2) before changing to a new password. In the second, the user must change the password within 300 days (-x 300). In the next example, the user is warned 10 days before the password expires (-w 10). In the last example, the user account is disabled 14 days after the password expires (-i 14).

To **view password expiration**, you can use the chage command as follows:

```
$ sudo chage -l vern             View password expiration information
Last password change                 : Aug 04, 2007
Password expires                     : May 31, 2008
Password inactive                    : Jun 14, 2008
Account expires                      : never
```

```
Minimum number of days between password change        : 2
Maximum number of days between password change        : 300
Number of days of warning before password expires     : 10
```

As system administrator, you can also use the chage command to manage password expiration. Besides being able to set minimum (-m), maximum (-M), and warning (-w) days for password expiration, chage can also set the day when a user must set a new password or a particular date the account becomes inactive:

$ **sudo chage -I 40 frank**   *Make account inactive in 40 days*
$ **sudo chage -d 5 perry**   *Force user's password to expire in 5 days*

Instead of five days (-d 5), you could set that option to 0 and cause the user to have to set a new password the next time he or she logs in. For example, the next time the user perry logged in, if -d 0 had been set, perry would be prompted for a new password as follows:

```
login: perry
Password: ********
You are required to change your password immediately (root enforced)
Changing password for perry.
(current) UNIX password:
New UNIX password: *********
Retype new UNIX password: *********
```

Adding Groups

Each new user is assigned to one or more groups. You can create groups at any time and add users to those groups. The permissions that each group has to use files and directories in Linux depend on how the group permission bits are set on each item. Assigning users to a group allows you to attach ownership to files, directories, and applications so that those users can work together on a project or have common access to resources.

Commands similar to those for working with users are available for managing your groups. You can add groups (groupadd), change group settings (groupmod), delete groups (groupdel), and add and delete members from those groups (groupmems). Here are some examples for **adding new groups** with the groupadd command:

$ **sudo groupadd marketing**   *Create new group with next available GID*
$ **sudo groupadd -g 1701 sales**   *Create new group with GID of 1701*
$ **sudo groupadd -o -g 74 mysshd**   *Create group with existing GID*

With the groupmod command, you can **change the name or group ID** of an existing group. Here are examples:

$ **sudo groupmod -g 491 myadmin**   *Modify myadmin to use GID 491*
$ **sudo groupmod -n myad myadmin**   *Change name of myadmin group to myad*

To remove an existing group, use the `groupdel` command. Here is an example:

```
$ sudo groupdel myad          Remove existing myad group
```

Keep in mind that removing a group or user doesn't remove the files, directories, devices, or other items owned by that group or user. If you do a long listing (`ls -l`) of a file or directory assigned to a user or group that was deleted, the UID or GID of the deleted user or group is displayed.

Checking on Users

After you have created user accounts, and let those users loose on your computer, there are several different commands you can use to keep track of how they are using your computer. Commands for checking on user activity on your Linux system that are covered in other chapters include the following:

❑ Use the `find` command (see Chapter 4) to search the system for files anywhere on the system that are owned by selected users.

❑ Use the `du` command (see Chapter 7) to see how much disk space has been used in selected users' home directories.

❑ Use commands such as `fuser`, `ps`, and `top` (Chapter 9) to find out which processes users are running.

Aside from the commands just mentioned, there are commands for checking such things as who is logged into your system and getting general information about the users with accounts on your system. Here are examples of commands for getting information about people logging into your system:

```
$ last                        List the most recent successful logins
greek    tty3                         Sun Aug  5 18:05   still logged in
chris    tty1                         Sun Aug  4 13:39   still logged in
root     pts/4     thompson           Sun Aug  5 14:02   still logged in
chris    pts/1     :0.0               Sat Aug  4 15:47   still logged in
jim      pts/0     10.0.0.50          Fri Aug  3 13:46 - 15:40  (01:53)
francois pts/2                        Thu Aug  2 11:14 - 13:38 (2+02:24)
$ last -a                     Makes it easier to read the remote client hostname
$ sudo lastb                  List the most recent unsuccessful logins
julian   ssh:notty  ritchie            Mon Aug  6 12:28 - 12:28  (00:00)
morris   ssh:notty  thompson           Tue Jul 31 13:08 - 13:08  (00:00)
baboon   ssh:notty  10.0.0.50          Sun Jul  8 09:40 - 09:40  (00:00)
francois ssh:notty  000db9034dce.cli Fri Jun 22 17:23 - 17:23  (00:00)
$ who -u                      List who is currently logged in (long form)
greek    tty3    2007-08-05 18:05 17:24    18121
jim      pts/0   2007-08-06 12:29    .     20959 (server1.example.com)
root     pts/3   2007-08-04 18:18 13:46    17982 (server2.example.com)
```

```
francois pts/2   2007-07-31 23:05  old    4700  (0a0d9b34x.example.com)
chris   pts/1   2007-08-04 15:47  old    17502 (:0.0)
$ users              List who is currently logged in (short form)
chris francois greek jim root
```

With the last command, you can see when each user logged in (or opened a new shell) and either how long they were logged in or a note that they are "still logged in." The tty1 and tty3 terminal lines show users working from virtual terminals on the console. The pts lines indicate a person opening a shell from a remote computer (thompson) or local X display (:0.0). We recommend you use the -a option for improved readability. The lastb command shows failed login attempts and where they are from. The who -u and users commands show information on currently logged-in users.

Here are some commands for finding out more about individual users on your system:

```
$ id                 Your identity (UID, GID and group for current shell)
uid=1000(chris) gid=1000(chris) groups=4(adm),20(dialout),24(cdrom),25(floppy),
29(audio),30(dip),44(video),46(plugdev),104(scanner),112(netdev),113(lpadmin),
115(powerdev),117(admin),1000(chris)
$ who am i            Your identity (user, tty, login date, location)
chris   pts/0   Aug 3 2140 (:0.0)
$ finger -s chris    User information (short)
Login   Name        Tty    Idle   Login Time   Office   Office Phone
chris   Chris Negus tty1   1d     Aug  4 13:39  A-111    555-1212
$ finger -l chris    User information (long)
Login: chris                        Name: Chris Negus
Directory: /home/chris              Shell: /bin/bash
Office: A-111, 555-1212             Home Phone: 555-2323
On since Sat Aug  4 13:39 (CDT) on tty1    2 days idle
New mail received Mon Aug  6 13:46 2007 (CDT)
     Unread since Sat Aug  4 09:32 2007 (CDT)
No Plan.
```

Besides displaying basic information about the user (login, name, home directory, shell, and so on), the finger command will also display any information stored in special files in the user's home directory. For example, the contents of the user's ~/.plan and ~/.project files, if those files exist, are displayed at the end of the finger output. With a one-line .project file and multi-line .plan file, output could appear as follows:

```
$ finger -l chris    User information (long, .project and .plan files)
     ...
Project:
My project is to take over the world.
Plan:
My grand plan is
to take over the world
by installing Linux on every computer
```

Configuring the Built-In Firewall

A firewall is a critical tool for keeping your computer safe from intruders over the Internet or other network. It can protect your computer by checking every packet of data that comes to your computer's network interfaces, then making a decision about what to do with that packet based on the parameters you set. The firewall facility built into the current Linux kernel is called iptables. (You may also hear of ipchains, which was the predecessor of iptables in kernel 2.2 and below.) Ubuntu comes with iptables fully started and configured when you install Linux.

The iptables facility (www.netfilter.org) is extraordinarily powerful, yet complex to use from the command line. For that reason, many people set up their basic firewall rules using a graphical interface. To get a graphical interface, install the firestarter package. Firestarter provides a wizard to configure and set up your firewall. To run Firestarter, select System ⇨ Administration ⇨ Firestarter. You can also try add-on packages such as FWBuilder (fwbuilder package) and Shorewall (shorewall package) for graphically configuring firewalls.

When you installed Ubuntu, you installed a firewall on your system. Ubuntu generates an iptables configuration that is a good starting point for simple desktop firewalling, which consists of opening just a few ports for running daemons and blocking the rest. You can customize this default configuration by running the commands shown in the following sections.

> **NOTE** *Before you go much further, read the IpTables HowTo document for Ubuntu, at* https://help.ubuntu.com/community/IptablesHowTo. *This document provides a lot of useful information for using iptables on Ubuntu, as this usage differs a lot from other versions of Linux such as Fedora.*

For more complex needs, as when iptables is used as the firewall in front of multiple machines, we recommend using one of the graphical tools mentioned above. However, there are times when either you don't have a GUI available or you need a firewall rule that isn't available through a GUI. In those cases, it's useful to know the syntax of the iptables command to list current rules and add a new rule yourself.

Before you start messing around with your firewall in Ubuntu, you should check how the firewall is set up on your system. Here is how to **list the current rules set** on your Linux system's firewall:

```
$ sudo iptables -L
Chain INPUT (policy ACCEPT)
target     prot opt source              destination

Chain FORWARD (policy ACCEPT)
target     prot opt source              destination

Chain OUTPUT (policy ACCEPT)
target     prot opt source              destination
```

When you install Ubuntu, you see this output for the preceding command, which means no rules have been defined. After some changes, you may see a more customized rule set like the following:

```
$ sudo iptables -L                 Display current iptables filter table
Chain INPUT (policy ACCEPT)
target     prot opt source     destination
 ...
ACCEPT     udp  --  anywhere   anywhere   udp dpt:ipp
ACCEPT     tcp  --  anywhere   anywhere   tcp dpt:ipp
ACCEPT     0    --  anywhere   anywhere   state RELATED,ESTABLISHED
ACCEPT     tcp  --  anywhere   anywhere   state NEW tcp dpt:ftp
ACCEPT     tcp  --  anywhere   anywhere   state NEW tcp dpt:ssh
ACCEPT     tcp  --  anywhere   anywhere   state NEW tcp dpt:http
REJECT     0    --  anywhere   anywhere   reject-with icmp-host-prohibited


Chain FORWARD (policy ACCEPT)
target   prot opt source     destination
REJECT   0    --  anywhere   anywhere   reject-with icmp-host-prohibited


Chain OUTPUT (policy ACCEPT)
target     prot opt source         destination
```

The example illustrates the default *filter* iptables firewall table. It shows that for packets coming into the computer's network interfaces, packets for Internet Printing Protocol (ipp) on udp and tcp protocols are allowed. Likewise, tcp packets matching the FTP (ftp), Secure Shell (ssh), and Web (http) destination ports are accepted. Packets are also accepted if they are associated with an established connection. Next you can **look at the nat table:**

```
$ sudo iptables -t nat -L          Display current iptables nat table
Chain PREROUTING (policy ACCEPT)
target  prot opt source      destination
DNAT    tcp  --  0.0.0.0/0   11.22.33.44  tcp dpt:8785 to:10.0.0.155:22
DROP    tcp  --  0.0.0.0/0   0.0.0.0/0    tcp dpt:135
DROP    udp  --  0.0.0.0/0   0.0.0.0/0    udp dpt:135


Chain POSTROUTING (policy ACCEPT)
target      prot opt source         destination
MASQUERADE  all  --  0.0.0.0/0       0.0.0.0/0


Chain OUTPUT (policy ACCEPT)
target      prot opt source         destination
```

The nat table just shown applies to a feature called Network Address Translation. NAT allows you to do such things as use private addresses behind your firewall. As the packets from internal LAN machines exit the firewall, the source private address is rewritten with the IP address of the firewall's external interface. The firewall keeps track of these sessions in order to allow the return traffic through to the LAN machines. All this is configured with the MASQUERADE line on the POSTROUTING chain.

In the example above, the DNAT line in the PREROUTING chain causes any requests to port 8785, at IP address 11.22.33.44, to be forwarded to the internal LAN IP address 10.0.0.155 on port 22 (a trick to let someone ssh into a computer behind the firewall through a non-standard port).

Here are other examples for **listing information about your firewall**. The iptstate command is part of the iptstate package.

```
$ sudo iptables -n -L            Filter rules, IP numbers (no DNS lookup)
$ sudo iptables -v -L            Verbose output (with packet/byte counts)
$ sudo iptables -L --line-numbers   Show line number in chain for each rule
$ sudo iptables -nvL --line-numbers  Our tech editor's favorite combination
```

Here is how you can **stop or flush all iptables rules** on an Ubuntu system:

```
$ sudo iptables -F               Flush all iptables rules
```

This command removes all the rules, so be careful when running it. You'll want to immediately add new rules.

Here are some examples of how the iptables command can be used to **change rules on an active firewall**:

```
$ sudo iptables -A INPUT -p TCP  \   Add filter input rule for TCP packets
    -i eth0                      \   on the first Ethernet interface
    --destination-port 25        \   destined for mail service port (25)
    -j ACCEPT                        to accept those packets when encountered

$ sudo iptables -t nat           \   Add nat rule
    -A POSTROUTING               \   POSTROUTING chain
    -o eth1                      \   for packets received on eth1 interface
    -j SNAT                      \   jump to network address translation
    --to-source 11.22.33.1           using outgoing address 11.22.33.1
```

Of the two examples shown, the first example creates a rule that allows new incoming requests to your system on port 25. This is presumably because you have configured your computer as a mail server (with sendmail, postfix, or other SMTP service). The second example creates a nat table rule to allow the firewall to do Source Network Address Translation (SNAT). The SNAT feature lets you have private IP addresses behind your firewall that can communicate to the public Internet using the firewall's external IP address.

To use SNAT or any other form of NAT, you must **also enable IP forwarding** on the machine. This can be done by editing the /etc/sysctl.conf file and uncommenting the following variable:

```
net.ipv4.conf.default.forwarding=1
```

In cases where you have an Internet-facing service offered on a machine behind your firewall, you can instruct the firewall to **forward requests for that service** to that machine. The following example uses a feature called *port forwarding* to pass requests for a service through the firewall to the destination machine behind the firewall:

```
$ sudo iptables -t nat -A PREROUTING \     Add nat PREROUTING rule
    -p tcp -d 11.22.33.1        \          accepts tcp requests on 11.22.33.1
    --dport 80                  \          for port 80 (Web service)
    -j DNAT                     \          jump to the DNAT target
    --to-destination 10.0.0.2              forward those packets to 10.0.0.2
```

There are many other types of rules you can create to change how your firewall behaves. Refer to the iptables man page or the Netfilter web site (www.netfilter.org) for further information on using the iptables facility.

After making the above changes, you'll see the following rules defined:

```
$ sudo iptables -t nat -L
Chain PREROUTING (policy ACCEPT)
target     prot opt source                destination
DNAT       tcp  --  anywhere              11.22.33.1    tcp dpt:www to:10.0.0.2

Chain POSTROUTING (policy ACCEPT)
target     prot opt source                destination
SNAT       0    --  anywhere              anywhere      to:11.22.33.1

Chain OUTPUT (policy ACCEPT)
target     prot opt source                destination
```

All of the changes to the iptables rules apply only for this session. When you next reboot Ubuntu, you will get the default set of no rules, which is generally not what you want. To preserve your iptables rules, run iptables-save:

```
$ sudo iptables-save > iptables.rules     Save rules to a file in the
                                           current directory
$ sudo cp iptables.rules /etc             Copy the saved rules to /etc
```

The two-step process is required due to the restrictions on the /etc directory. (You can change those restrictions, but that probably isn't a good idea.) Thus far, the rules are saved for later usage.

Next, you can configure Ubuntu to load these saved rules each time it enables an Ethernet interface (this is specific to each network card or interfaces on your system). Edit the /etc/network/interfaces file. After the iface configuration for an Ethernet interface, such as eth0, make a call to iptables-restore, as shown in this snippet:

```
auto eth0
iface eth0 inet dhcp
  pre-up iptables-restore < /etc/iptables.rules
```

This addition to the interfaces files calls iptables-restore to restore the rules saved previously to the file /etc/iptables.rules.

285

Working with System Logs

Most Linux systems are configured to log many of the activities that occur on those systems. Those activities are then written to log files located in the /var/log directory or its subdirectories. This logging is done by the Syslog facility.

Ubuntu uses the syslogd (system log daemon) and klogd (kernel log daemon) from the sysklogd and klogd packages to manage system logging. Those daemons are started automatically from the syslog init script (/etc/init.d/sysklogd). Information about system activities is then directed to files in the /var/log directory such as messages, secure, cron, and boot.log, based on settings in the /etc/syslog .conf file.

Automatic log rotation is handled by logrotate, based on settings in the /etc/ logrotate.conf file and /etc/logrotate.d directory. The /etc/cron.daily/ logrotate cronjob causes this daily log rotating to take place.

You can check any of the log files manually (using vi or another favorite text editor). However, if you install the logwatch package, highlights of your log files will automatically be mailed to your root user's mailbox every day. You can change both the recipient and the sender address of that mail by editing the /etc/cron.daily/ 0logwatch file. To prevent e-mail loops, you should change the sender address to a real e-mail address when the recipient is not on the local machine. Another way to change the recipient is to forward root's e-mail to another address by editing /etc/ aliases and running newaliases to enact the changes. Otherwise, just log in as root and use a mail client, as described in Chapter 12, to read the logwatch email messages:

You can **send your own messages to the syslogd logging facility** using the logger command. Here are a couple of examples:

```
$ logger Added new video card          Message added to messages file
$ logger -p info -t CARD -f /tmp/my.txt  Priority, tag, message file
```

In the first example, the words *Added new video card* are sent to the messages file. In the second example, the priority of the message is set to info, and a tag of CARD is added to each line in the message. The message text is taken from the /tmp/my.txt file. To see these log entries in real time, use tail -f or less as described in Chapter 5.

Using Advanced Security Features

A dozen or so pages covering security-related commands are not nearly enough to address the depth of security tools available to you as a Linux system administrator. Beyond the commands covered in this chapter, here are descriptions of some features you may want to look into to further secure your Linux system:

❑ **Security Enhanced Linux (SELinux)** — The SELinux feature provides a means of securing the files, directories, and applications in your Linux system in such a way that exploitation of one of those areas of your system cannot be used to breach other areas. For example, if intruders were to compromise your web daemon, they wouldn't necessarily be able to compromise the rest of the system.

SELinux was developed by the U.S. National Security Agency (NSA), who hosts a related FAQ at www.nsa.gov/selinux/info/faq.cfm.You need to install SELinux as separate packages. See https://wiki.ubuntu.com/SELinux for details.

❑ **Central logging** — If you're managing more than a couple of Linux servers, it becomes preferable to have all your systems log to a central syslog server. When you implement your syslog server, you may want to explore using syslog-ng. Also, if you outgrow logwatch, you should consider using a log parser such as Splunk.

❑ **Tripwire** — Using the tripwire package, you can take a snapshot of all the files on your system, then later use that snapshot to find if any of those files have been changed. This is particularly useful to find out if any applications have been modified that should not have been. First, you take a baseline of your system file. Then at regular intervals, you run a tripwire integrity check to see if any of your applications or configuration files have been modified.

❑ **APT database** — Another way to check if any of your applications have been modified is by using the APT commands to validate the applications and configuration files you have installed on your system. See Chapter 2 for information on using the APT and dpkg commands to verify the contents of installed packages.

❑ **chkrootkit** — If you suspect your system has been compromised, download and build chkrootkit from www.chkrootkit.org. This will help you detect rootkits that may have been used to take over your machine. We recommend you run chkrootkit from a LiveCD or after mounting the suspected drive on a clean system.

Summary

While there are many tools available for securing your Linux system, the first line of security starts with securing the user accounts on your system and the services that run on your system. Commands such as useradd, groupadd, and password are standard tools for setting up user and group accounts.

Because most serious security breaches outside your organization can come from intruders accessing your systems on public networks, setting up secure firewalls is important for any system connected to the Internet. The iptables facility provides the firewall features that are built into the Linux kernel.

To keep track of activities on your system, the Syslog facility logs information about nearly every aspect of the actions that take place on your system. Packages that are installed by default, such as logrotate and logwatch, make it easy to manage and do daily checks on your system logs.

A

Using vi or Vim Editors

Although easy-to-use graphical text editors (such as gedit and kedit) are readily available with Linux, most power users still use vi or Emacs to edit text files. Besides the fact that vi and Emacs will work from any shell (no GUI required), they offer other advantages such as your hands never having to leave the keyboard and integration with useful utilities. And unlike GUI editors, text-based editors are usable over slow Internet connections such as dial-up or satellite.

This appendix focuses on features of the vi editor that can not only help you with basic editing, but also help you do some advanced text manipulation. We chose to cover vi rather than Emacs because vi is more universal and leaner, and also because vi keyboard shortcuts only require two arms. Because many Linux systems use the Vim (Vi IMproved) editor in place of the older vi editor, the descriptions in this appendix are extended to cover Vim as well. Some features in Vim that are not in vi include multiple undo levels, syntax highlighting, and online help.

IN THIS APPENDIX

Using the vi editor

Starting/quitting the vi editor

Moving around in vi

Changing and deleting text

Using Ex commands

Using visual mode

NOTE *If you have never used vi or Vim before, try out the tutor that comes with the* vim-enhanced *package. Run the* vimtutor *command and follow the instructions to step through many of the key features of vi and Vim.*

Starting and Quitting the vi Editor

If you want to experiment with using vi, you should copy a text file to practice on. For example, type:

```
$ cp /etc/passwd /tmp
```

Then open that file using the vi command as follows:

```
$ vi /tmp/passwd
```

To benefit from all the improvements of Vim, make sure you have the vim-enhanced package installed (which gets installed by default on Ubuntu). On many systems, `vi` is aliased to the `vim` command. On Ubuntu, both commands launch `vim`. You may want to double-check that using the `alias` command.

```
/bin/vi /tmp/text.txt
```

Here are a few other ways you can **start vi**:

```
$ vi +25 /tmp/inittab      Begin on line 25
$ vi + /tmp/inittab        Begin editing file on the last line
$ vi +/tty /tmp/inittab    Begin on first line with word "tty"
$ vi -r /tmp/inittab       Recover file from crashed edit session
$ view /tmp/inittab        Edit file in read-only mode
```

When you are done with your vi session, there are several different ways to save and quit. To **save the file before you are ready to quit**, type **:w**. To **quit and save changes**, type either **zz** or **:wq**. To **quit without saving changes**, type **:q!**. If you find that you can't write to the file you are editing, it may be opened in read-only mode. If that's the case, you can try forcing a write by typing **:w!** or you can **save the contents of the file to a different name**. For example, type the following to save the contents of the current file to a file named `myfile.txt`:

```
:w /tmp/myfile.txt
```

The vi editor also enables you to **line up several files at a time to edit**. For example, type:

```
$ cd /tmp
$ touch a.txt b.txt c.txt
$ vi a.txt b.txt c.txt
```

In this example, `vi` will open the `a.txt` file first. You can **move to the next file** by typing **:n**. You may want to **save changes before moving to the next file (:w)** or **save changes as you move to the next file (:wn)**. To **abandon changes while moving to the next file**, type **:n!**.

You will probably find it easier to open multiple files by splitting your vi screen. When you're in vi and have a file open, you can **split your screen multiple times** either horizontally or vertically:

```
:split /etc/motd.tail
:vsplit /etc/motd.tail
```

Use <*Tab*> to complete the path to the files, just like you would in a bash shell. To **navigate between split windows**, press Ctrl+w, followed by the w key. To close the current window, use the usual vi exit command (:q).

Moving Around in vi

The first thing to get used to with vi is that you can't just start typing. Vi has multiple modes that enable you to perform a different set of tasks. You start a vi session in Normal mode, where vi is waiting for you to type a command to get started. While you are in Normal mode, you can move around the file, to position where you want to be in the file. To enter or modify text, you need to go into Insert or Replace modes.

Assuming vi is open with a file that contains several pages of text, Table A-1 shows some keys and combinations you can type to **move around the file while in normal mode.**

Table A-1: Keystroke Commands for Moving Around

Key	Result	Key	Result
PageDown or Ctrl+f	Move down one page	PageUp or Ctrl+b	Move up one page
Ctrl+d	Move down half page	Ctrl+u	Move up half page
Shift+g	Go to last line of file	:1	Go to first line of file (use any number to go to that line)
Shift+h	Move cursor to screen top	Shift+l	Move cursor to screen bottom
Shift+m	Move cursor to middle of screen	Ctrl+l	Redraw screen (if garbled)
Enter	Move cursor to beginning of the next line	-	Move cursor to beginning of the previous line
Home or $	Move cursor to end of line	End or ^ or 0	Move cursor to line beginning
(	Move cursor to beginning of previous sentence	)	Move cursor to beginning of next sentence
{	Move cursor to beginning of previous paragraph	}	Move cursor to beginning of next paragraph
w	Move cursor to next word (space, new line, or punctuation)	Shift+w	Move cursor to next word (space or new line)

Continued

291

Table A-1: Keystroke Commands for Moving Around (*continued*)

Key	Result	Key	Result
b	Move cursor to previous word (space, new line, or punctuation)	Shift+b	Move cursor to previous word (space or new line)
e	Move cursor to end of next word (space, new line, or punctuation)	Shift+e	Move cursor to end of next word (space or new line)
Left arrow or Backspace	Move cursor left one letter	Right arrow or l	Move cursor right one letter
k or up arrow	Move cursor up one line	j or down arrow	Move cursor down one line
/*string*	Find next occurrence of *string*	?*string*	Find previous occurrence of *string*
n	Find same string again (forward)	Shift+n	Find same string again (backwards)

Changing and Deleting Text in vi

To begin changing or adding to text with vi, you can enter Insert or Replace modes, as shown in Table A-2. When you enter Insert or Replace mode, the characters you type will appear in the text document (as opposed to being interpreted as commands).

Press the Esc key to exit to normal mode after you are done inserting or replacing text.

Table A-2: Commands for Changing Text

Key	Result	Key	Result
i	Typed text appears before current character	Shift+i	Typed text appears at the beginning of current line
a	Typed text appears after current character	Shift+a	Typed text appears at the end of current line

Table A-2: Commands for Changing Text (*continued*)

Key	Result	Key	Result
o	Open a new line below current line to begin typing	Shift+o	Open a new line above current line to begin typing
s	Erase current character and replace with new text	Shift+s	Erase current line and enter new text
c?	Replace ? with l, w, $, or c to change the current letter, word, end of line, or line	Shift+c	Erase from cursor to end of line and enter new text
r	Replace current character with the next one you type	Shift+r	Overwrite as you type from current character going forward

Table A-3 contains keys you type to delete or paste text.

Table A-3: Commands for Deleting and Pasting Text

Key	Result	Key	Result
x	Delete text under cursor	Shift+x	Delete text to left of cursor
d?	Replace ? with l, w, $, or d to cut the current letter, word, or end of line from cursor or entire line	Shift+d	Cut from cursor to end of line
y?	Replace ? with l, w, or $ to copy (yank) the current letter, word, or end of line from cursor	Shift+y	Yank current line
p	Pastes cut or yanked text after cursor	Shift+p	Pastes cut or yanked text before cursor

Using Miscellaneous Commands

Table A-4 shows a few miscellaneous, but important, commands you should know.

Table A-4: Miscellaneous Commands

Key	Result
u	Type **u** to undo the previous change. Multiple u commands will step back to undo multiple changes.
.	Typing a period (.) will repeat the previous command. So, if you deleted a line, replaced a word, changed four letters, and so on, the same command will be done wherever the cursor is currently located. (Entering input mode again resets it.)
Shift+j	Join the current line with the next line.
Esc	If you didn't catch this earlier, the Esc key returns you from an input mode back to command mode. This is one of the keys you will use most often.

Modifying Commands with Numbers

Nearly every command described so far can be modified with a number. In other words, instead of deleting a word, replacing a letter, or changing a line, you can delete six words, replace 12 letters, and change nine lines. Table A-5 shows some examples.

Table A-5: Modifying Commands with Numbers

Command	Result
7cw	Erase the next seven words and replace them with text you type
5, Shift+d	Cut the next five lines (including the current line)
3p	Paste the previously deleted text three times after the current cursor
9db	Cut the nine words before the current cursor
10j	Move the cursor down ten lines
y2)	Copy (yank) text from cursor to end of next two sentences
5, Ctrl+f	Move forward five pages
6, Shift+j	Join the next six lines

From these examples, you can see that most vi keystrokes for changing text, deleting text, or moving around in the file can be modified using numbers.

Using Ex Commands

The vi editor was originally built on an editor called Ex. Some of the vi commands you've seen so far start with a semicolon and are known as *Ex* commands. To enter Ex commands, start from normal mode and type a colon (:). This switches you to command line mode. In this mode, you can use the Tab key to complete your command or file name, and the arrow keys to navigate your command history, as you would in a bash shell. When you press Enter at the end of your command, you are returned to normal mode.

Table A-6 shows some examples of Ex commands.

Table A-6: Ex Command Examples

Command	Result
:!bash	Escape to a bash shell. When you are done, type exit to return to vi.
:!date	Run date (or any command you choose). Press Enter to return.
:!!	Rerun the command previously run.
:20	Go to line 20 in the file.
:5,10w abc.txt	Write lines 5 through 10 to the file abc.txt.
:e abc.txt	Leave the current file and begin editing the file abc.txt.
:.r def.txt	Read the contents of def.txt into the file below the current line.
:s/RH/RedHat	Substitute Red Hat for the first occurrence of RH on the current line.
:s/RH/Red Hat/g	Substitute Red Hat for all occurrences of RH on the current line.
:%s/RH/Red Hat/g	Substitute Red Hat for the all occurrences of RH in the entire file.
:g/Red Hat/p	List every line in the file that contains the string "Red Hat".
:g/gaim/s//pidgin/gp	Find every instance of gaim and change it to pidgin.

From the ex prompt you can also see and change settings related to your vi session using the set command. Table A-7 shows some examples.

Table A-7: set Commands in ex Mode

Command	Result
:set all	List all settings.
:set	List only those settings that have changed from the default.
:set number	Have line numbers appear left of each line. (Use set nonu to unset.)
:set ai	Sets autoindent, so opening a new line follows the previous indent.
:set ic	Sets ignore case, so text searches will match regardless of case.
:set list	Show $ for end of lines and ^I for tabs.
:set wm	Causes vi to add line breaks between words near the end of a line.

Working in Visual Mode

The Vim editor provides a more intuitive means of selecting text called *visual mode*. To begin visual mode, move the cursor to the first character of the text you want to select and press the v key. You will see that you are in visual mode because the following text appears at the bottom of the screen:

```
-- VISUAL --
```

At this point, you can use any of your cursor movement keys (arrow keys, Page Down, End, and so on) to move the cursor to the end of the text you want to select. As the page and cursor move, you will see text being highlighted. When all the text you want to select is highlighted, you can press keys to act on that text. For example, d deletes the text, c lets you change the selected text, :w /tmp/test.txt saves selected text to a file, and so on.

B

Shell Special Characters and Variables

Ubuntu provides bash as the default shell. Chapter 3 helps you become comfortable working in the shell. This appendix provides a reference of the numerous characters and variables that have special meaning to the bash shell. Many of those elements are referenced in Table B-1 (Shell Special Characters) and Table B-2 (Shell Variables).

IN THIS APPENDIX

Using special shell characters

Using shell variables

Using Special Shell Characters

You can use special characters from the shell to match multiple files, save some keystrokes, or perform special operations. Table B-1 shows some shell special characters you may find useful.

Table B-1: Shell Special Characters

Character	Description
*	Match any string of characters.
?	Match any one character.
[...]	Match any character enclosed in the braces.
' ... '	Remove special meaning of characters between quotes. Variables are not expanded.
" ... "	Same as simple quotes except for the escape characters ($ ` and \ ) that preserve their special meaning.
\	Escape character to remove the special meaning of the character that follows.

Continued

Table B-1: Shell Special Characters (*continued*)

Character	Description
~	Refers to the $HOME directory.
~+	Value of the shell variable PWD (working directory).
~-	Refers to the previous working directory.
.	Refers to the current working directory.
..	Refers to the directory above the current directory. Can be used repeatedly to reference several directories up.
$param	Used to expand a shell variable parameter.
cmd1 `cmd2` or cmd1 $(cmd2)	cmd2 is executed first. Then the call to cmd2 is substituted with the output of cmd2, and cmd1 is executed.
cmd1 >	Redirects standard output from command.
cmd1 <	Redirects standard input to command.
cmd1 >>	Appends standard output to file from command, without erasing its current contents.
cmd1 | cmd2	Pipes the output of one command to the input of the next.
cmd &	Runs the command in the background.
cmd1 && cmd2	Runs first command, then if it returns a zero exit status, runs the second command.
cmd1 || cmd2	Runs first command, then if it returns a non-zero exit status, runs the second command.
cmd1 ; cmd2	Runs the first command and when it completes, runs the second command.

Using Shell Variables

You identify a string of characters as a parameter (variable) by placing a $ in front of it (as in $HOME). Shell environment variables can hold information that is used by the shell itself, as well as by commands you run from the shell. Not all environment variables will be populated by default. Some of these variables you can change (such as the default printer in $PRINTER or your command prompt in $PS1). Others are managed by the shell (such as $OLDPWD). Table B-2 contains a list of many useful shell variables.

Table B-2: Shell Variables

Shell Variable	Description
BASH	Shows path name of the bash command (/bin/bash).
BASH_COMMAND	The command that is being executed at the moment.
BASH_VERSION	The version number of the bash command.
COLORS	Path to the configuration file for ls colors.
COLUMNS	The width of the terminal line (in characters).
DISPLAY	Identifies the X display where commands launched from the current shell will be displayed (such as :0.0).
EUID	Effective user ID number of the current user. It is based on the user entry in /etc/passwd for the user that is logged in.
FCEDIT	Determines the text editor used by the fc command to edit history commands. The vi command is used by default.
GROUPS	Lists groups of which the current user is a member.
HISTCMD	Shows the current command's history number.
HISTFILE	Shows the location of your history file (usually located at $HOME/.bash_history).
HISTFILESIZE	Total number of history entries that will be stored (default, 1000). Older commands are discarded after this number is reached.
HISTCMD	The number of the current command in the history list.
HOME	Location of the current user's home directory. Typing the cd command with no options returns the shell to the home directory.
HOSTNAME	The current machine's host name.
HOSTTYPE	Contains the computer architecture on which the Linux system is running (i386, i486, i586, i686, x86_64, ppc, or ppc64).
LESSOPEN	Set to a command that converts content other than plain text (images, RPMs, zip files, and so on) so it can be piped through the less command.
LINES	Sets the number of lines in the current terminal

Continued

Table B-2: Shell Variables (*continued*)

Shell Variable	Description
LOGNAME	Holds the name of the current user.
LS_COLORS	Maps colors to file extensions to indicate the colors the ls command displays when encountering those file types.
MACHTYPE	Displays information about the machine architecture, company, and operating system (such as i686-redhat-linux-gnu)
MAIL	Indicates the location of your mailbox file (typically the user name in the /var/spool/mail directory).
MAILCHECK	Checks for mail in the number of seconds specified (default is 60).
OLDPWD	Directory that was the working directory before changing to the current working directory.
OSTYPE	Name identifying the current operating system (such as linux or linux-gnu)
PATH	Colon-separated list of directories used to locate commands that you type (/bin, /usr/bin, and $HOME/bin are usually in the PATH).
PPID	Process ID of the command that started the current shell.
PRINTER	Sets the default printer, which is used by printing commands such as lpr and lpq.
PROMPT_COMMAND	Set to a command name to run that command each time before your shell prompt is displayed. (For example, PROMPT_COMMAND=ls lists commands in the current directory before showing the prompt).
PS1	Sets the shell prompt. Items in the prompt can include date, time, user name, hostname, and others. Additional prompts can be set with PS2, PS3, and so on.
PWD	The directory assigned as your current directory.
RANDOM	Accessing this variable generates a random number between 0 and 32767.
SECONDS	The number of seconds since the shell was started.
SHELL	Contains the full path to the current shell.
SHELLOPTS	Lists enabled shell options (those set to on)

C

Getting Information from /proc

Originally intended to be a location for storing information used by running processes, the /proc file system eventually became the primary location for storing all kinds of information used by the Linux kernel. Despite the emergence of /sys to provide a more orderly framework for kernel information, many Linux utilities still gather and present data about your running system from /proc.

If you are someone who prefers to cut out the middleman, you can bypass utilities that read /proc files and read (and sometimes even write to) /proc files directly. By checking /proc, you can find out the state of processes, hardware devices, kernel subsystems, and other attributes of Linux.

Viewing /proc information

Checking out information in files from the /proc directory can be done by using a simple cat command. In /proc, there is a separate directory for each running process (named by its process ID) that contains information about the process. There are also /proc files that contain data for all kinds of other things, such as your computer's CPU, memory usage, software versions, disk partitions, and so on.

The following examples describe some of the information you can get from your Linux system's /proc directory:

```
$ cat /proc/cmdline     Shows options passed to the boot prompt
root=UUID=db2dac48-a62e-4dbe-9529-e88a57b15bac ro quiet splash

$ cat /proc/cpuinfo         Shows information about your processor
Processor     : 0
vendor_id     : GenuineIntel
cpu family    : 6
model         : 8
```

```
model name      : Pentium III (Coppermine)
stepping : 3
cpu MHz         : 648.045
cache size      : 256 KB
   ...
```

In the example above, the MHz speed may be well below your actual system speed if a CPU governor such as cpuspeed is running.

```
$ cat /proc/devices        Shows existing character and block devices
Character devices:
  1 mem
  4 /dev/vc/0
  4 tty
  4 ttys
  5 /dev/tty
   ...
Block devices:
  1 ramdisk
  8 sd
  9 md
$ cat /proc/diskstats      Display disks, partitions, and statistics
    1    0 ram0 0 0 0 0 0 0 0 0 0 0 0
    1    1 ram1 0 0 0 0 0 0 0 0 0 0 0
   ...
    8    0 sda 2228445 1032474 68692149 21672710 1098740 4003143
47790770 101074392 0 15385988 122799055
    8    1 sda1 330077 13060510 188002 8443280
    8    1 sda2 1491 1759 50 162
   ...
    7    0 loop0 0 0 0 0 0 0 0 0 0 0 0
```

In the diskstats output just shown, you can see ramdisk (ram0, ram1, and so on) and loopback devices (loop0, loop1, and so on) devices. For hard disk partitions, the example shows statistics for the whole hard disk (sda) and each partition (sda1, sda2, and so on).

The 11 fields for the entire hard disk show (from left to right): total number of reads, number of reads merged, number of sectors read, number of milliseconds spent by all reads, number of writes completed, number of writes merged, number of sectors written, number of milliseconds spent writing, number of input/output requests currently in progress, number of milliseconds spent doing input/output, and weighted number of milliseconds spend doing input/output. Fields for a particular partition show (from left to right): number of reads issued, number of sectors read, number of writes issued, and number of sectors written.

```
$ cat /proc/filesystems      List filesystem types supported by current kernel
nodev    sysfs               nodev means type is not currently used by any device
nodev    rootfs
   ...
         ext3                ext3 is used on a mounted block device
         iso9660             iso9660 is used on a mounted block device
```

```
$ cat /proc/interrupts        View IRQ channel assignments
        CPU0
  0:  198380901   XT-PIC-XT      timer
  1:     28189    XT-PIC-XT      i8042
  2:        0     XT-PIC-XT      cascade
  6:   3770197    XT-PIC-XT      Ensoniq AudioPCI
  7:       660    XT-PIC-XT      parport0
    ...
$ cat /proc/iomem             Show physical memory addresses
00000000-0009fbff : System RAM
  00000000-00000000 : Crash kernel
0009fc00-0009ffff : reserved
000a0000-000bffff : Video RAM area
000c0000-000c7fff : Video ROM
000c8000-000c8fff : Adapter ROM
000f0000-000fffff : System ROM
00100000-0febffff : System RAM
    ...
$ cat /proc/ioports           Show virtual memory addresses
0000-001f : dma1
0020-0021 : pic1
0040-0043 : timer0
0050-0053 : timer1
0060-006f : keyboard
0070-0077 : rtc
0080-008f : dma page reg
00a0-00a1 : pic2
00c0-00df : dma2
00f0-00ff : fpu
    ...
$ cat /proc/loadavg           Shows 1, 5, and 15 minute load averages,
1.77 0.56 0.19 2/247 1869       running processes/total and highest PID
$ cat /proc/meminfo           Shows available RAM and swap
MemTotal:       482992 kB
MemFree:         25616 kB
Buffers:         12204 kB
Cached:          64132 kB
SwapCached:     117472 kB
Active:         321344 kB
Inactive:        93168 kB
HighTotal:           0 kB
HighFree:            0 kB
LowTotal:       482992 kB
    ...
$ cat /proc/misc              Shows name/minor number of devices
229 fuse                        registered with misc major device (10)
 63 device-mapper
175 agpgart
144 nvram
    ...
$ cat /proc/modules           Shows loaded modules, memory size,
nls_utf8 6209 1 - Live 0xd0c59000     instances loaded, dependencies
cifs 213301 0 - Live 0xd0e3b000       load state, and kernel memory
```

```
nfs 226861 0 - Live 0xd0e02000
nfsd 208689 17 - Live 0xd0d8a000
exportfs 9537 1 nfsd, Live 0xd0cfb000
lockd 62409 3 nfs,nfsd, Live 0xd0d45000
nfs_acl 7617 2 nfs,nfsd, Live 0xd0c56000
fuse 45909 2 - Live 0xd0d24000
vfat 16193 0 - Live 0xd0cf6000
       ...
```

$ **cat /proc/mounts**   *Show mounted local/remote file system info*
```
rootfs / rootfs rw 0 0
none /sys sysfs rw,nosuid,nodev,noexec 0 0
none /proc proc rw,nosuid,nodev,noexec 0 0
udev /dev tmpfs rw 0 0
/dev/disk/by-uuid/db2dac48-a62e-4dbe-9529-e88a57b15bac / ext3 rw,data=
  ordered 0 0
/dev/disk/by-uuid/db2dac48-a62e-4dbe-9529-e88a57b15bac /dev/.static/dev
ext3 rw,data=ordered 0 0
tmpfs /var/run tmpfs rw,nosuid,nodev,noexec 0 0
tmpfs /var/lock tmpfs rw,nosuid,nodev,noexec 0 0
tmpfs /lib/modules/2.6.20-16-generic/volatile tmpfs rw 0 0
tmpfs /dev/shm tmpfs rw 0 0
devpts /dev/pts devpts rw 0 0
usbfs /dev/bus/usb/.usbfs usbfs rw 0 0
udev /proc/bus/usb tmpfs rw 0 0
usbfs /proc/bus/usb/.usbfs usbfs rw 0 0
fusectl /sys/fs/fuse/connections fusectl rw 0 0
tmpfs /var/run tmpfs rw,nosuid,nodev,noexec 0 0
tmpfs /var/lock tmpfs rw,nosuid,nodev,noexec 0 0
/dev/disk/by-uuid/4f419cb8-a920-4b6e-a8fd-b3946f9bf644 /boot ext3
rw,data=ordered 0 0
/dev/disk/by-uuid/91ae7a92-ca5c-4ef0-9729-ba0cdcf2a07f /home2 ext3
rw,data=ordered 0 0
nfsd /proc/fs/nfsd nfsd rw 0 0
rpc_pipefs /var/lib/nfs/rpc_pipefs rpc_pipefs rw 0 0
binfmt_misc /proc/sys/fs/binfmt_misc binfmt_misc rw 0 0
```
$ **cat /proc/partitions**   *Show mounted local disk partitions*
```
major minor  #blocks  name

   8    0    40031712  sda
   8    1      200781  sda1
   8    2    10241437  sda2
   8    3     6160927  sda3
   ...
   7    0      682998  loop0
```

$ **cat /proc/mdstat**   *If using software RAID, show RAID status*
```
Personalities : [raid1]
read_ahead 1024 sectors
Event: 1
md0 : active raid1 sdb1[1] sda2[0]
      69738048 blocks [2/2] [UU]

unused devices: <none>
```

The /proc/mdstat file contains detailed status information on your software RAID devices, if you have set up such a software RAID device. In this example, md0 is a RAID1 (mirror) composed of the /dev/sdb1 and /dev/sda1 partitions. On the following line, there is one U for each healthy RAID member. If you lose a drive, the output would appear as [U_].

```
$ cat /proc/stat                    Shows kernel stats since system boot
cpu  1559592 1488475 710279 218584583 1446866 5486 16708
cpu0 1559592 1488475 710279 218584583 1446866 5486 16708
intr 215956694 200097282 28242 0 1 3 0 3770197 660 1 1 0 3753340  ...
ctxt 281917622
btime 1181950070
processes 519308
procs_running 1
procs_blocked 0
```

The /proc/stat file contains statistics related to CPU and process activities. The cpu line shows totals for all CPUs, while separate lines for each processor (cpu0, cpu1, and so on) show stats for each CPU on the computer. There are seven fields (from left to right) of CPU information: number of normal processes executed in user mode, niced processes executed in user mode, kernel mode processes, idle processes, iowait processes (waiting for input/output to finish), servicing interrupts (IRQ), and servicing soft IRQs.

```
$ cat /proc/swaps               List information about swap space
Filename      Type      Size      Used    Priority
/dev/sda2     partition 1020088   201124  -1
$ cat /proc/uptime          Seconds since system booted/total seconds idle
2300251.03 2261855.31
$ cat /proc/version         List kernel version and related compiler
Linux version 2.6.20-16-generic (root@terranova) (gcc version 4.1.2 (Ubuntu
4.1.2-0ubuntu4)) #2 SMP Fri Aug 31 00:55:27 UTC 2007
```

Changing /proc information

On some versions of Linux, some values in the /proc/sys directory can actually be changed on the fly. For /proc/sys files that accept binary values (0 disabled or 1 enabled) people would often simply echo a value to any files they wanted to change. Ubuntu does not allow this feature, though.

The preferred method of changing /proc/sys information on the fly is using the sysctl command. To change those settings on a more permanent basis, you should add entries to the /etc/sysctl.conf file. Here are some examples of the sysctl command:

```
$ sudo sysctl -A | less               Display all kernel runtime parameters
$ sudo sysctl -w net.ipv4.ip_forward=1  Turn on IPV4 packet forwarding
```

See Chapter 10 as well as the sysctl and sysctl.conf man pages for further information.

Index

D

J

K

L

317

N

Take a look inside the Linux® toolbox.

Check out other books available in the series.

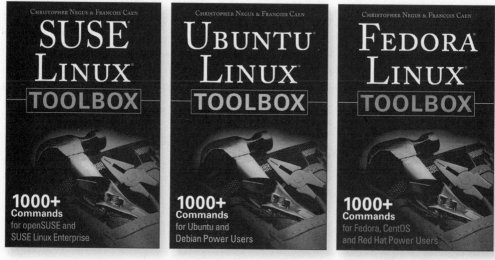

978-0-470-08292-8   978-0-470-08293-5   978-0-470-08291-1

Available now at www.wiley.com